Darwell Stone

Holy Baptism

Darwell Stone

Holy Baptism

ISBN/EAN: 9783337285807

Printed in Europe, USA, Canada, Australia, Japan

Cover: Foto ©Lupo / pixelio.de

More available books at **www.hansebooks.com**

The Oxford Library
of
Practical Theology

EDITED BY THE

REV. W. C. E. NEWBOLT, M.A.
CANON AND CHANCELLOR OF S. PAUL'S

AND THE

REV. F. E. BRIGHTMAN, M.A.
LIBRARIAN OF THE PUSEY HOUSE, OXFORD

HOLY BAPTISM

BY

DARWELL STONE, M.A.

Principal of
Dorchester Missionary College

LONGMANS, GREEN, AND CO.
39 Paternoster Row: London
New York, and Bombay
1899

CAROLO O. BECKER

PIGNUS AMICITIAE

HOC OPUSCULUM

AUCTOR DEDICAVIT

EDITORS' PREFACE

The object of the Oxford Library of Practical Theology is to supply some carefully considered teaching on matters of Religion to that large body of devout laymen, who desire instruction, but are not attracted by the learned treatises which appeal to the theologian. One of the needs of the time would seem to be, to translate the solid theological learning, of which there is no lack, into the vernacular of everyday practical religion; and while steering a course between what is called plain teaching on the one hand and erudition on the other, to supply some sound and readable instruction, to those who require it, on the subjects included under the common title 'The Christian Religion,' that they may be ready always to give an answer to every man that asketh them a reason of the hope that is in them, with meekness and fear.

The Editors, while not holding themselves precluded from suggesting criticisms, have regarded their proper task as that of editing, and accordingly they have not interfered with the responsibility of each writer for his treatment of his own subject.

W. C. E. N.
F. E. B.

PREFATORY NOTE

THE following pages are an attempt to give a clear and simple account of the history of the administration of Holy Baptism, and of the Christian doctrine of Baptism. It is hoped that the relegation of references and of quotations in Greek or Latin, and of the discussion of some difficult matters, to the notes at the end of the book, may make it more useful to the general reader than it would otherwise be, and that any inconvenience thus caused to theological students may be but slight. For the sake of the general reader, also, translations of the Greek and Latin quotations in the notes have been added in all cases except where the passages have been fully quoted in English in the text; and dates and brief descriptions have been attached to the names in the index of authors and books referred to.

The author can hardly hope to have avoided all mistakes. He would only say that he has not willingly passed by anything in Holy Scripture or in Catholic theology which seemed within the scope of the present work, and that in matters the detailed discussion of which has been impossible within the limits of such a book, he has not rejected any opinion, with regard either to doctrine or to history, without attempting to present it to his own mind in its strongest possible form.

If the book should prove of use to any, the author would make his own the words in which, at the end of the earliest existing treatise on Holy Baptism, Tertullian addresses the baptized: 'Ye have sought and ye have found; ye have knocked and to you it has been opened. This only I ask that, when ye pray, ye will remember the sinner Tertullian.'

D. S.

CONTENTS

CHAP.		PAGE
I.	PREPARATION FOR THE INSTITUTION OF CHRISTIAN BAPTISM	1
II.	ADMINISTRATION OF CHRISTIAN BAPTISM IN THE NEW TESTAMENT	13
III.	THE SCRIPTURAL DOCTRINE OF HOLY BAPTISM	25
IV.	THE TEACHING OF THE CHURCH ON THE DOCTRINE OF HOLY BAPTISM	40
V.	THE BAPTISMAL GIFT OF THE HOLY SPIRIT	67
VI.	HOLY BAPTISM A SACRAMENT	86
VII.	THE BAPTISM OF INFANTS	96
VIII.	THE NECESSITY OF HOLY BAPTISM	110
IX.	THE MINISTER OF HOLY BAPTISM	117
X.	THE MATTER AND FORM OF HOLY BAPTISM	131
XI.	THE TIME AND PLACE OF THE ADMINISTRATION OF HOLY BAPTISM	141
XII.	PREPARATION OF CANDIDATES FOR HOLY BAPTISM	151
XIII.	THE CEREMONIAL OF THE ADMINISTRATION OF HOLY BAPTISM	162
XIV.	REASONABLE AND MORAL ASPECTS OF THE DOCTRINE OF HOLY BAPTISM	192
	NOTES	218
	INDEX OF SUBJECTS	293
	INDEX OF PASSAGES IN HOLY SCRIPTURE REFERRED TO	296
	INDEX OF AUTHORS REFERRED TO	299

CHAPTER I

PREPARATION FOR THE INSTITUTION OF CHRISTIAN BAPTISM

It was a saying of S. Augustine that 'the New Testament lies hid in the Old.'[1] In other words, the religion of the Jews contained anticipations of the work of Christ and formed a preparation for the coming of the incarnate life of the eternal Word. Anticipations and preparation were not confined to any short space of time or to the people with the record of whose history the Old Testament is chiefly concerned. They were vouchsafed by God during a period which lasted for centuries; they were to be found in many places; and in the course and development of them manifold agencies were employed. Parts of this work were carried out among heathen peoples, as in the attempts of philosophers to attain to truth, in struggles after a higher morality, in the process of civilisation, and in codes of law. Yet the forms of it which were

[1] The numbers refer to notes at the end of the book.

highest and under the most direct working of Almighty God were found among the Jews. To the latter many truths which were unknown or dimly known to the heathen were clearly manifested.

Some among the heathen had observed natural indications of the will of God to make use of human and material instrumentalities. The fact which was thus seen formed part of the system of truth revealed to the Jews. To mention some of the more striking instances contained in the Old Testament of supernatural works accomplished through what was intermediate,—the rod of Moses was the means by which miracles in the domain of nature were wrought; his uplifted hands formed the instrument by which victory over the Amalekites was won by Israel; the serpent of brass was employed to cure fatal sickness; and a seven-fold bath in the waters of Jordan availed to heal the disease of leprosy.

The use of intermediate agencies was not limited to cases in which physical results were to be produced. The ministry of the prophets and of the priests filled a large place in the Old Testament dispensation; religion was carefully organised; an elaborate system of sacrifice was appointed. That which is material was made to be the instrument of that which is spiritual. Much which God did for the souls of men was accomplished by means of some person or thing utilised to convey spiritual benefit. Sometimes He showed His power of acting outside His appointed methods, as sometimes also He spoke directly to individual souls by a miraculous voice. For the most part, instrumental means were used to carry out His purposes and accomplish His divine will.[2]

'The Old Testament,' S. Augustine went on to say, ' is explained in the New.' The divine employment of human and material means was more fully revealed when the Son of God took our flesh and soul and spirit, and used the nature which He thus completely possessed for the purposes of His ministry on earth, the offering of His Sacrifice, and the completion of His work in His risen and ascended Manhood. In the course of His ministry He used instruments and agencies. His disciples were given wonderful powers. The touch of His Sacred Humanity or of His garments had healing force. Highest of all, His human nature was made the means of the accomplishment of His mighty work in His passion, death, resurrection, and ascension into heaven.

In so acting, the divine wisdom and love have treated man in view of what he is. He possesses faculties of body and mind which respond to appeals made to the natural senses. God Himself, in using intermediate agencies, has respected the nature of the creature whom He has made. In so doing, He has also conformed to those essential and eternal principles which are ultimately grounded upon His own Being and have their temporal expression in the fundamental laws by which creation and human life are ruled. Moreover, in the same plan of action, He has deigned to employ that which is practically useful. It is a mark of the kindly providence of Him Who orders all that 'in the Christian dispensation, as much as in the natural scheme of things, means are made use of to accomplish ends.'[3]

The Old Testament prefigured, not only the sacramental principle, but also particular Sacrments. Using the word Sacrament in its wider sense, Christian theologians have not hesitated to apply it to the ordinances of the Jewish religion.[4] The manna in the wilderness was referred to by our Lord as having spiritual significance, and in view of His teaching may reasonably be regarded as a type of the Eucharistic bread. S. Peter described the water on which the ark of Noah floated as a figure of Baptism; and S. Paul said that the Jews were baptized in the cloud and in the sea. Various acts of purification by means of washing were appointed in the Jewish law, which not only were valuable as tests of obedience, but also were indications of mysterious efficacy to be attached to the use of water. Indeed, God had not left Himself without witness even among the heathen, and, using the things that are seen as tokens of His invisible blessings, allowed the ceremonial lustrations of the pagan rites to be signs of the need of purification and grace.[5]

So too, the rite of circumcision was full of preparatory teaching pointing on to the Christian religion. It was essential for any who was to be within the covenant made by God with the Jewish nation and to receive its blessings. It was received, in ordinary cases, at the age of eight days. Thus it showed that an external ceremony, performed without any act of will on the part of the person receiving it, might profoundly affect the soul.[6]

This foreshadowing of the Sacraments, reaching as it does a distinctive force in the Old Testament, was in harmony with very much in the purpose of the Jewish religion. 'The law,' says S. Paul, 'hath been our tutor to bring us unto Christ.' God gave to His people from time to time what they were able to bear. Not till the 'term appointed of the Father' could the Redeemer come.[7] Before He came there were indications of the truth and methods which He was to reveal and employ. These were sufficient to show those who, at the time of His coming, were morally capable of receiving Him that the teaching of the Old Testament and that given by Himself and His apostles were different parts of the one revelation of the true God. Thus, the doctrine of the Holy Trinity was dimly foreshadowed and the second and third Persons of the Godhead occasionally referred to in the Old Testament. In the New Testament this doctrine was clearly revealed. So, also, the truth of the immortality and future destinies of the human soul was but slightly hinted at in the greater part of the Old Testament, and the gradually growing teaching about it which some parts of the Old Testament contain fall very far short of the fulness and clearness of the New Testament revelation of the life to come. In the same way, the sacramental principle and particular Sacraments were dimly indicated in the older dispensation; the clear revelation of them was not made until after the Incarnation of our Lord.

It is necessary to take care neither to exaggerate nor to ignore the differences between the Old Testament and the New Testament dispensations. Both dispensations are those of a priestly religion. The Jews were described as a 'kingdom of priests and a holy nation.' S. Peter quoted this description and applied it to Christians. The priestly Jewish nation needed a ministerial priesthood by means of which its sacerdotal functions could be performed. A ministerial priesthood is no less necessary to the 'elect race,' the 'royal priesthood,' the 'holy nation' of the people of Christ. Our Lord appointed His apostles and through them others to form the ministry of His Church. It was to 'fulfil,' not to 'destroy,' that He came.[8] Yet the fulfilment of the Jewish religion was on an altogether higher level than Judaism itself. The sacrifices of the Jews were valuable because they tested obedience, were full of teaching, and were means whereby the faithful soul might lay hold of the promises of God. The Sacrifice of Christ to which they pointed was itself full of divine power; the Christian Church is actually the storehouse of grace.

The characteristic features of Christian Baptism imply that it could only follow and could not precede the accomplishment of the work of Christ. This is a result of its necessary dependence on the Manhood of the Son of God, the offering of the Sacrifice of Calvary, the resurrection and ascension of Christ, and the gift of the Holy Spirit to the Church. Yet ceremonies of baptism were not unknown before the Incarnation. It was laid down in the Mosaic Law that those who were defiled must undergo a washing of purification before approaching the worship of God. From this enactment the Rabbis evolved a rule that a Gentile could not become a 'proselyte of righteousness' unless, in addition to receiving circumcision and taking part in a sacrifice, he was baptized.[9] This ceremony signified that the defilement connected in the eyes of the Jews with Gentile race was washed away, and that thus it became possible for the proselyte to be associated with the holy nation of the people of God. Moreover, parts of the teaching of the prophets appear to have led to a Jewish belief that the forerunner of the Messiah and the Messiah Himself would baptize. Isaiah had foretold that the servant of the Lord would sprinkle many nations; Ezekiel had described how God in His pity would sprinkle clean water upon His people and they should be clean; Zechariah had prophesied the fountain which should be opened for sin and for uncleanness; S. John's Gospel shows that to come baptizing with water was thought to be a sign that he who should do so was either the Messiah or His forerunner.[10]

Thus, the idea of baptism was familiar to the Jews when S. John the Baptist 'came into all the region round about Jordan, preaching the baptism of repentance unto remission of sins.'[11] This baptism of S. John, like the Jewish sacrifices, was a sign of spiritual desires and effort on the part of those who submitted to it. Administered by divine commission, it signified also the will of God to bestow good gifts on men. It pointed on to the remission of sins which was to be the outcome of the life and ministry, the passion and death, the resurrection and ascension of Christ, of which an anticipatory touch might even then be obtained. It was a preparation for the Baptism of regeneration which Christ was to institute. It necessitated confession of sins. 'They were baptized of him in the river Jordan, confessing their sins.' It led on to submission of life. 'The multitudes asked him, saying, What then must we do?' It was accompanied by a prophecy that He of whom S. John the Baptist was the forerunner should baptize with the Holy Ghost and with fire. Coming before the beginning of our Lord's ministry, and consequently before His passion and death, His resurrection, ascension, and gift of the Spirit, it was not identical with the Baptism subsequently instituted by Christ and was not in itself a means of grace or of the forgiveness of sins.[12]

The baptism administered by S. John the Baptist was received by our Lord Himself. In His infancy the Redeemer had submitted to the rite of circumcision, which in all other cases was a mark of the need of redemption. Similarly, on approaching His ministry, in spite of His perfect holiness, He received the 'baptism of repentance.' In so doing, it was His divine purpose that in contact with sinful men and in the path of humiliation He might 'fulfil all righteousness.' His baptism may also be regarded as a dedication of His ministry to the service of His Father, and as pointing on to the sanctification of water which would be possible after His death and resurrection and was to be found in the Sacrament of Christian Baptism. After the reception of the 'baptism of repentance,' the Divine Person of God the Holy Ghost manifested and bestowed anew His Presence in the Sacred Manhood of the Son, and the voice of the Father was heard from heaven declaring 'This is My beloved Son, in whom I am well pleased.'[13]

There were anticipations of the institution of Christian Baptism during our Lord's ministry and at the time of His passion. He told Nicodemus, 'Except any one be begotten anew' (or 'from above') 'he cannot see the kingdom of God.' He explained His meaning by adding the words, 'Except any one be begotten of water and the Spirit, he cannot enter into the kingdom of God.'[14] A little later, under His instructions, His disciples, though not their Master Himself, administered a ceremony of baptism which appears to have differed from the subsequent Christian Baptism and to have resembled the baptism of S. John the Baptist, since, like the latter, it preceded the accomplishment of the atoning work of our Lord.[15] The account by S. John the Evangelist of the stream of blood and water which flowed from Christ's side on the cross implies that this event had more than a merely natural significance as an evidence of His death. It may reasonably be thought to have been of a mysterious import. Part of the explanation of it may be seen in the connection between the efficacy of the Sacrifice on Calvary and the sacramental use of water.

Between the resurrection and the ascension our Lord commissioned His apostles to make disciples of all the nations, and, as a means of doing so, to baptize them into the Name of the Father and of the Son and of the Holy Ghost. The New Testament does not record whether, on this occasion, or on any other, He Himself baptized those who were thus to be the first ministers of Christian Baptism. That He did so must be regarded as unlikely. So far as an external ceremony was concerned, some of them, at any rate, had been disciples of S. John the Baptist, and consequently would have received his baptism. So far as the reception of Christian grace is concerned, it is difficult to see how this could have been bestowed before the descent of the Holy Spirit on the day of Pentecost. The probability is that the apostles received in the outpouring of God the Holy Ghost gifts which included anything which they could have obtained by a baptism personally administered by our Lord Himself. When he sent forth the Holy Spirit from the Father after His ascension into heaven, He bestowed, in addition to gifts for the life of the apostles themselves, the power to obey all His commands and consequently to baptize. Therefore after the descent of the Holy Spirit the apostles proceeded to carry out the commission which He had given.[16]

It may thus be seen that for the institution of the Christian Sacrament of Holy Baptism, as for the Incarnation itself, there was a long and gradual preparation. The divine wisdom was careful that so great a blessing should not come suddenly into the world. If it had so come, there might have been none capable of receiving it. In such a matter, human nature being what it is and human history what it has been, delay was the condition of success. 'Men are impatient, and for precipitating things: but the Author of nature appears deliberate throughout His operations; accomplishing His natural ends by slow successive steps.'[17] In the works of revelation and grace He is no less deliberate, no less One who slowly accomplishes His ends and uses fitting preparatory means. His patience is not the least wonderful of the manifestations of His wisdom and His love.

CHAPTER II

ADMINISTRATION OF CHRISTIAN BAPTISM IN THE NEW TESTAMENT

The instructions given by our Lord to His apostles before His ascension included the command 'not to depart from Jerusalem but to wait for the promise of the Father.' That promised gift they were to receive when they should be 'baptized with the Holy Ghost.' At His coming they were to be 'clothed with power from on high.' In obedience to this command they continued waiting from the ascension to the day of Pentecost. On the day of Pentecost they received the baptism 'with the Holy Ghost and with fire' which the forerunner of our Lord, in administering the baptism of repentance, had foretold and our Lord Himself had promised. This descent of God the Holy Ghost placed the apostles in full possession of Christian life. It was this reception of divine grace through divine indwelling which conferred on them the gifts of Christian Baptism and rendered effective that authority for the work of the Christian Ministry which our Lord before His ascension had bestowed upon them. They were now able to put in practice what they had learned from Him. The time had come for them to obey His final instructions, to make disciples and baptize.[1]

Accordingly, from the beginning of Christian preaching Baptism was spoken of as being, as a matter of course, the means of becoming a disciple. On the day of Pentecost the hearts of those who heard S. Peter's speech were 'pricked,' they asked the apostles what they were to do, and received the answer, 'Repent ye and be baptized.' The reception of Baptism led to their being associated with the Christian company. 'Now when they heard this, they were pricked in their heart, and said unto Peter and the rest of the apostles, Brethren, what shall we do? And Peter said unto them, Repent ye, and be baptized every one of you in the Name of Jesus Christ unto the remission of your sins; and ye shall receive the gift of the Holy Ghost. For to you is the promise, and to your children, and to all that are afar off, even as many as the Lord our God shall call unto Him. And with many other words he testified and exhorted them, saying, Save yourselves from this crooked generation. They then that received his word were baptized: and there were added unto them in that day about three thousand souls.' In Samaria, belief in the Gospel which S. Philip the Deacon preached concerning the kingdom of God and the Name of Jesus Christ caused both men and women to be baptized, and the Baptism of a notable convert, Simon, is mentioned as if it were the natural consequence of his having believed. 'When they believed Philip preaching good tidings concerning the kingdom of God and the Name of Jesus Christ, they were baptized, both men and women. And Simon also himself believed: and being baptized he continued with Philip.' When S. Philip preached the Gospel of Jesus to the 'man of Ethiopia,' who was an official of high rank under Queen Candace, as they journeyed together in the chariot, the eunuch pointed to water by the wayside and asked why he should not be baptized. 'And they both went down into the water, both Philip and the eunuch; and he baptized him.' When Saul of Tarsus had been converted, and after three days' blindness received his sight by the ministry of Ananias, the personal and miraculous dealing of the Lord Jesus with his soul culminated in the fact that 'he arose and was baptized.' Even though the gift of the Holy Ghost had been poured out on

Cornelius and his company, S. Peter 'commanded them to be baptized.' 'While Peter yet spake these words, the Holy Ghost fell on all them which heard the word. And they of the circumcision which believed were amazed, as many as came with Peter, because that on the Gentiles also was poured out the gift of the Holy Ghost. For they heard them speak with tongues, and magnify God. Then answered Peter, Can any man forbid the water, that these should not be baptized, which have received the Holy Ghost as well as we? And he commanded them to be baptized in the Name of Jesus Christ.' At Philippi the 'heart' of the proselyte Lydia was 'opened' to 'give heed' to the things which S. Paul spake, and she and her household were baptized. At the same place the gaoler asked S. Paul and S. Silas what he must do to be saved, and after receiving the answer, 'Believe on the Lord Jesus and thou shalt be saved' and hearing 'the word of the Lord,' he was baptized, as also were 'all his.' During S. Paul's stay at Corinth the Corinthians who believed were baptized. Disciples at Ephesus who had received the baptism of S. John the Baptist were taught by S. Paul that the purpose of this baptism was to be preliminary to the acceptance of Christ, and as a result of the apostle's teaching they received

Christian Baptism by being 'baptized into the Name of the Lord Jesus.' 'It came to pass that, while Apollos was at Corinth, Paul having passed through the upper country came to Ephesus and found certain disciples: and he said unto them, Did ye receive the Holy Ghost when ye believed? And they said unto him, Nay, we did not so much as hear whether there is a Holy Ghost. And he said, Into what then were ye baptized? And they said, Into John's baptism. And Paul said, John baptized with the baptism of repentance, saying unto the people that they should believe on Him which should come after him, that is, on Jesus. And when they heard this, they were baptized into the Name of the Lord Jesus.' In various Epistles S. Paul addresses those to whom he writes as if he assumed, as a matter of course, that they all had been baptized, and does not appear to contemplate the presence of unbaptized persons in the Christian community. S. Peter speaks of Baptism in such a way as to imply that those who were being saved from destruction had received it. In the Epistle to the Hebrews the 'doctrine of baptisms' is mentioned as having an elementary place in the Christian Faith in common with 'repentance from dead works,' 'faith towards God,' the 'laying on of hands,' the 'resurrection of the dead,' and 'eternal judgment.' Thus, both in act and by teaching Baptism was represented as essential to Christian life.²

It is not recorded whether the first Baptisms were administered by the apostles themselves, or by other disciples, or partly by the apostles, partly by others. The inspired historian only says, 'They then that received his word were baptized: and there were added unto them in that day about three thousand souls.' S. Philip the Deacon apparently baptized in Samaria, since, though S. Luke in recording the history simply says, 'they were baptized, both men and women,' there is no indication of his having been accompanied on his journey by any other Christian; and that he was not accompanied by one of the apostles is made clear by the account of the subsequent visit to Samaria of S. Peter and S. John. S. Philip certainly baptized the Ethiopian eunuch. Ananias, a Christian disciple, baptized S. Paul. Cornelius and his company appear to have been baptized by 'brethren from Joppa.' No statement is made in the Acts of the Apostles as to who baptized Lydia, or the Corinthians, or the disciples at Ephesus. The Philippian gaoler and his household apparently were baptized either by S. Paul or by S. Silas. In his First Epistle to the Corinthians, S. Paul lays some emphasis on the fact that, though in some cases he had baptized, it had not been his ordinary custom himself to do so.³ It is a reasonable inference from these facts that Baptism was administered in the apostolic period by the apostles themselves, by the deacons, and by Christian laymen.

In most cases recorded in the Acts it is stated that those who were to receive Baptism 'believed,' and it is evident that the belief referred to included the acceptance of our Lord. In the case of the Ethiopian eunuch a very early reading, apparently not part of the original text of the Acts, represents that the confession, 'I believe that Jesus Christ is the Son of God,' preceded Baptism. It is probable that this reading gives substantially the act of belief required before the administration of the earliest Baptisms, which thus corresponded to the confession of belief made by S. Peter on behalf of the apostles during our Lord's ministry.⁴

It is nowhere expressly mentioned in the New Testament that infants were baptized in the days of the apostles. S. Peter's words on the day of Pentecost declaring that 'the promise' of the gifts of Baptism 'is to you' 'and to your children, and to all that are afar off, even as many as the Lord our God shall call unto Him,' might conceivably suggest such a possibility. It has with much reason been thought likely that there were infants in the households of which it is said that they received Baptism; and these Baptisms of households were probably recorded as representative instances of what was customary in the earliest days of the Church. The analogy of circumcision and the custom of children being made proselytes together with their parents would naturally lead to any infants which formed part of a household being baptized. S. Paul's way of addressing children and speaking of their duties and of those of their parents towards them evidently implies that they were reckoned as part of the Christian body to which Baptism gave admission; and his description of children as holy would not be in accordance with his usual phraseology unless it was the custom that they should be baptized. He refers to the passage of the Red Sea as a type of Baptism, and says that all who crossed the Sea were included in this type; and the Israelites who came out from Egypt included many children. It would probably be realised in the first days of the Church, as it has been since, that if infants, without act of their own, inherit loss from the sin of Adam, they are capable also, without act of their own, of receiving grace. The sanctification of the prophet Jeremiah before his birth, and the gift of the Holy Spirit to S. John the Baptist even from his mother's womb, would naturally be held to support this belief. And it could hardly fail to be felt that our Lord's action in blessing little children, which would be robbed of a great part of its meaning if they could not unconsciously receive spiritual gifts, supplied a powerful reason for admitting them to Baptism.[5]

In the cases of the Ethiopian eunuch and of Cornelius and his company water is specified as the matter with which Baptism was administered. 'As they went on their way, they came to a certain water; and the eunuch saith, Behold, here is water: what doth hinder me to be baptized? And he commanded the chariot to stand still: and they both went down into the water, both Philip and the eunuch; and he baptized him.' 'Then answered Peter, Can any man forbid the water, that these should not be baptized?' Obviously, it is throughout the New Testament assumed that water was a necessary part of Baptism. The language employed by S. Paul and in the Epistle to the Hebrews implies its use. Thus, writing to the Ephesians, S. Paul describes the Church as being sanctified through being cleansed 'by the washing of water.' The writer of the Epistle to the Hebrews speaks of Christians having their 'hearts sprinkled from an evil conscience, and' their 'body washed with pure water.'

The history of the Baptism of the Ethiopian eunuch may imply that in this case the person baptized was immersed in the water. Such a custom would give special significance to passages about Baptism in the writings of S. Paul in which he compares it to the descent of our Lord into the earth in His burial and the being raised from the dead in His resurrection.

There is also evidence that immersion, however usual, was not universal or held to be necessary. While the Greek word translated 'baptize' naturally suggests the idea of dipping, there are indications both in the use of it elsewhere and in the records of Baptisms that this was not its only sense. When S. Luke, in saying that the Pharisee marvelled that our Lord 'had not first washed before dinner,' used this word, he plainly did so in a sense other than that of immersion. Three thousand persons were baptized on one day in Jerusalem. The Baptisms at Cæsarea and Philippi were administered apparently in the houses, or close to the houses, of Cornelius and the gaoler, and under circumstances which make immersion improbable.[6] A comparison of the different passages thus appears to indicate that if immersion was usual, it was not the invariable practice.

In S. Peter's words to the first converts Christian Baptism is described as being 'in' or 'upon' 'the Name of Jesus Christ.' Those to whom S. Philip preached in Samaria are said to have been 'baptized into the Name of the Lord Jesus.' S. Peter's command was that Cornelius and those with him should be 'baptized in the Name of the Lord' or 'of Jesus Christ.' The disciples at Ephesus were 'baptized into the Name of the Lord Jesus.' This phraseology has led some writers to suppose that the actual words used in the time of the apostles were 'into the Name of Jesus.' This opinion has little probability. Our Lord's command to baptize 'into the Name of the Father and of the Son and of the Holy Ghost' was very clear. The phrase 'into the Name of Jesus' may very well mean that the baptized were enrolled among the servants of Jesus. This interpretation receives some support from passages in the early book entitled *The Teaching of the Twelve Apostles*. This book, using a somewhat similar phrase to those in the Acts, says that Christians were baptized 'into the Name of the Lord,' apparently denoting by this expression the Name of the Holy Trinity, while in describing the administration of Baptism it gives the words used as being 'Into the Name of the Father and of the Son and of the Holy Ghost.' There is nothing in the Epistles which supplies evidence on this point.[7]

There are several passages in the New Testament in which reference is made to the anointing and sealing of Christians. It has sometimes been thought that these passages imply that those who were baptized in the days of the apostles were anointed with oil and signed with the sign of the cross. An examination of the use of the words 'anoint' or 'anointing' and 'seal' in the New Testament does not support this view; and it is probable that in these, as in other details of ceremonial, the early Church was rather putting into action principles of apostolic teaching than performing acts which the apostles had performed.[8]

To sum up, then, the evidence which the New Testament supplies, there is no doubt that in the days of the apostles Baptism was the means of entrance into the Christian Church for Jews and Jewish proselytes and Gentiles alike, and was held to be necessary for those who had received the baptism of S. John the Baptist; that the persons who administered Baptism included a deacon and those who appear to have been Christian laymen; that in the case of adults some profession of belief was required from those who were to be baptized; and that in the administration of the Sacrament water was used. It affords a high probability that children as well as adults were baptized; that the words employed were, 'Into the Name of the Father and of the Son and of the Holy Ghost'; and that immersion, if sometimes practised, was not universal. The fuller consideration of the various questions which these facts suggest must be left until they can be viewed in the light of the history and teaching and practice of the Christian Church.[9]

CHAPTER III

THE SCRIPTURAL DOCTRINE OF HOLY BAPTISM

Holy Baptism is described in the New Testament as the means of a new and spiritual birth. In His discourse with Nicodemus our Lord declared that those only could 'see' or 'enter into' the kingdom of God' who should be 'begotten anew,' or, as He Himself explained this phrase, 'begotten of water and the Spirit.' A common-sense view of this passage, taken in connection with the subsequent command to baptize, is that in these words He was referring to Christian Baptism. That this is the true explanation of them may be held to be fully proved by the fact that for fifteen centuries they were uniformly interpreted in this sense by Christian teachers, and that no other interpretation of them earlier than the writings of Calvin has been found. As they thus refer to Baptism the doctrine that to be baptized is to be 'begotten anew' forms part of the teaching of our Lord.[1]

A new birth in Baptism is implied also in the passage in which S. Paul speaks of the 'washing of regeneration.' The word 'washing' would almost certainly recall Baptism to the mind of any to whom this rite was a familiar ceremony; and the natural interpretation of the passage is that the reference is to Baptism. Here again the commonsense view of the words is borne out by the historical treatment of them. They are held to refer to Baptism alike in the treatises of the Fathers and in the services of the Church. Any other explanation earlier than the sixteenth century has been sought for in vain. It may then be concluded that S. Paul here refers to Baptism and describes it as the means of regeneration.[2]

It is in harmony with this description of Baptism as a new birth that to be begotten or born is sometimes used in Holy Scripture as a phrase which denotes to be made a Christian; and the truth which is thus referred to gives a reasonable aspect to the fact that Baptism is regarded as the means of entrance into the Christian Church.[3]

Being thus begotten anew in Holy Baptism, Christians are made to be the sons of God. The Scriptural use of the word 'Name' in connection with God as denoting His attributes and Being as well as His revelation, and the natural sense of the word 'into,' concur in indicating that to be baptized 'into the Name of the Father and of the Son and of the Holy Ghost' conveys a close relation to Almighty God.[4] The teaching of S. Paul throws fuller light on the words of our Lord. He refers to the Baptism of the Galatians as supplying the proof that they are sons of God. 'Ye are all sons of God, through faith, in Christ Jesus. For as many of you as were baptized into Christ did put on Christ.' He speaks of the Romans having received the 'Spirit of adoption whereby we cry, Abba, Father' at some definite past moment, evidently the time when they were made Christians.[5] These distinct statements, no less than the habitual interpretation of the early Church, warrant us in believing that where elsewhere in the New Testament Christians are spoken of as children of God or as having been begotten of God, they are regarded as having this relation by virtue of their Baptism.[6]

Baptism, again, is the means of being made sons of God because by it Christians are united to Christ and become members of Him. S. Paul, in the passage just quoted, tells the Galatians that when they were baptized into Christ they put on Christ. Writing to the Corinthians, he expressly connects the truth that Christians are members of the body of Christ with the fact that they have been baptized. 'As the body is one, and hath many members, and all the members of the body, being many, are one body; so also is Christ. For in one Spirit were we all baptized into one body, whether Jews or Gentiles, whether bond or free.' His strong assertion in the Epistle to the Ephesians that Christians are members of the body of Christ immediately follows a reference to the cleansing and sanctifying of the Church by the washing of water. 'Christ,' he says, 'loved the Church and gave Himself up for it; that He might sanctify it, having cleansed it by the washing of water with the word, that He might present it to Himself a glorious Church, not having spot or wrinkle or any such thing; but that it should be holy and without blemish. . . . We are members of His body, of His flesh, and of His bones.' The intimate character of this union with Christ is further shown by the description of Baptism as the means whereby Christians are partakers of the death and burial and resurrection of their Lord. 'All we who were baptized into Christ Jesus were baptized into His death. We were buried therefore with Him through Baptism into death, that like as Christ was raised from the dead through the glory of the Father, so we also might walk in newness of life.'[7]

By means of Baptism, also, the gift of the Holy Spirit is received. The agency of the Spirit is a mark of the Baptism of Christ, as distinguished from that of S. John the Baptist. 'I,' said S. John, 'baptized you with water, but He shall baptize you with the Holy Ghost.' The Spirit is described as given as well as acting. S. Peter promised that those who should be baptized should 'receive the gift of the Holy Ghost.' Ananias told S. Paul, with evident allusion to his coming Baptism, that he was to be 'filled with the Holy Ghost.' In the Epistle to S. Titus S. Paul connects the 'renewing of the Holy Ghost' with the 'washing of regeneration.' The whole Church is indeed the habitation of the Holy Ghost, since the whole Church is the mystical Body of Christ and the gift of Pentecost is an abiding possession. It is no less true that the soul of each baptized person is a temple in which He dwells. Individual Christians are members of Christ's mystical Body, and are spoken of by S. Paul as the shrines of God. Thus, there is reason to believe that it is the moment of Baptism which is referred to when it is said that Christians were 'made to drink of one Spirit,' or that 'God sent forth the Spirit of His Son into' their 'hearts,' or that God 'gave' the Spirit, or 'made' Him 'to dwell' in Christians.[8]

These specific effects of Baptism carry with them the gift of salvation. It would indeed be inconceivable that God would bestow on the soul so great gifts and should not purpose that they should be the means of obtaining salvation. A new birth through grace, sonship to God, union with Christ, the reception of the Holy Spirit, could have as their appointed result nothing less than the saving of the soul of him on whom so great privileges should be conferred. What may thus be seen to be in accordance with reason is found to be expressly asserted in the New Testament. Our Lord declared that he who believed and was baptized should be saved. Those who by means of Baptism were admitted into the Christian Church were described by S. Luke in the Acts of the Apostles as being in the way of salvation. 'They then that received his word were baptized: and there were added unto them in that day about three thousand souls.' 'The Lord added to them day by day those that were being saved.' The inquiry of the Philippian gaoler what he must do that he might be saved led to his being baptized. S. Peter speaks of regeneration as leading to an 'inheritance incorruptible and undefiled and that fadeth not away, reserved in heaven,' and asserts that 'Baptism now saves.' S. Paul associates with Baptism the outpouring of the Holy Spirit upon Christians, that 'being justified by the grace' of

God they ' may be made heirs according to the hope of eternal life.'

Baptism, again, is the means whereby the soul of man obtains forgiveness of sins from the mercy of Almighty God. The general teaching of the Bible in itself implies that since Baptism affords the entrance into the way of salvation all past sin must be forgiven to those who receive it. That this is one of its effects is more directly taught in S. Paul's account of the words of Ananias to him at the time of his Baptism, ' Arise and be baptized, and wash away thy sins.' [9]

To understand the teaching of the New Testament on the subject of Baptism, it is necessary to consider other Scriptural truths. It was characteristic of the nature of man that by his creation he possessed the image of God. He was granted also supernatural gifts by virtue of which he was endowed with moral likeness to God. By the sin of Adam he lost the moral likeness which he had thus received, but still retained the image of God in which he had been created. Subsequent sin plunged him more deeply in alienation from God. As time went on his state grew worse and worse, as natural efforts failed and the revelation and law given to the Jews tended rather to emphasize the inability of man to serve God in his own strength than to provide a remedy. When the disease of sin seemed to men to be incurable, the Son of God became man. The purposes of the Incarnation included the forgiveness of sins, the restoration of man to the moral likeness of God which he had lost, and the eventual gift to each individual of perfected holiness. Great as were the sin and degradation of man, he was yet capable of receiving from God these great benefits because he had retained, in however distorted and stained a condition, the divine image which was his by creation and distinguished him from the beasts. From the time of the Fall to the time of the Incarnation the divine treatment of man is always that of one for whom, though as yet unredeemed, redemption and holiness are by the gift of God possible. The histories contained in the Old Testament, the utterances of the psalmists, and the anticipations of the prophets are all filled with the spirit of the hope which is based upon the beliefs that God is willing to help man, and that man is capable of being helped.

The making of an atonement for sin is everywhere in Holy Scripture ascribed to the death of our Lord Jesus Christ. The spotless holiness of His Sacred Manhood made the offering of His human life one which the righteous Father could accept. His complete possession of human nature, and the fact that His Humanity and His Godhead were united in His one Divine Person enabled His offering to be truly representative of all mankind. His true Deity gave infinite efficacy to all that He did as Man. In the accurate language of the English Order of Holy Communion, He 'made' 'upon the cross' 'a full, perfect, and sufficient sacrifice, oblation, and satisfaction, for the sins of the whole world.' Not only did He accomplish by His death the forgiveness of sins. As S. Paul says, 'He was delivered up' to death 'for the sake of our transgressions, and He was raised for the sake of our justification.'[10] When raised from the dead His Manhood was enriched with new powers. His resurrection was no mere recovery of the life which had been surrendered. His body as it rose from the dead was the body which He had taken from the flesh of the Blessed Virgin. But it was now in a spiritual condition, endowed with supernatural gifts. These new and rich powers were not for Himself alone. The new life which was His was a life which not only transcended natural laws, but also was capable of being spiritually communicated to others. As the sin of Adam was a source of death to the whole human race, so Christ became a source of life. Each soul by the mere possession of its natural life is maimed by the touch of the spiritual death which had its source in the sin of Adam. Each Christian in receiving Baptism is brought into union with the life which is in Christ. In His Incarnation He took the nature of the race of mankind; His resurrection endowed His human body with spiritual capacities; by means of Baptism He unites each baptized person to Himself; and in union with Him alone can man truly live. Thus, the gift of the new birth is the gift of the true life which man needs. 'Where sin abounded, grace did abound more exceedingly, that as sin reigned in death, even so might grace reign through righteousness unto eternal life through Jesus Christ our Lord. What shall we say then? Shall we continue in sin that grace may abound? God forbid. We who died to sin, how shall we any longer live therein? Or are ye ignorant that all we who were baptized into Christ Jesus were baptized into His death? We were buried therefore with Him through Baptism into death, that like as Christ was raised from the dead through the glory of the Father, so we also might walk in newness of life. For if we have become united with Him by the likeness of His death, we shall be also by the likeness of His resurrection, knowing this, that our old man was crucified with Him, that the body of sin might be done away, that so we should no longer be in bondage to sin; for he that hath died is justified from sin. But if we died with Christ, we believe that we shall also live with Him; knowing that Christ being raised from the dead dieth no more; death no more hath dominion over Him. For the death that He died, He died unto sin once; but the life that He liveth, He liveth unto God. Even so reckon ye also yourselves to be dead unto sin, but alive unto God in Christ Jesus.'[11]

Regeneration is one thing; conversion is another. S. Paul was converted when he spoke the words, 'What shall I do, Lord?' He was regenerated when, three days later, he was baptized. The Philippian gaoler was converted when he asked what he must do that he might be saved. He was regenerated when, a little afterwards, he received Baptism.[12] Conversion is the act whereby, in response to and by the power of divine grace, the soul turns to God in the desire to accept and do His will. Regeneration is the gift which God bestows on the soul by producing in its nature such a change as imparts to it the forgiveness of original sin and makes it to be accepted by God instead of under His wrath. To have kept clear a distinction which the facts and teaching contained in the New Testament undoubtedly express might have saved many from confusions of thought which have led to complete misunderstanding of the doctrine of Holy Baptism.

Regeneration, further, does not necessarily imply perseverance in goodness or ultimate salvation. Simon of Samaria—if, indeed, in his case, bad faith had not at the first deprived him of benefits which, in ordinary cases, Baptism conveyed—could, after Baptism, so far fall from grace as to merit S. Peter's rebuke, 'Thy heart is not right before God. Repent therefore of this thy wickedness, and pray the Lord, if perhaps the thought of thy heart shall be forgiven thee. For I see that thou art in the gall of bitterness, and in the bond of iniquity.' S. Paul repeatedly addressed those who were evidently baptized in terms which implied that eternal life might be forfeited by them. 'Know ye not that ye are a temple of God, and that the Spirit of God dwelleth in you? If any man destroyeth the temple of God, him shall God destroy; for the temple of God is holy, which temple ye are.' 'I verily, being absent in body but present in spirit, have already, as though I were present, judged him that hath so wrought this thing, in the Name of our Lord Jesus, ye being gathered together, and my spirit, with the power of our Lord Jesus, to deliver such a one unto Satan for the destruction of the flesh, that the spirit may be saved in the day of the Lord Jesus.' 'If ye receive circumcision, Christ will profit you nothing.' 'Ye are severed from Christ, ye who would be justified by the law: ye are fallen away from grace.' 'The works of the flesh are manifest . . . of the which I forewarn you, even as I did forewarn you, that they which practise such things shall not inherit the kingdom of God.' He contemplated the abstract possibility that he himself might be lost. 'I therefore so run, as not uncertainly; so fight I, as not beating the air: but I buffet my body, and bring it into bondage: lest by any means, after that I have preached to others, I myself should be rejected.' He spoke of the possession of baptismal privileges as a reason for real and energetic struggle to do what is right. 'But ye were washed, but ye were sanctified, but ye were justified in the Name of the Lord Jesus Christ, and in the Spirit of our God. . . . Know ye not that your bodies are members of Christ? Shall I then take away the members of Christ, and make them members of a harlot? God forbid. . . . Know ye not that your body is a temple of the Holy Ghost which is in you, which ye have from God? and ye are not your own, for ye were bought with a price: glorify God therefore in your body.'[13] The fact of the reception of grace is altogether distinct from any question of continuance in grace.

Here, again, confusions of thought have been numerous and harmful. It has been supposed by many that, if regeneration is bestowed in Baptism, there cannot subsequently be any departure from holiness or the grace of God. Such an idea has caused thoughtful persons to fail to grasp the Scriptural teaching that the baptized are regenerate, because they are convinced that many of the baptized commit sins of the most grievous kind. This fact was certainly not unknown to or ignored by the writers of the New Testament; but they viewed it in its proper light as not contradictory of but parallel to the truth that Baptism is the means of regeneration. Indeed, a moment's consideration should be sufficient to show any one that a person may receive a gift and may yet fail to answer to the responsibilities or use the powers which the gift confers. One who has been freed from original sin may yet commit actual sin; a nature which has been made holy may yet by sin become unholy; the child of God may, by the wrong use of the divinely given power of free-will, act as though he were still the child of wrath. The facts of life are to be explained, not by the rejection of the Scriptural doctrine of regeneration in Baptism, but by viewing it in connection with other truths which are no less Scriptural.

Christian Baptism, then, according to the teaching of Holy Scripture, by making the baptized person a member of Christ and a child of God and imparting to him the gift of the Holy Spirit, causes him to partake of the merits of Christ's life and death and the power of His resurrection. It thereby enables him to live a Christian life and attain to eternal glory. Yet he may subsequently depart from grace and fall into sin by the act of his will choosing evil, and, if evil be finally chosen, he may be involved in eternal sin,[14] and consequently in eternal loss. Baptism confers a position of high privilege and great responsibility. The free-will of the baptized person has to determine to what use this position is to be put. Holy Baptism affords the beginning of the possibility of the highest holiness; it supplies also the measure of the terrible character of sins committed by the baptized.

CHAPTER IV

THE TEACHING OF THE CHURCH ON THE DOCTRINE OF HOLY BAPTISM

The source of the teaching of the Church is to be found in Holy Scripture, the doctrine of which, on the subject of Holy Baptism, has been considered in the last chapter. The voice of the Church has been expressed also in the decisions of Councils universally accepted throughout the whole Church, in the common teaching of representative theologians, and in practices of worship universally adopted by the orthodox Christian body.

The original Creed of the Council of Nicæa ended with the words 'the Holy Ghost.' Among the additions made to this Creed, which, whether first formally adopted at the Council of Constantinople in 381 A.D. or at the Council of Chalcedon in 451 A.D., have been accepted by the Universal Church, are the words, 'One Baptism for the remission of sins'; and these words are contained in the Creed as it is used at the present time in the Liturgies of the East, in the Roman Mass, and in the Order of Holy Communion in the English Book of Common Prayer. If it is asked whether this phrase means that in Baptism the sins of the baptized person are forgiven, or that Christian Baptism, like the baptism of S. John the Baptist, is merely a preparatory rite leading on towards some subsequent remission of sins, the answer must be sought in the teaching about Baptism of those whose beliefs the Creed summarised and those who in turn regarded the Creed as truth.

The teaching of the Fathers on the subject of Holy Baptism is voluminous and rich. Yet the fulness of its meaning does no more than express and explain the doctrine clearly stated or necessarily implied in the New Testament. With great strength and unanimity it describes Baptism as the means of regeneration, of adoption to be the sons of God, of union with Christ, of partaking of the Holy Ghost, of receiving forgiveness of sins and eternal life.

From the earliest times all orthodox writers regarded Baptism as the means of entrance into the Church of Christ. To reject Baptism was a mark of an heretical sect.[1] But it was not looked upon merely as thus admitting into the visible society of Christians, or as a mark by which a Christian might be distinguished from one who was not a Christian. The high view taken of it is shown by words in which it was described. It was the 'seal' which was believed to correspond spiritually to the bodily mark made by circumcision, and to exist in the soul no less really than circumcision existed in the bodies of those who had been circumcised. It was held to have been impressed upon the soul by Christ Himself through the operation of God the Holy Ghost. It was regarded as denoting the soldiers of the King and the servants of the Lord. It was described as the 'illumination' which was not only accompanied by instruction but also conveyed light. It was called the 'key of the kingdom of heaven,' the 'water of life,' the 'garment of immortality,' the 'shining robe,' the 'chariot to God.'[2] If some of these expressions, taken separately and isolated from their context, might be thought to mean no more than that Baptism showed the baptized person to have been admitted into the external communion of the Church on earth, such an explanation of them may be seen to be impossible when they are taken in connection with one another and viewed in their context.

The sense of the value of Baptism may be seen also in the tendency of the Fathers to recognise signs of it everywhere. When the 'waters of comfort' of the Twenty-third Psalm are interpreted of it; or the 'blessedness of him to whom the Lord imputeth no sin' of the Thirty-second Psalm is explained of its effects; or almost any mention of water in Holy Scripture is taken to be a figure of this Sacrament, it may be possible to hold different opinions as to the soundness of this exegesis; there can be no doubt that those who habitually accepted and used it were strongly impressed with the importance of that which they supposed to be so continually alluded to in the Bible.[3]

The express teaching of the Fathers bears out what might thus be inferred. Hermas describes Baptism as bringing out into life those who were involved in death; and adds that those who are baptized go down into the water 'in a state of death,' and come up 'in a state of life.' The *Epistle of Barnabas* speaks similarly of going down 'full of sins and pollution,' and coming up 'bearing fruit.' S. Justin Martyr says that those who are baptized are begotten anew and obtain forgiveness of sins. S. Irenæus teaches that our Lord gave to His disciples the 'power of regeneration' when He commanded them to baptize, and he speaks of 'our bodies' receiving that 'union' with Christ 'which is unto incorruption by means of the washing,' and 'our souls' receiving it 'by means of the Spirit.' Tertullian begins his book

On Baptism by describing it as the 'happy Sacrament by being washed in which we are set free from the offences of our former blindness unto eternal life.' In his treatise *On the Resurrection of the Flesh* he connects the washing of the flesh and the deliverance of the soul from the stains of sin. To put together some only of the phrases he uses about it: in the water we are born; by the font death is washed away; in Baptism the spirit is healed, eternal life is restored, both the guilt and the penalty of sin are destroyed, and man is restored to his likeness to God by the reception of the Spirit. The *Canons of Hippolytus* describe Baptism as the means whereby God bestows the remission of sins, as regeneration, and as the rite in which the Holy Spirit perfumes the body of the Christian and wholly cleanses it. Clement of Alexandria exclaims, 'Being baptized, we are enlightened; being enlightened, we are adopted as sons; being adopted, we are made complete; being made complete, we are rendered immortal. "I," says the Scripture, "have said, Ye are gods and ye are all sons of the Most High." But this work bears various names—the gift of grace, and enlightenment, and completion, and washing; the washing, by means of which we are cleansed from the filth of our sins; the gift of grace, by which the penalties due to our sins are remitted;

enlightenment, by means of which that holy light which is our salvation is set before our eyes, that is, by means of which our eyes are made keen to behold that which is divine; by completion we understand the lack of nothing, for what is still wanting to one who knows God?' Origen describes Baptism as the 'washing of regeneration' and the 'beginning and source of divine gifts.' The writings of S. Cyprian are full of testimonies to his belief: he regards Baptism as the 'beginning of all faith and the saving entrance into the hope of eternal life'; it is the means of receiving the 'remission of sins' and becoming a 'temple of God'; it conveys 'regeneration' and adoption to be the 'sons of God'; it bestows salvation; by means of it 'the Holy Spirit is received'; in his description of the effects of his own Baptism he tells how 'by the help of the life-giving wave the stain of former time was washed away.' 'For me,' he says, writing to his friend Donatus shortly after his Baptism, 'while I yet lay in darkness and bewildering night, and was tossed to and fro on the billows of this troublesome world, ignorant of my true life, an outcast from truth and light, I used to think that second birth, which divine mercy promised for my salvation, a hard saying according to the life I then led: as if a man could be so quickened to a new life in the bath of healing water as to put off his natural self, and keep his former tabernacle, yet be changed in heart and soul! How is it possible, said I, for so great a change to be accomplished, so that both the obstinate defilement of our natural substance and old and engrained habits should be suddenly and rapidly put off, evils whose roots are deeply seated within? When does he learn frugality, to whom fine feasts and rich banquets have become a habit? or he who in gay sumptuous clothes glitters with gold and purple, when does he reduce himself to ordinary and simple raiment? Another, whose bent is among public distinctions and honours, cannot bear to become a private and unnoticed man; while one who is surrounded by a phalanx of dependents, and accompanied by the overflowing attendance of an obsequious host, thinks it punishment to be alone. The temptation still unrelaxed, need is it that, as before, wine should entice, pride inflate, anger inflame, covetousness disquiet, cruelty stimulate, ambition delight, and lust lead headlong. Such were my frequent musings; for whereas I was encumbered with the many sins of my past life, which it seemed impossible to get rid of, so I had used myself to give way to my clinging infirmities, and, from despair of better things, to humour the evils of my heart, as slaves born in my house, and my proper offspring. But after that by the help of the life-giving wave the stain of former time was washed away, and the light which comes from heaven was poured into my cleansed and hallowed breast, after that I drank in the Heavenly Spirit and was created into a new man by a second birth—then marvellously what before was doubtful became plain to me, what was hidden was revealed, what was dark began to shine, what was before difficult now had a way and means, what had seemed impossible now could be achieved, what was in me of the guilty flesh now confessed that it was earthly, what was quickened in me by the Holy Ghost now had a growth according to God. Thou knowest well, thou canst recollect as well as I, what was then taken from me, and what was given by that death of sin, that quickening power of holiness. . . . From God, I say, from God is all we can be; from Him we live, from Him we grow, and by that strength which is from Him accepted and ingathered, we learn beforehand, even in this present state, the foretokens of what is yet to be.'

According to S. Hilary of Poitiers, those who are baptized are 're-born'; they 'receive the Holy Spirit'; they feel within them 'some beginnings of the Holy Spirit.' S. Athanasius speaks of those who are 'being begotten again by means of the laver of regeneration.' S. Cyril of Jerusalem describes Baptism as 'ransom' and 'remission' and 'regeneration'; he tells his catechumens that in Baptism 'the Holy Spirit is about to seal' their 'souls,' and that they are to 'accept salvation by the operation of the Holy Spirit'; he says that those who have been baptized have 'put on Christ,' have 'become conformed to the Son of God,' have 'become partakers of Christ,' and that the 'water of salvation' was to them 'both a grave and a mother.' S. Basil declares that 'by means of the washing of regeneration and renewing of the Holy Ghost we are adopted as sons of God.' S. Gregory of Nazianzus asserts that 'sin is buried' 'in the water,' and that Baptism is the 'acquiring of the Spirit.' S. Gregory of Nyssa teaches that the 'mystery of regeneration is accomplished' by means of 'prayer to God and the invocation of heavenly grace and water and faith.' S. Ambrose compares the operation of the Holy Spirit in the conception of our Lord and His action in Baptism in which 'He accomplishes the reality of regeneration.' S. Chrysostom, to quote one sentence as representative of many, affirms that 'we have the chief of good things in Baptism; we received remission of sins, sanctification, participation of the

Spirit, adoption, eternal life.' S. Cyril of Alexandria regards the water as receiving 'a kind of divine inexpressible power, so as to hallow those upon whom it may come,' and describes 'him who has been baptized' as 'partaker of the divine nature,' 'having the Holy Spirit within him,' 'already bearing the title of a temple of God.' S. Ephraim the Syrian refers to a man 'who has not received Baptism' as 'like unto a house made ready for a king in which the king has never dwelt.' To the mind of S. Augustine, who had occasion repeatedly to refer to the effects of Baptism, the Holy Spirit accomplished by means of it the remission of sins; it was itself regeneration; and in it God bestowed the Holy Spirit. S. Jerome spoke of it as purifying the soul and making the soul to be 'a shrine of the Holy Trinity.' It was to S. Leo the 'sacrament of regeneration'; by means of it, he says, a Christian is made to be 'a temple of the Holy Spirit' as well as a 'member' of the 'Body' of 'Christ'; 'the font of Baptism makes them innocent, and the election of adoption confirms them as heirs'; the 'baptismal child-bearing' produces 'an innumerable multitude of children of God'; 'the body of the regenerate becomes the flesh of the Crucified.'[4]

Witness is thus borne to the reality of the baptismal gifts by the unvarying voice of the Fathers of

East and West. Their testimony cannot fairly be set aside by a supposition that they were speaking metaphorically, or because in some instances their language is of a rhetorical character. There is no indication that, in their statements about Baptism, they were making use of metaphor. If such assertions as that 'in Baptism we received remission of sins,' or that Baptism is 'the saving entrance into the hope of eternal life' are metaphorical, it is difficult to see what the metaphor represents. Some of the patristic utterances on the subject of Baptism are indeed expressed in glowing rhetoric. This fact illustrates the strength of the conviction of the value of this Sacrament by which the Fathers were animated. That it affords no justification for minimising the meaning of what they say is shown by the presence of like teaching in calmly given instruction, and by the agreement of Fathers of widely differing temperaments and ways of speech. If, indeed, in some passages, for a reason to be explained in a later chapter, it is not clear whether particular details refer to Baptism or to Confirmation, it is still abundantly plain that the teaching about Baptism which has been described as contained in the New Testament is echoed by the Fathers.

Not less significant was the practice of the early Church. There was a long course of careful preparation for Baptism; the ceremonial of the administration of it was of an elaborate character; there was a strong sense of the heinous guilt of the sins of baptized persons; and the difference between the baptized and the unbaptized was emphatically marked. All this served to indicate the strength of the Church's belief that by means of Baptism an objective gift of the highest value was bestowed upon the soul. And the language used in connection with the rite always represented it as a passage from death unto life.

The Church of the Fathers clearly distinguished the gift of divine grace in Holy Baptism from the acts of the human will. Their language may not always have the clear and exact and detailed precision which is characteristic of the later West and to a large extent the outcome of experience in controversies and the application of philosophical and logical methods to the subjects with regard to which it is used; but there is no more trace in their writings of any confusion between regeneration and conversion or between regeneration and ultimate perseverance than in Holy Scripture itself.

S. Augustine was converted when he heard the child's voice which came to him as an omen from heaven and read in the words of S. Paul so clear a message for his own soul that 'the light of peace seemed to be shed upon' his 'heart, and every shadow of doubt melted away'; it was in Baptism that he sought and found the gift of regeneration. After he became a Christian he was careful in his teaching to distinguish between the regeneration of which Baptism is the Sacrament and the conversion which is the act of the will; he explains that in the case of those baptized as infants regeneration in the administration of the Sacrament goes first and conversion in the heart follows at a later time. The 'Sacrament of Baptism,' he adds, 'is one thing; the conversion of the heart is another; the salvation of man is completed by both.'[5]

Similarly, the grace conferred in Baptism is nowhere regarded as in itself necessarily causing a good life or ensuring ultimate salvation. Both in theological teaching and in practical appeals the baptized are frequently spoken of and to as capable of falling, as needing to be warned, as having become sinful. The carefully organised and elaborate penitential system of the early Church was necessary because of the sins of the baptized; the painful and humiliating penances inflicted by it were gladly borne because in bearing them lay the hope of deliverance from eternal loss. It would have been altogether unmeaning if a baptized person could not sin, or could not fail to obtain ultimate salvation. There was need of effort, of submission to discipline, of divine grace, if the standard described in the *Apostolical Constitutions* was to be maintained: 'Let him who is baptized be estranged from all impiety, free from sin, the friend of God, the enemy of the devil, the heir of God the Father, the co-heir with His Son, one who has renounced Satan and his evil spirits and his deceits, holy, pure, pious, loving God, the son of God, praying as a son to the Father.'

In two splendid passages, to the teaching of which there are many parallels in his writings and in those of the other Fathers, S. Leo describes the obligations of the baptized: 'Let us put off the old man with his deeds, and having obtained a share in Christ's birth, let us renounce the works of the flesh. Acknowledge, O Christian, thine own dignity, and, having been made partaker of the divine nature, do not by degenerate conduct return to thine old evil deeds. Bethink thee of what a Head and of what a Body thou art a member. Remember that thou hast been rescued from the power of darkness, and translated into the light and kingdom of God. By the sacrament of Baptism thou hast been made a temple of the Holy Ghost; do not by evil deeds drive away from thyself so great an inmate, and subject thyself again to the bondage of the devil. For thy ransom is the blood of

Christ; for He Who redeemed thee in mercy will judge thee in truth.' 'In order that we may hold fast immovably, dearly beloved, to this sacred fact' (that is, of the Incarnation and the resurrection), 'we must strive with a great effort both of mind and body, seeing that, while it is a very grievous offence to neglect the Paschal festival, it is still more dangerous to take our place in church assemblies without also having our part in the fellowship of our Lord's passion. For, since our Lord says, "He that taketh not up his cross and followeth Me not, is not worthy of Me," and the apostle, "If we suffer with Him, we shall also reign with Him," who does truly honour Christ as having suffered, died, and been raised, save he who suffers and dies and rises again with Him? And indeed in all the children of the Church these events have already been begun in the very mystery of regeneration, wherein the death of sin is the life of the new-born, and the three days' death of the Lord is imitated by trine immersion, so that, as if by the removal of a burial mound, those whom the bosom of the font receives in their old state are brought forth in a new condition by the baptismal wave. But nevertheless, that which has been celebrated in the Sacrament must be fulfilled in deed; and those who have been born of the Holy Spirit must not spend whatever remains to them of the bodily life of this world without taking up the cross. For although the strong and cruel tyrant has been despoiled of the vessels of his ancient plunder through the power of the cross of Christ, and the rule of the prince of this world has been cast out from the bodies of the redeemed, yet does the same malignant one persist in plotting even against the justified, and in many ways attacks those in whom he does not reign; so that, if he finds any souls negligent and careless, he again entangles them in more cruel snares, snatches them out of the paradise of the Church, and brings them into the fellowship of his own condemnation. Therefore, when any one feels that he is passing beyond the bounds fixed by Christian vigilance and that the direction of his desires is towards what may make him go astray from the straight path, let him have recourse to the cross of the Lord and nail to the wood of life the motions of a hurtful will: let him cry out in the prophet's words to the Lord, and say, "Pierce my flesh with nails from the fear of Thee, for I have been afraid of Thy judgments."' So also, to quote one brief saying of S. Augustine, 'Who does not know that if one who has been baptized in his infancy does not believe when he attains an age of reason and does not keep himself from unlawful lusts, what he received when he was young will profit him nothing?' Or as S. Cyprian says immediately after the passage already quoted from his treatise to Donatus *On the Grace of God*, 'Let only fear be a guard upon innocency, that the Lord, Who by the influence of His heavenly mercy has graciously shone into our hearts, may be detained by righteous obedience in the hostel of a mind which pleases Him, that the security imparted to us may not beget slothfulness, nor the former enemy steal upon us anew.'[6]

The truths of the high privileges and powers of the baptized, and of the need of the co-operation of human will with divine grace if the privileges and powers are to produce their due effect, were not obscured in the later years of the Church. In the mediæval period, especially in the West, a system of accurate terminology and the use of technical forms of expression were highly developed. The exactness of expression which was thus gained does not altogether compensate for the loss of the richness and glowing force of patristic language. But it was certainly the object of this clear-cut phraseology to maintain and defend the Scriptural and historical teaching that in the Sacrament of Holy Baptism are to be found the beginning of Christian life, the ground of Christian virtues, and the hope of eternal joy. 'By means of Baptism,' says S. Thomas Aquinas, 'all sin is taken away.' 'To every one who is baptized,' he says again, 'the passion of Christ is communicated for a remedy'; 'the passion of Christ is a complete satisfaction for all the sins of all men; and therefore he who is baptized is set free from the guilt of the whole penalty which is due to him for his sins'; 'it is the result of Baptism that the baptized are incorporated in Christ as His members'; 'from the Head, which is Christ, there flows into all His members the fulness of grace and virtue'; 'an effect of Baptism is the opening of the gate of the kingdom of heaven.'[7] The whole system of worship, of prayer, of the use of other rites, concurred with practical and moral teaching and exhortations in showing that the mediæval Church, like the Church of the Fathers and the writers of Holy Scripture, believed that this beginning needed to be developed by new gifts of divine grace and by the co-operating action of the human will.

The sixteenth century was a time of storm and conflict for the Christianity of the West. During this conflict some who became separated from the Church lost the true doctrine of Baptism, and some even who remained within her fold may have missed parts of it, yet nowhere was it abandoned or modified in the teaching of the Church herself. Confused theories, which retained assertions of Baptismal grace, were adopted by Luther.[8] Zwingli denied that Baptism was more than a sign.[9] The 'Confessions' of the 'Reformed' used some phrases of a more satisfactory kind as well as others which tended in a Zwinglian direction.[10] The opinions of Calvin, if not without inconsistencies somewhat resembling parts of the teaching of Luther, approximated closely to those of Zwingli.[11] The doctrine of Holy Scripture and the Fathers was carefully affirmed in the official declarations of the Church of Rome at the Council of Trent,[12] and, with even greater distinctness, in the Book of Common Prayer of the Church of England.

In spite of strong pressure from determined opponents of the truth, the Church in England, both in the sixteenth and in the seventeenth century, was careful to maintain the doctrine of Baptism which, as enshrined in Scripture and taught by the Universal Church, may rightly be called Catholic. It might well be anticipated that in the Orders for the Ministration of Baptism there would be a very full and clear indication of the mind of the Church in England on this subject. In them the Catholic teaching referred to is again and again affirmed or implied. This holy rite is regarded as the means of being 'regenerate and born anew,' of being 'washed' and 'sanctified' 'with the Holy Ghost,' 'delivered from' the 'wrath' of God, 'received into the ark of Christ's Church,' of receiving 'remission of' 'sins by spiritual regeneration,' of being given 'the blessing of eternal life,' and made 'partaker of' the 'everlasting kingdom' of 'our Saviour Christ,' of receiving the Holy Spirit, of being 'born again' and 'made an heir of everlasting salvation'; the priest is directed to pray that the water may be sanctified 'to the mystical washing away of sin,' and that those baptized may 'receive the fulness of' the 'grace' of God; after the Baptism it is declared that those who have been baptized are 'regenerate and grafted into the body of Christ's Church,' that they have been made 'regenerate' with the 'Holy Spirit,' received as the children of God 'by adoption,' incorporated into the 'holy Church,' and that they have 'by Baptism put on Christ.' Special emphasis is laid on the effects of Baptism in the words used at the reception of infants who have been privately baptized in which it is said, 'Seeing now' 'that this child is by Baptism regenerate and grafted into the body of Christ's Church.' In no place is there any indication that this language, or any part of it, is of an hypothetical character or is to be figuratively explained. And it may be noticed that when, at the Savoy Conference in the reign of Charles II., the Puritans objected to the teaching of the services that all baptized infants are regenerate the bishops asserted and defended the doctrine that 'Baptism is our spiritual regeneration' and proceeded to say that 'every child that is baptized' 'is regenerated by God's Holy Spirit.'[13]

The Catechism, again, drawn up for the instruction of children, may well be regarded as a dependable statement of the mind of the English Church, expressed in language intended to be understood in its literal and most obvious sense. Here the child is directed to say that in his Baptism he 'was made a member of Christ, the child of God, and an inheritor of the kingdom of heaven,' to describe the 'inward and spiritual grace' of Baptism as 'a death unto sin and a new birth unto righteousness,' and to add that 'being by nature born in sin and the children of wrath we are hereby' (*i.e.* by Baptism) 'made the children of grace.'

Both the general character and the nature and extent of the obligation of the Thirty-nine Articles of Religion differ greatly from those of the Baptismal Offices and of the Catechism. They were drawn up, not as a complete expression of the mind of the Church in England for all her children, but as a concordat intended to facilitate the comprehension of individuals rather than to exactly define truth. As such, they are accepted by the clergy as a condition of receiving office within her fold, and consequently as containing in their express and positive statements a minimum of doctrine which no bishop, priest, or deacon is allowed by the Church to deny in his public teaching. In them the Zwinglian view of Baptism is unmistakably rejected; and, if the language subsequently used partakes of the obscurity common in documents of the kind, it is at least altogether consistent with the fuller and clearer teaching contained in the Prayer Book. Baptism is described as one of the Sacraments which are 'not only badges or tokens of Christian men's profession, but rather' 'certain sure witnesses and effectual signs of grace and God's goodwill towards us, by the which He doth work invisibly in us, and doth not only quicken, but also strengthen and confirm our faith in Him,' which are 'effectual because of Christ's institution and promise'; it is declared to be 'not only a sign of profession and mark of difference whereby Christian men are discerned from others that be not christened but' 'also a sign of regeneration or new birth,' and 'an instrument' for the reception of high gifts from God.

Moreover, the Baptismal Offices and the Catechism exhibit in a marked degree the characteristic of the New Testament and the teaching of the Fathers by which the privileges which Christians receive in Baptism are regarded as the starting-point of their lives in the service of God. The priest is directed to say to those who are baptized as adults: 'As for you who have now by Baptism put on Christ, it is your part and duty also, being made the children of God and of the light, by faith in Jesus Christ, to walk answerably to your Christian calling, and as becometh the children of light'; and, in the case both of infants and of adults, the solemn words are used, 'remembering always that Baptism representeth' (or 'doth represent') 'unto us our profession, which is, to follow the example of our Saviour Christ, and to be made like unto Him; that, as He died and rose again for us, so should we, who are baptized, die from sin, and rise again unto righteousness; continually mortifying all our evil and corrupt affections, and daily proceeding in all virtue and godliness of living.' In the Catechism the child says, 'I heartily thank our heavenly Father, that He hath called me to this state of salvation' (*i.e.* the state of salvation conferred in Baptism), 'through Jesus Christ our Saviour. And I pray unto God to give me His grace, that I may continue in the same unto my life's end'; the duties of faith and obedience are explained at length; the catechist explains to the baptized child, 'Thou art not able to do these things of thyself, nor to walk in the commandments of God, and to serve Him, without His special grace; which thou must learn at all times to call for by diligent prayer'; the child rehearses that those baptized as infants, 'when they come to age,' 'are bound to perform' the 'promise' made in their name by 'their sureties'; and the duty of a continuous life of fulfilment of the will of God is implied in the final answer, that those 'who come to the Lord's Supper' are 'required' 'to examine themselves whether they repent them truly of their former sins, steadfastly purposing to lead a new life; have a lively faith in God's mercy through Christ, with a thankful remembrance of His death; and be in charity with all men.'

The laxity and rationalism of the eighteenth century did much to obscure the truth which the English Church had carefully guarded in the sixteenth and seventeenth centuries. In popular teaching little was heard of the true doctrine of Baptism, and belief in it among English Churchmen grew gradually less. The restoration of the doctrine by calling attention to the teaching of Holy Scripture, of the Fathers, and of the English formularies, was one of the great works of the Tractarian movement of the present century; and a characteristic part of the Tractarian teaching was the stress laid on the greatness both of the gifts conferred by God in Baptism and of the responsibilities of the baptized.

Eastern Christianity, with its different history, has maintained no less steadfastly than the West the reality of the grace conferred in the Sacrament of Baptism and its place in the Church's system as the beginning of Christian life. The Synod of Bethlehem, which contains the authorised teaching of the Greek Church, and has been accepted, with certain modifications which do not affect this subject, by the Russian Church, thus described the effects of Baptism :—' First, it is the remission of original sin, and of whatever sins he that is baptized hath committed. Secondly, it delivers him from the eternal penalty to which he is liable on account of original sin, or of any deadly sin he has himself committed. Thirdly, it gives immortality to the baptized persons, for it justifies them from their sins and makes them the temples of God.' *The Longer Catechism of the Russian Church* defines the 'virtue' of Baptism as consisting in the fact that in it 'man is mysteriously born to a spiritual life,' speaks of Baptism as 'spiritual birth,' and asserts that in it the baptized receive 'from God special help to do well.'[14]

The significance of the teaching of which representative illustrations have been given is of the most momentous kind. It would call for very great consideration even apart from a belief that the

Church of God is, in the language of S. Paul, the 'pillar and ground of the truth,' and that the promise of our Lord 'The gates of Hades shall not prevail against it' implies the Providential preservation of the Universal Church from such errors on matters of vital doctrine as would amount to a failure to hold fast that which has been committed to her charge. It is teaching not characteristic merely of some particular time, but found throughout nearly nineteen centuries. It is not confined to any particular place, but declared in the utterances of Christians of all parts of the East and of the West. It is not due to the influence of any special type of mind, for it is held by writers of most different lines of thought. It is as much part of the belief of mediæval schoolmen in the West as it is of Eastern Fathers in the early days of the Faith. It was no less jealously guarded by the Church in England in the sixteenth century than by the primitive or mediæval Church. It is found alike in authorised office-books and in the writings of representative theologians. At the present time it is the official doctrine of Eastern Christians, of Western Christians in communion with the See of Rome, and of Western Christians in the Church of England. Looked at merely as a human phenomenon, the unanimity of minds differing so greatly under circumstances of such different character would of necessity demand the most careful attention to the doctrine thus affirmed. For those who believe that the Holy Ghost teaches and guides the whole Church, it is impossible to doubt that the doctrine thus affirmed comes to us with the authority of God Himself.

In the Reformation, which extended through a great part of the sixteenth and seventeenth centuries, the Church in England made a twofold appeal. She appealed, in the first place, to the teaching contained in Holy Scripture. She appealed, in the second place, to the teaching of the Universal Church, especially as presented by the undivided Church before the division of East and West. To such an appeal on the subject of Baptism, the same response comes from the Bible and from the Church. Those who are baptized are regenerated with the new birth which makes them Christians. They are adopted to be the sons of God with the high Christian sonship which nature cannot give. They are united to the Sacred Manhood of the Son of God, and consequently are in mystical union with His Divine Person and with the Holy Trinity. They have received the Holy Ghost. Their sins have been forgiven. On them the gift of eternal life has been bestowed.

CHAPTER V

THE BAPTISMAL GIFT OF THE HOLY SPIRIT

It has been stated in the preceding chapters that the New Testament and the Fathers concur in teaching that in Baptism there is a gift of God the Holy Ghost to the souls of the baptized. In the Church of England in recent years there has been discussion as to the nature of this gift. It was formerly the almost universal belief of those English Churchpeople who held the doctrine of Baptismal regeneration that the gift in Baptism is that of the personal indwelling of the Holy Spirit in the soul of the baptized person. Of late years an opinion that the gift in Baptism is merely an operation of the Holy Spirit from without the soul, and that His personal indwelling is not received until those who have been baptized are also confirmed, has been brought into notice, and has been received with no little approval.

In considering this question, it may be well to observe at the outset that the Church in England is committed with some definiteness to the belief that the gift of the Holy Spirit in Baptism is of a very real kind, and has used language which it would be difficult to reconcile with a denial of the personal indwelling in those who have been baptized but have not yet been confirmed. To pass by expressions in the Baptismal Offices which only speak, with greater or less definiteness, of the operation of the Holy Ghost in Baptism, prayers are offered 'that all things belonging to the Spirit may live and grow in' the baptized, and that God will 'give' His 'Holy Spirit to this infant' (or 'these persons') 'that he' (or 'they') 'may be born again and be made an heir' (or 'heirs') 'of everlasting salvation'; and in the case of the Baptism of adults it is declared with great clearness, 'Doubt ye not, therefore, but earnestly believe, that He will favourably receive these present persons, truly repenting, and coming unto Him by faith; that He will grant them remission of their sins, and bestow upon them the Holy Ghost; that He will give them the blessing of eternal life, and make them partakers of His everlasting kingdom.' The suggestion of a well-known scholar that by the words 'that he may be born again' the preceding phrase, 'Give Thy Holy Spirit to this infant,' is so restricted as to mean simply an operation of the Holy Spirit from without the soul to regenerate it, and not the personal indwelling, is of too forced a character to be accepted; and even without considering the express assertions of English Churchmen contemporary with the official language of the Prayer Books of the reign of King Edward VI.,[1] or laying emphasis on the fact that the words quoted from the Office for the Baptism of adults, like the whole of that office, were added at the revision of 1662, it may be concluded that a reasonable interpretation of the English formularies leads to their being regarded as teaching that in Baptism the personal indwelling of the Holy Spirit is received by the soul of the baptized. 'Bestow upon them the Holy Ghost,' 'that all things belonging to the Spirit may live and grow in them,' are not phrases which can rightly be explained as meaning less than that at the reception of Baptism the Divine Person of God the Holy Ghost Himself enters into and abides in the human spirits of those persons to whom the rite is administered.

It must then be asked whether the Church in England, in thus connecting the personal indwelling of God the Holy Ghost with the reception of Baptism, has been faithful to the authorities to which she appeals, Holy Scripture and the undivided Church, or has gone beyond them in ascribing to

Baptism a gift which they restrict to Confirmation.

It may be well, before proceeding to the evidence supplied on this point by the New Testament and the writings of the Fathers, to mention several considerations of a theological character which cannot rightly be ignored.

In the first place, it is very difficult to grasp in thought any clear distinction between the operation of the Holy Spirit upon the human spirit from outside it and His personal dwelling within it. There are, of course, manifold differences in the divine methods and in the divine presence. These differences may well be thought to be greater rather than less than human language can adequately convey. The personal indwelling is certainly a far more precious gift than any degree of an operation of the Divine Spirit which falls short of indwelling. Still, when it is remembered that we are considering the action of the Holy Spirit upon the spiritual part of the nature of man, it must be acknowledged that there is no small danger of a passion for definition leading logical minds to an undue assertion of difference.

In the second place, there is a marked harmony between the doctrine that the personal indwelling of the Holy Spirit is received in Baptism and the facts recorded about our Lord Jesus Christ taken in connection with the revealed truth about Baptism itself. The life of our Blessed Lord presents the ideal of Christian life. Part of the divine purpose of the Incarnation was that human life should be exhibited in its highest perfection. It is involved in this truth that there is a real analogy between the life of Christ and that of the Christian. In detail there is such an analogy between our Lord's Baptism and the Christian's Confirmation, and between our Lord's ascension and the Christian's attaining to his reward in heaven. The Holy Spirit was outpoured upon the Sacred Manhood of Our Lord after His baptism and at His ascension. These gifts to His Humanity may be compared with the gifts of the Holy Spirit to the Christian at his Confirmation and after his resurrection. But it is not to be supposed by serious believers in the truth of the Incarnation that the Sacred Humanity of our Divine Lord was without the personal indwelling of God the Holy Ghost between His conception and His Baptism, and that the Divine Spirit came upon the holy Mother of our Saviour to enable her to conceive her Son without communicating His personal indwelling to the Sacred Manhood of the Child Who at the time of His conception and of His birth was, by virtue of His Divine Person, the eternal Son of God. And if He Who thus possessed this gift in His Manhood from the first moment of His human life received fresh outpourings of it on special occasions, it may well be that the Christian receives the personal indwelling when he is made a Christian at Baptism, although there are to be to him fresh gifts when he is confirmed and when he rises from the dead. If it be so, the analogy between the life of Christ and that of Christians is of a very significant kind. In Baptism, wherein the Christian life begins to be, the Christian receives the personal indwelling of the Holy Ghost, as Christ received it at His conception when His human life began to be. In Confirmation, the Christian receives a fresh gift of the same divine indwelling to strengthen him for the battle of life, as Christ received a like fresh gift at the time of His baptism before His ministry began. At the resurrection, the Christian is again to receive a fresh gift of the same indwelling to grant him the beatitude of the life of heaven, as Christ received the gift of the Holy Spirit at the time of His ascension to convey to His Manhood the joy of His ascended glory. Such successive outpourings of the Holy Ghost on the same person would be parallel also to the succession by which the baptized and confirmed have received the Holy Ghost but can yet, if ordained priests, be the recipients of the gift described and conferred in the words, 'Receive the Holy Ghost for the office and work of a priest in the Church of God'; or, if consecrated bishops, obtain the extended powers of their new function by being again the recipients of the same Divine Person when it is said to them, 'Receive the Holy Ghost for the office and work of a bishop in the Church of God.'

It is further to be considered that Holy Baptism confers the grace of regeneration. By thus being begotten again and made sons of God, the baptized become Christians. It is difficult to suppose that one who thus is, in the Christian sense, a child of God, is not also a temple of God the Holy Ghost, filled by His personal indwelling.

Regeneration and sonship are closely connected with the fact that the baptized are made members of Christ and are united to the risen, ascended, and glorified humanity of our Lord. United to Him, they are united to One Who possesses perpetually in His Sacred Manhood the personal indwelling of the Holy Spirit. This union can hardly fail to carry with it the gift to the baptized of the same personal indwelling. With great force it has been said, 'It is hard to see how the recipient of Baptism as such could be a child of

God, yet destitute of that "assurance of sonship" which comes from the spirit of adoption; could be "in" Christ, yet not "in" the Holy Spirit; could be incorporated into the body mystical, yet not really "inhabited" by the "Giver of life," Who is the very informing and vitalising principle of that body. Such incoherences and anomalies, involved in a theory which would restrict His indwelling to Confirmation, should deter a consistent believer in Baptismal regeneration from adopting it.'[2]

Such considerations as these are of very great importance, and cannot lightly be set aside. No discussion could approach completeness without paying attention to them. Yet the fundamental question undoubtedly is, what is the teaching on the subject contained in Holy Scripture and the works of the theologians of the undivided Church?

The writer of the Acts of the Apostles, in describing the Confirmation of those who had been baptized, says, 'When the apostles which were at Jerusalem heard that Samaria had received the word of God, they sent unto them Peter and John: who, when they were come down, prayed for them that they might receive the Holy Ghost (for as yet He was fallen upon none of them: only they had been baptized into the Name of the Lord Jesus): then laid they their hands on them, and they received the Holy Ghost'; 'when Paul had laid his hands upon them, the Holy Ghost came on them.'[3] These passages unquestionably assert that at Confirmation the Holy Spirit is received. Do they also imply that His personal indwelling is not given to the baptized before their Confirmation? More writers than one of undisputed ability and learning have maintained that they do, and especially that the words 'as yet He was fallen upon none of them: only they had been baptized into the Name of the Lord Jesus,' conclusively prove that this personal indwelling of God the Holy Ghost is not possessed by those who have been baptized but have not been confirmed. If these passages stood by themselves, this inference would be open to question, since 'as yet He was fallen upon none of them' might well mean that the Samaritans had not yet received the special Confirmation gifts of the Holy Spirit, and 'the Holy Ghost came upon them' might well mean that He came upon them with these same special Confirmation gifts.

When these passages are compared with other statements in the Acts, strong reasons may be seen for interpreting them in this latter way. On the day of Pentecost the sermon of S. Peter caused those who heard it to ask what they were to do, and they received the answer, 'Repent ye and be baptized every one of you in the Name of Jesus Christ unto the remission of your sins, and ye shall receive the gift of the Holy Ghost.'[4] There is no indication in this passage of the meaning which some have attached to it so as to understand its teaching to be that by some further ceremony subsequent to Baptism, namely Confirmation, the 'gift of the Holy Ghost' was to be received. Neither is there anything to show that by 'be baptized' S. Peter meant, 'Receive the whole rite, afterwards divided into Baptism and Confirmation,' that is, 'Be baptized with water and receive also the laying on of hands.' The 'gift of the Holy Ghost,' in such a context, can hardly mean less than His personal indwelling. It is the natural interpretation, then, to regard the promise of S. Peter as affirming that the baptized should in their Baptism receive the personal indwelling of God the Holy Ghost. Moreover, when Ananias, who, it must be noticed, did not possess the power to confirm, told S. Paul 'the Lord' 'hath sent me that thou mayest receive thy sight and be filled with the Holy Ghost,'[5] the gift referred to is evidently that received in Baptism, and there is no good reason for supposing that the phrase 'be filled with the Holy Ghost' does not mean that His personal indwelling was to be given.

Further, in view of the Baptismal grace of

regeneration carrying with it, as has been already pointed out, the Christian privilege of sonship to God, it can hardly be contended that one who has been baptized and has not been confirmed is not a Christian or does not belong to Christ; and S. Paul, when he is writing of the indwelling of the Spirit, says expressly, 'If any man hath not the Spirit of Christ, he is none of His.'[6]

Comparison, then, of the different passages in the Acts of the Apostles, as well as due regard to the teaching of S. Paul, leads naturally to the conclusion that the Holy Spirit personally indwells those who have been baptized, although they have not yet been confirmed. And, in the light of this conclusion, ratification is seen of the belief already expressed that various passages in other parts of the New Testament which speak of Christians being 'made to drink of one Spirit,' or of the Holy Ghost being 'given' to us, or 'received' by us, or 'made to dwell in us,' or which say that 'God sent forth the Spirit of His Son into our hearts,' are rightly taken as referring to Baptism.[7]

If the teaching of the Prayer Book of the Church in England is thus in accordance with the New Testament, it has next to be asked whether it is also consonant with the doctrine taught in the early Church? In the last chapter some of the quotations made from the Fathers were to the effect that in Baptism the Holy Spirit comes to dwell in the soul. If it were clear that in all these and similar passages the word Baptism was used to denote Baptism without Confirmation, there could be no doubt as to the answer to this inquiry. In the early Church, however, Baptism and Confirmation were in ordinary cases administered at the same time, and it is sometimes a matter of no little difficulty to determine, when a patristic writer speaks of Baptism, whether he means Baptism simply, or the whole rite of which Baptism and Confirmation were component parts. And, in favour of interpreting Baptism in these passages in the more extended sense, it has been pointed out that there are statements in the Fathers which appear to deny the reception of the Holy Spirit prior to Confirmation. Thus, Cornelius, Bishop of Rome in the third century, said that Novatian, in consequence of his not having been confirmed, had not 'obtained the Holy Ghost.' Tertullian used the words, 'Not that we obtain the Holy Spirit in the waters, but having been cleansed in the water under the ministry of the angel, we are prepared for the Holy Spirit.' S. Cyprian spoke of Baptism as making a man 'fit to receive the Holy Ghost,' and said that to be regenerated in Baptism was to be prepared for the reception of the Spirit. It has been urged, moreover, that S. Chrysostom interpreted the words of S. Paul 'were all made to drink of one Spirit' not of Baptism but of Confirmation.[8] These passages have been thought by some to afford sure proof that the belief held by these writers was that the personal indwelling of the Holy Ghost is not received by a baptized person until he is confirmed.

There is no doubt that the Fathers habitually thought and spoke of Baptism in close connection with Confirmation. Yet it will, on investigation, be found that when they distinguish the two, they by no means deny that the gift of the indwelling Spirit is conferred in Baptism. S. Chrysostom's interpretation of 1 Corinthians xii. 13 as referring to the descent of the Holy Spirit which is a result of Baptism may or may not affirm the unquestionable truth that the Christian is made to drink of the Holy Spirit in Confirmation; in either case it does not deny that the Holy Spirit has already been received by the Christian when he was baptized. The words of Cornelius and of Tertullian may both refer to a special Confirmation gift of the Holy Ghost, and it is far less difficult to assign this interpretation to them than to explain passages in other writers in such a way as to be harmonious with a denial of the indwelling of the Holy Ghost in all the baptized. And the explanation thus suggested of Tertullian's language is very strongly supported by considering the evidence afforded by S. Cyprian, who in many respects was the disciple of Tertullian. S. Cyprian, as referred to above, says that Baptism makes a man 'fit to receive the Holy Ghost,' and regeneration prepares for the reception of the Spirit. At first sight, these statements might be taken to mean that in Baptism by itself the Holy Spirit is not received. That this would be a wrong interpretation is distinctly shown by the fact that S. Cyprian, in speaking definitely of those who had been baptized on a sick-bed and had therefore not been confirmed, denies that they have obtained a 'more scanty and smaller measure of the divine gift and the Holy Spirit' than those baptized in health, and says with reference to them that 'the Holy Spirit is not given by measure but is poured out upon the believer in His fulness,' and that in them 'the Holy Spirit begins to dwell.'[9] This important statement makes it clear that S. Cyprian believed that the personal indwelling of the Holy Spirit is conferred at Baptism, and shows that his view of Baptism as preparing for the reception of the Holy Spirit at Confirmation was substantially the same as that which has been expressed by a modern theologian, well known for his intimate acquaintance with the doctrine of the Holy Ghost as taught in Holy Scripture and by the Fathers, 'We must be careful, whilst we affirm that the Holy Spirit is given in Confirmation, not to forget that in Baptism the same Spirit has already made the soul His temple. . . . The qualification to receive "the plenitude of the Holy Spirit" is the possession already of the gift of the Spirit. In Confirmation there is a second largess of the Holy Spirit, the "complement" of the Baptismal Gift.'[10] What may thus be stated about S. Cyprian is probably true of Tertullian also. Even if it were not so, a peculiarity of individual writers of the North African Church, especially in view of marked features of North African Christianity, could not properly be allowed great weight in opposition to teaching from different parts of the Church. S. Basil and S. Athanasius, as well as Origen, link the receiving of the Holy Ghost with the 'water' or with regeneration.[11]

In view of this fact and of what has been said about the teaching of S. Cyprian, it may be concluded that the passages quoted in the last chapter from the Fathers assigning the gift of the Holy Spirit to Baptism are rightly interpreted as meaning that the baptized who as yet are unconfirmed have received the personal indwelling of the Holy Ghost. In the frequently quoted words of a Gallican homily of the fifth or sixth century, ' The Holy Spirit, who comes down upon the waters of Baptism with health-giving descent, in the font gives His fulness to produce innocence, in Confirmation affords an increase to produce grace. In Baptism we are regenerated so as to attain to life; after Baptism we are strengthened for battle. In Baptism we are washed; after Baptism we are made strong.' Or, as expressed in the middle ages by Peter Lombard, ' The virtue in Confirmation is the gift for strength of the Holy Spirit who was given in Baptism for remission.'[12]

In spite, then, of certain difficulties which it is fair to recognise, it may be truly said that the English Baptismal Offices are in accordance with the doctrine of the early Church as well as with the teaching of the New Testament.

It has, again, been thought that, however fully the Church in England may in this matter correspond with the rest of Western Christendom, and with the teaching of early writers in the East, she yet differs from the accredited doctrine of Eastern Christians at the present day. There are, indeed, individual Eastern theologians who restrict the indwelling of the Holy Spirit to the confirmed. To quote from one writer, who in many matters is representative of the Russian Church, Macarius, Bishop of Vinitza, wrote, 'In Baptism we are only purified from all sin and regenerated by the power of the Holy Ghost, but we are not yet worthy to receive that Spirit in us and to become His temples; by Unction' (*i.e.* Confirmation) 'He is communicated to us with all the gifts of His grace which are indispensable for the spiritual life.'[13] In such teaching writers of the Eastern Churches do not appear to follow their authorised formularies. The Synod of Bethlehem, the decisions of which have long been regarded as authoritative in the Greek Church and have more recently been accepted by the Church in Russia, described the baptized as temples of God.[14] The Greek Baptismal Office connects the 'gift of the Holy Spirit' with the water used in Baptism.[15]

It would not be in accordance with the teaching of the New Testament, or of the Fathers, or of the best traditions of the Church, to make little of the importance and effects of Confirmation. Neither is it right, in emphasising these, to rob Baptism of one of its great gifts, or unduly limit the spiritual privileges of those who have been baptized but as yet are unconfirmed, by denying to them the distinctively Christian possession of the personal indwelling of God the Holy Ghost.[16]

The question discussed in this chapter is one of great practical importance. It affects not only the theoretical completeness of a part of Christian truth, but also the methods of pastoral work. The Christian pastor who believes the true doctrine of Baptism makes the fact of baptism the starting-point in all his relations to the baptized. If Baptism indeed conferred only the other gifts which are rightly regarded as bestowed by means of it, and did not convey also the personal indwelling of the Holy Ghost, there would still be very much of priceless value to which he could appeal and on which he could build in those who, having been baptized, were still unconfirmed. But the loss would be neither small nor unimportant. If the personal indwelling is received at Baptism, it is possible to regard and treat and appeal to all the baptized as temples of the Holy Ghost. Without this indwelling, the baptized but unconfirmed would be without the special power and the highly sacred character which, if they have received the gift of the indwelling, they all possess, however little they have responded to it or however greatly they have sinned against it. And the importance of this consideration is vastly increased for English people by the great numbers of persons in this country who have been baptized but have not been confirmed.

Yet the discussion which has here been referred to has its consoling side. That it should have been thought worth while to discuss what is the nature of the gift of the Holy Ghost to the soul of those who are baptized marks the reality and strength of the conviction, on the part of any who have entered into the discussion, that the grace conferred in Baptism is of high value and includes the bestowal of regeneration and adoption. It illustrates the fact that, although the doctrine of Baptism contained in the Book of Common Prayer may have been greatly obscured in England in careless days, yet now there is a very numerous body of English Churchmen who would take as a starting-point in any discussion of details in connection with the baptismal gifts that the baptized receive a new birth unto eternal life, are made to be members of Christ and sons of God in no figurative sense, and receive, if not the personal indwelling, at least the special operation, of God the Holy Ghost.

CHAPTER VI

HOLY BAPTISM A SACRAMENT

The Latin word 'sacramentum' has passed through many meanings. Among the senses in which it was used in its pre-Christian history were those of a sum of money deposited in a court of law as a guarantee of good faith before the hearing of an action, the oath of obedience taken by a soldier, and any kind of solemn oath. The letter of Pliny, the Roman Governor of Bithynia, written about the year 110 A.D., appears to show that the word was used by Christians in connection with the Holy Eucharist in some way which he had failed to understand. Christians, he said, whom he had examined, 'declared that this was the whole of their fault or error, that they were accustomed to assemble on a fixed day before daybreak and to sing antiphonally a hymn to Christ as to a god, and to bind themselves by a sacrament, not to some crime but that they should not commit theft or robbery or adultery, that they should not break faith or deny what had been deposited with them when asked for it; that, when this was over, it was their custom to disperse, and to assemble again for a meal taken in common, and innocent.'[1]

In the writings of Christians of the early Church, this word is used in a vague general sense to denote a sacred event or thing. Reference has already been made to the application of it to ordinances of the Jewish dispensation. In connection with the Christian system and rites the use of it is extensive and indefinite. Thus it is applied, for instance, to the Incarnation and the Holy Eucharist and the blessed salt given to catechumens.[2]

As time went on, the tendency of Christian thought was in the direction of more closely defining and limiting this word. In the mediæval theology an important restriction was introduced into the definition of it. ·S. Thomas Aquinas, for instance, says that a Sacrament is 'a sign of a sacred thing in so far as it sanctifies men.' The Catechism of the Council of Trent, embodying in this matter the theology of the middle ages, spoke of a Sacrament as 'a thing subjected to the senses which, from the institution of God, has the power both of signifying and of effecting sanctity and righteousness.'[3] Following the same line of thought, the twenty-fifth of the English Articles of Religion defined Sacraments as 'certain sure witnesses, and effectual signs of grace and God's goodwill towards us, by the which He doth work invisibly in us, and doth not only quicken, but also strengthen and confirm our faith in Him'; and the English Catechism explained a Sacrament to be 'an outward and visible sign of an inward and spiritual grace given unto us, ordained by Christ Himself, as a means whereby we receive the same, and a pledge to assure us thereof.'

The question, which, as it would seem, has stirred much needless controversy, as to the number of the Sacraments is closely connected with the definition of the word. When it was used in the vague sense customary in the early Church, no limit could be put to the number. As, in the course of time, the word came to have a more restricted meaning, there were corresponding restrictions in the possibilities of its application. It is believed that the earliest writer to fix the number as seven was Gregory of Bergamo in the first half of the twelfth century. In his treatise *On the Reality of the Body of Christ* he spoke of these seven in three groups: the first group, which he described as 'more worthy than the other Sacraments,' consisted of Baptism, Confirmation, and the Eucharist; the second group comprised Ordination and Matrimony; the third group, to which he applied the name Sacraments with more hesitation, was that of Holy Scripture and an oath. A little later the great schoolman, Peter Lombard, the 'Master of the Sentences,' adopting the same number seven, gave the name Sacrament to Baptism, Confirmation, the Eucharist, Penance, the Last Unction, Holy Orders, and Matrimony. His influence led to this restriction and classification being adopted by the schoolmen generally, and it thus passed into and came to be taken for granted in all Western theology. The first formal decree now known which asserts it is the decree of Pope Eugenius IV. to the Armenians, which was issued in the year 1439. This restriction was confirmed by the Council of Paris in 1528, and it appears, some twenty years later, in the first canon of the seventh session of the Council of Trent. In the seventeenth century the same limitation was expressed in the East by the Synod of Constantinople and the Synod of Bethlehem.[4] Since that time it has been generally recognised in the East. It has been customary among those who have asserted that the number of the Sacraments is seven to make distinctions between them, whether as to the general necessity of some of them in distinction from the particular and individual need of others, or as to the different degrees of dignity attaching to different Sacraments, or as to the definition of Baptism and Penance as 'Sacraments of the dead,' *i.e.* to be administered to persons dead by reason of sin, and of the others as 'Sacraments of the living,' *i.e.* to be administered to those in a state of grace and spiritual life.[5]

The Church in England in her authorised formularies has used great caution with regard to the number of the Sacraments. The Catechism, in answer to the question, 'How many Sacraments hath Christ ordained in His Church?' adds to the words 'Two only' the careful statement 'as generally necessary to salvation'; and it is a matter of some significance, as showing in what sense the word Sacrament was used in the limitation of the Sacraments to two, that the attempt on the part of the Puritans, at the time of the Savoy Conference in the reign of Charles II., to obtain the omission of this clause was successfully resisted.[6]

In the twenty-fifth of the Articles of Religion it is first said that 'Confirmation, Penance, Orders, Matrimony, and Extreme Unction, are not to be counted for Sacraments of the Gospel,' and then added that they 'have not like nature of Sacraments with Baptism and the Lord's Supper, for that they have not any visible sign or ceremony ordained of

God'; the careful phrases, 'Sacraments of the Gospel,' 'like nature of Sacraments,' being apparently used to avoid a denial that other rites than Baptism and the Eucharist are in any sense Sacraments.

The two books of the Homilies are not authoritative declarations of the doctrine of the English Church. They possess whatever importance may be implied in their having been composed by divines of the times of the publication of the English Prayer Books of the reigns of King Edward VI. and Queen Elizabeth, and of the Articles. Parts of their contents have received general approval in the statement of the thirty-fifth article that they 'contain a godly and wholesome doctrine.'

In the first part of the homily entitled *A sermon against swearing and perjury* it is stated that 'the Sacrament of Matrimony knitteth man and wife in perpetual love,' and in the *Homily wherein is declared that Common Prayer and Sacraments ought to be ministered in a tongue that is understood of the hearers* Absolution and Holy Orders are referred to as Sacraments and there is a long explanation of the different senses in which the word Sacrament may be used: 'As for the number of them,' it is said, 'if they should be considered according to the exact signification of a Sacrament, namely, for the visible signs expressly commanded in the New

Testament, whereunto is annexed the promise of free forgiveness of our sins, and of our holiness and joining in Christ, there be but two; namely, Baptism and the Supper of the Lord. For although Absolution hath the promise of forgiveness of sin, yet by the express word of the New Testament it hath not this promise annexed and tied to the visible sign, which is imposition of hands. For this visible sign (I mean laying on of hands) is not expressly commanded in the New Testament to be used in Absolution, as the visible signs in Baptism and the Lord's Supper are: and therefore Absolution is no such Sacrament as Baptism and the Communion are. And though the Ordering of ministers hath this visible sign and promise, yet it lacks the promise of remission of sin, as all other Sacraments besides the two above-named do. Therefore, neither it nor any other Sacrament else, be such Sacraments as Baptism and the Communion are. But in a general acceptation the name of a Sacrament may be attributed to any thing, whereby an holy thing is signified. In which understanding of the word, the ancient writers have given this name, not only to the other five commonly and of late years taken and used for supplying the number of the seven Sacraments, but also to divers and sundry other ceremonies, as to oil, washing of feet, and such like, not meaning thereby to repute them as Sacraments in the same signification that the two fore-named Sacraments are.' Thus the limitation of the word to Baptism and the Holy Communion is viewed as being only a limitation of it as used in a special sense.

In whatever sense the word Sacrament is used, Holy Baptism is certainly a Sacrament. From at any rate the time of Tertullian it has been so called. As will be explained in a later chapter, it is 'generally necessary to salvation.' As has already been pointed out, it was 'ordained by Christ Himself.' It has the 'outward and visible sign' in the use of water and the invocation of the Father and the Son and the Holy Ghost. It has the 'inward and spiritual grace' in the gifts of 'a death unto sin and a new birth unto righteousness.' It is, to use a wider definition, 'a thing subjected to the senses which, from the institution of God, has the power both of signifying and of effecting sanctity and righteousness.'

One of the distinctions commonly made between different Sacraments by those who affirm that the Sacraments are seven in number is that Baptism, Confirmation, and Holy Orders differ from the others because they can only be received once, and any attempt to confer or receive them a second time is a sacrilegious act. The reason is that these three rites confer what theologians describe as 'character,' that is, an indelible impression made upon the soul which permanently distinguishes all those who have received it from all those who have not. Thus, a person who has once been baptized can never become an unbaptized person. He can never cease to be one who has been regenerated by divine grace, united to Christ so as to be a member of His mystical Body, made to be a son of God. His virtues, if he lives well, are grounded upon his Baptism. They are but the expansion and development of the life which Baptism was the means of communicating to him. His sins, if he lives badly, are offences against Baptismal grace. They result, not in the destruction of the gifts which have been received from God, but in the perversion of them, so that the powers which were bestowed for good deepen the offence of him who uses them ill. However deeply he may, subsequently to his Baptism, have fallen into sin, his path of repentance can never include a fresh Baptism. Even in the extreme case of an adult baptized without either faith or repentance, he is still a baptized person in whom the fruits of Baptism are lying dormant, and if, at a later time, he attain to the faith and repentance through which Baptismal grace begins to take effect in him, he is not again to be baptized. If, indeed, the rite be administered to any adult under violent compulsion in defiance of his expressed will, it is reasonable to suppose that in such a case the opposition of the will makes the act null and void. In all other cases, including those in which Baptism is received without knowledge or comprehension on the part of the person baptized, the mere administration of the rite constitutes a valid Sacrament. If there is doubt whether a person has received valid Baptism, a conditional form of words saying, 'If thou art not already baptized' is to be used.[7] In the language of the ancient Church, there is 'one Baptism for the remission of sins.' In the words of S. Paul, 'One Lord, one Faith, one Baptism, one God and Father of all.'[8]

CHAPTER VII

THE BAPTISM OF INFANTS

There is no express statement in the New Testament that infants were baptized in the days of the apostles. The high probability that children were among those whose Baptisms are recorded in the Acts of the Apostles has already been pointed out. This high probability that in the earliest Christian times Baptism was not restricted to adults becomes a practical certainty when the evidence afforded by early Christian writers is impartially considered. The words ascribed to S. Polycarp in the *Letter of the Smyrnæans* describing his martyrdom, 'Fourscore and six years have I been His servant,' probably denote that this saint had been baptized in infancy or, at any rate, in early childhood. The most reasonable interpretation of the words of S. Justin Martyr that there were many 'who from the time when they were children had been the disciples of Christ' implies the Baptism of children. S. Irenæus speaks of 'infants and little ones, and boys and youths, and older people' being 'regenerated unto God,' and other passages in his writings show that he connects regeneration with Baptism. The treatise of Tertullian *On Baptism* and the *Canons of Hippolytus* show that it was customary in the Church to baptize infants. S. Cyprian, writing in the name of a Carthaginian Council, urges that Baptism be not delayed till the eighth day, but be administered when children are only two or three days old. Clement of Alexandria mentions 'little children that are drawn up out of the water.' Origen asserts and defends the custom of the Church in baptizing infants, and says that this practice is a 'tradition' which 'the Church has received from the apostles.' In the *Apostolical Constitutions* the Baptism of infants is enjoined.[1]

It is unnecessary to refer to other writers to establish the unquestionable fact that the undivided Church was convinced of the lawfulness of infant Baptism. Tertullian, indeed, wrote in disapproval of the Baptism of children; but, as mentioned above, the language which he used shows that the practice thus condemned was the custom of the Church. S. Gregory of Nazianzus also advised that, in ordinary cases, Baptism should be postponed till children were three years old; but he excepted from the rule he thus wished to establish any who might be in peril of death.² In the fourth century, it was common enough for Christian parents to hold back their children from Baptism; but this was due, not to any doubt as to the lawfulness of the Baptism of infants, but to the tremendous sense of the enormity of the sin of a baptized person as committed against grace and the fear that their children, if baptized, might fall into so terrible an offence; and the practice, wherever it obtained, was caused by this hesitancy on the part of parents and not by any shrinking on the part of the authorities of the Church from baptizing infants.³

The general sense of the Church has been in the direction of the Baptism of infants being administered at an early age. S. Cyprian, as has been said, thought it better not to wait, as thereby appears to have been customary in his time, until the child had attained the age of eight days. The ecclesiastical laws of Ine, king of the West Saxons, of the year 693, order that a child be baptized within thirty days of its birth. The English Book of Common Prayer directs that 'the curate of every parish shall often admonish the people that they defer not the Baptism of their children longer than the first or second Sunday next after their birth, or other Holy-day falling between, unless upon a great and reasonable cause, to be approved by the curate.' In the Church of Rome the parish priest is still ordered to exhort the people to bring their children to be baptized at the earliest possible time. In the East the child is to be brought to the church to receive a name and to be blessed eight days after birth, and is to be baptized on the fortieth day. 'On the fortieth day,' says the Archpriest Peter Smirnoff, 'in compliance with the example of the Lord and Saviour, the child is brought into the temple and therein dedicated to God as His property bought with the priceless blood of Jesus Christ.'[4]

Infant Baptism has been rejected by some modern sects. This rejection has been defended on the grounds that the commission of our Lord associates the work of teaching with the work of baptizing and implies that none but the taught are to be baptized; that the Baptisms recorded in the New Testament are those of adults; and that the ceremony of Baptism is meaningless unless the person baptized has already been converted by the grace of God. This position misinterprets the words of our Lord in the institution of Baptism. An accurate translation of them shows that His command was not to teach and baptize, but to make disciples by means of Baptism. Apart from this, the commission given in the earliest days of Christianity would necessarily contemplate chiefly the admission of adults into the Church. That the instances of Baptism recorded in the New Testament were in all cases the Baptisms of adults is, as has been said, unlikely. The argument that conversion must precede Baptism is due to error as to the effects of the Sacrament and to a strangely persistent misconception by which the gift of regeneration and the act of conversion have been confused. In the case of a person who has been living in unbelief or sin, conversion of heart is unquestionably necessary before it can be right or beneficial for any religious ordinance to be received. In the case of infants, who inherit the taint and distortion of original sin, the love of God provides that they may be unconsciously set free from that which they have unconsciously received, and that they may possess grace which may enable them from their earliest years to respond to the teaching of divine truth and the voice of conscience. The Baptism of infants, so far from minimising the need of moral effort and of holiness of life, makes provision that children, as they grow in years, may be continuously enabled to live in accordance with divine law.

Sponsors are mentioned by Tertullian, in the

Canons of Hippolytus, and in the *Apostolical Constitutions*.⁵ They were needed, as was thus early seen, partly that there might be some to act as spokesmen for the infant recipients of Baptism and partly that there might be some guarantee for the Christian education of the baptized. In a true sense the Universal Church made declarations of faith and goodwill on behalf of those whom she received into her body, and in early days the Church herself made provision that those thus received should be brought up as Christians. Thus, the sponsors were rightly regarded as the representatives of the Church; and S. Augustine says of them: 'Infants are brought to receive spiritual grace, not so much by those in whose hands they are borne, although they are brought by those also, if they be good and faithful, as they are brought by the universal society of the saints and of the faithful; for they are rightly understood to be offered in Baptism by all who are pleased that they should be offered, by all through whose holy and inseparable love they are helped to participate in the Holy Spirit. This is done, therefore, by the whole mother Church, which is in the saints, because it is that Church as a whole which brings forth all, and that Church as a whole which brings forth individuals.'⁶

In early times one sponsor was regarded as sufficient. In the middle ages in the West more sponsors than one were sometimes allowed. The mediæval English rubrics specified 'one man and one woman' or at the most three persons as the number which must not be exceeded. Mediæval English councils contemplated two men and one woman as sponsors at the Baptism of a boy, and one man and two women at the Baptism of a girl. In practice the allowed number was sometimes exceeded. The present rule of the Church of Rome requires one and allows two. In the East one sponsor is required.

Great stress has always been laid on the choice of suitable persons as sponsors. The Church of Rome still emphasizes the need of orthodoxy, knowledge of the elements of the Faith, and good character. In the Russian Church the authorised work entitled *On the Duty of Parish Priests* directs the priest 'to see that the godfather or godmother be an orthodox believer and know those articles of the faith which are necessary to salvation: inasmuch as the sponsor here stands in place of the infant baptized and makes answers for him to God, repeating the Creed, and so is bound, when his spiritual son, whom he receives from the font, begins to grow up and has no other instructors, to teach him the faith and God's law, and do his best to put him in mind of his vows made at Baptism and of the virtue of that Sacrament.'⁷

From at any rate the sixth century a theory of spiritual relationship as a result of Baptism has been held in the East and in the West. According to the earliest forms of this theory, a spiritual relationship, creating a barrier to marriage similar to that of natural relationship, was established in Baptism between the sponsors and the baptized. The code of Justinian prohibits marriage between the baptized person and a sponsor on the ground that 'nothing else can so much call out fatherly affection and the just prohibition of marriage as a bond of this kind by means of which, through the action of God, their souls are united to one another.' The later forms of the theory extended the relationship so as to include the parents and relatives of the baptized and the relatives of the sponsors. The mediæval teaching on this subject was fraught with complexity and excess, and led to great practical abuses, which were recognised and to a certain extent remedied by the Council of Trent. At the same time, it enshrined a truth which has been of late years too much forgotten, and emphasized the reality and deep solemnity of the relation between the sponsors and the baptized.[8]

The English Prayer Book, following a mediæval English custom,[9] directs that 'for every male child to be baptized two godfathers and one godmother; and for every female, one godfather and two godmothers' 'must be ready at the font' at the Public Baptism of Infants; assumes that 'godfathers and godmothers' are present to make the renunciation of sin and profession of faith and obedience, and to tell the name to the minister in the same Office and at the reception of children who have been baptized privately; and orders that, in the Baptism of 'such as are of riper years and able to answer for themselves,' 'the godfathers and godmothers' 'shall be ready to present them at the font' and shall tell the name to the minister. In the case of infants, the Office directs the sponsors to take care that the child is brought to the bishop to be confirmed, and implies that they are to see that he is taught the Creed, the Lord's Prayer, the Ten Commandments, and the rest of the Church Catechism.

The twenty-ninth canon of 1603 prohibited the father of a child from being sponsor. This action, though possibly to some extent influenced by mediæval theory and practice, was probably chiefly the result of a desire to secure as full a guarantee as possible for the Christian education of the baptized. This part of the canon was repealed by the Convocation of Canterbury in 1865, the action of which, however, did not receive any ratification by the Crown and was not followed by a corresponding decision of the Convocation of York.

The same canon of 1603 enacted that no one should 'be admitted godfather or godmother to any child' 'before the said person so undertaking hath received the Holy Communion.' It was thus implied that the sponsors must have been baptized and confirmed. This regulation was obviously intended to secure that they should be fitting representatives of the Church, and that in this matter all possible care should be taken to provide for the education of the baptized in the faith and laws of the Christian religion.

The care thus taken by the Church in England has not met with a due response in practice either from the clergy or from the laity. The clergy, as a body, cannot be said to have taken sufficient care in trying to secure the selection of communicants of suitable character as sponsors for the children who have been brought to them to be baptized. The choice of sponsors by the laity has frequently been dictated by considerations altogether apart from the Christian training of the child; in very many cases those chosen have been altogether unsuitable; often the existence of sponsors has been a mere formality; and the practical difficulties of the question have proved so great that children are habitually baptized with only two sponsors, or one sponsor, or no sponsor at all. For a large part of the period since the drawing up of the canons and the last revision of the Prayer Book, the needed guarantee for Christian training has in most parts of England been to a very large extent supplied by the parochial system and the existence of Church schools. At the present time, new conditions of life connected with the growth of great towns and the massing of the population in them, the re-organisation of Church methods, and the changing or changed aspect of education, are destroying this practical guarantee which older conditions afforded. It has become a very serious question whether it is right to place upon children the responsibilities of Christians without seeing that they are given also some possibility of knowing what they are and learning how to fulfil them, and to bring any within the Church without security that they will have the opportunity of being taught what is required from faithful members of the Church. On the one hand, it is a natural instinct of Christians to seek to extend as widely as possible the privileges of Baptism, and the children born within reach of Sacraments make a touching appeal; on the other hand, the special character of sins committed by the baptized is not to be ignored, and there is little doubt that the Church is weakened by the large numbers of those who are her members in nothing but their Baptism. Thus, clergy both at home and abroad do well to take proper precautions that they do not admit to Christian responsibilities those who from the conditions of their heathen surroundings are not likely to be able in the smallest degree to fulfil them. At the same time—to take an instance from a custom which has scandalised many, —it must be remembered that, in a majority of cases in this country where the promises of a sponsor in the person of a parish official may have been thought to be a meaningless formality, the children thus brought to the font have received to the letter through the Church the Christian instruction and influence which those promises are intended to guarantee. And, in all cases, it might matter less who the sponsors, regarded as representatives of the universal Church, individually are, if the Church herself, in the present and in the future, as in the past, could securely provide for the Christian training of the baptized.

It cannot reasonably be expected that any good result would be attained by sudden or violent action on the part of the bishops or the clergy in this matter of the selection of sponsors. Such action, coming after long tolerated and widely prevalent laxity, would be likely to produce harmful effects. But it may be hoped that clear and persistent teaching of the doctrine of Baptism and the meaning of sponsorship, combined with a gradual revival of much-needed discipline, will lead to a more healthy mind and a better practice among English Churchpeople. The worst offenders have frequently been found among the more educated classes, whose view of god-parents appears frequently to have been altogether social and not at all religious. Much that has been unsatisfactory among the poor and the uneducated has been due less to deliberate choice than to the exigencies of circumstances. As regards the latter class, it is a charitable work, which it may be hoped an increasing number of devout Churchpeople may be led to undertake, to accept the office of sponsor and to take care that its great responsibilities are fully recognised, and that the duties both of prayer and of action which it creates are adequately performed. Such acts of charity are often, under present circumstances, of high value to the Church and of spiritual benefit to those who perform them as well as of true kindness to the children who are baptized. Yet, in a country where Christianity as a system is securely established, they ought not to be regarded in ordinary cases as more than a temporary means of meeting a need. It is not likely that any satisfactory solution of existing difficulties will be found until a truly Christian spirit and a clear sense of the responsibilities of Baptism and sponsorship are more widely prevalent among those who are within the communion of the Church.

CHAPTER VIII

THE NECESSITY OF HOLY BAPTISM

It has been customary in theology to distinguish between the necessity which is comprised in a rite being the instrument by means of which a needed result is effected, and the necessity which exists because a rite has been authoritatively commanded as obligatory for Christians. Baptism is necessary for both reasons. Our Lord Himself commanded it when He said to His apostles, 'Go ye therefore and make disciples of all the nations, baptizing them into the Name of the Father and of the Son and of the Holy Ghost.' He both gave an implied command and asserted an inherent necessity when He told Nicodemus, 'Except any one be begotten of water and the Spirit, he cannot enter into the kingdom of God.' The doctrine that in Baptism the beginning of Christian life is bestowed upon the soul implies that this Sacrament is necessary as an instrumental means of conveying needed grace. In the New Testament no other means of becoming a Christian than by being baptized is anywhere mentioned or implied. The early Church saw in it the only appointed means of entrance into the kingdom of God. The same belief characterised the Church of the middle ages, and has continued to be held, with unbroken unanimity, by the various parts of the Christian Church unto the present day. The assertion of the Constitutions of an English Bishop early in the thirteenth century that Baptism is 'the gate of all the Sacraments and the first plank after shipwreck without which there is no salvation'; or of the Church in England at a later date that it is 'generally,' that is, universally or for all, 'necessary to salvation,' are but short expressions of the teaching which is found in the New Testament, in the writings of the Fathers and the schoolmen, and in the declarations of the Church throughout the world.[1]

Does it follow, from the assertion of the necessity of Baptism by Holy Scripture and the Church, that it is impossible for any person who dies unbaptized to be other than eternally lost? The only answer which we are qualified to make appears to be that we may not on the ground of general principles pass judgment on the eternal state of individual persons. The general law of God is plain. 'Make disciples of all the nations, baptizing them.' The general assertion of the consequences of want of compliance with that law are also plain. 'He cannot enter the kingdom of God.' Yet it is the teaching of the best theologians and in accordance with the principles of Holy Scripture that 'God is not bound by His own means.' We, on our part, have the obligation of obeying the commands of God. We are simply in ignorance to what extent or under what circumstances He may Himself relax His own law.[2]

The writers of the Church have commonly recognised two classes of exceptions to the necessity of receiving the Sacrament of Holy Baptism. The first class of exceptions is in the case of those who suffer martyrdom for Christ. They, it has been thought, are baptized in their own blood; and the general sense of Christendom has been well expressed in Richard Hooker's words: 'To think that a man whose Baptism the crown of martyrdom preventeth doth lose in that case the happiness which so many thousands enjoy, that only have had the grace to believe and not the honour to seal the testimony thereof with death, were almost barbarous.'[3] The second class of exceptions is in the case of those who, possessed of contrition and love, earnestly desire to be baptized and are unable to receive Baptism. On these, it has been believed, God Himself bestows what they cannot obtain from men. In S. Augustine's words, 'Invisibly is that which is necessary fulfilled, when it is not contempt for religion but some case of necessity which prevents Baptism.'

It was doubtless these exceptions which were in the minds of the English divines of the seventeenth century when they placed in the mouth of the priest administering Baptism to those of riper years the words, 'Ye hear in this Gospel the express words of our Saviour Christ that except a man be born of water and of the Spirit, he cannot enter into the kingdom of God. Whereby ye may perceive the great necessity of this Sacrament, where it may be had.'[4]

It is obvious that the principle underlying the two generally recognised exceptions is capable of extension. There are many who have never heard of Baptism, of whom it may be thought that, if they had known of it, they would have received it. There are others who have never been taught the fulness of Scriptural and Church truth, to whom clearer and more adequate teaching would have made a strong appeal. There are others, again, the circumstances of whose education or history have been of such a kind that, while earnestly desirous of knowing the truth and doing their duty, they have failed to understand the obligation of receiving this Sacrament without, as it would seem, any fault of their own. If the 'baptism of martyrdom' and the 'baptism of desire' are accepted by Almighty God when the 'baptism of water' cannot be obtained, there is no reasonable ground for supposing that in some cases of this kind it is impossible that He should, in the mercies of His uncovenanted grace, admit to salvation persons who by the strict law of the the covenant would be excluded from it. Such a consideration can never lessen the obligation of receiving Baptism on all to whom the divine law has been made clear, or the obligation upon Christian teachers of unflinchingly maintaining that Baptism is the appointed means of salvation, and is declared by our Lord Himself to be necessary if entrance into the kingdom of heaven is to be obtained. While it is not the work of men to pass sentence upon other men or to make rash assertions as to their eternal lot, it could not be regarded as a hopeful sign that any should be trusting to his being made an exception to general law. God alone can tell how far the conscience of any individual has become so distorted by his surroundings or his history that he has, while he

THE NECESSITY OF HOLY BAPTISM 115

desires to do what is right, become incapable of realising the truth on this subject. It is our task to affirm what Christ Himself has declared, to hand on the teaching of His Church, and to leave the difficulties of individual lives to Him who alone knows in their fulness the needs and the circumstances and the hearts of men.

A question of deep solemnity has often been raised about the state of infants who die unbaptized. With great wisdom the Church in England has declared, 'It is certain by God's Word that children which are baptized, dying before they commit actual sin, are undoubtedly saved,'[5] and made no statement about those who die without receiving Baptism. Yet the question must sometimes present itself to the minds of all thoughtful Christians, and there are those to whom personal history has brought it home with a sense of terrible pain. It can only be said again that such a matter is outside the limits of our present knowledge. If S. Augustine in his later teaching supposed that the exigencies of Christian theology and logic demanded that infants who die unbaptized should suffer, though in the lightest possible way, the pains of hell, there were others in the early Church who by no means agreed with this opinion. The scholastic view, as represented by S. Thomas Aquinas, that the conjoint lack of Baptism and absence of any act of will choosing to serve God, makes these infants incapable of entering into the joys of the Beatific Vision, but that they are free from pain and in enjoyment of natural bliss, has seemed probable to many.[6] In the presence of so deep a mystery, we can only rest in the certainty of the perfect wisdom and goodness of Almighty God. At the best, our knowledge goes but a little way; and 'Shall not the Judge of all the earth do right?'

CHAPTER IX

THE MINISTER OF HOLY BAPTISM

It has already been pointed out that the New Testament affords instances of Baptism being administered by those who appear to have been laymen as well as by those who were in the position of ordained ministers. It would not of necessity follow that what was possible in the emergencies of the earliest days of Christianity must be right at a later time when the system of the Church had become organised; but, as a matter of fact, we find in Christian history that others besides the ordained ministers have been regarded as capable of administering Baptism. Under ordinary circumstances, the administration of Baptism was restricted in the early Church to the bishops and the presbyters or priests; in cases of necessity, a deacon or even a layman might baptize.[1]

In the middle of the third century a view existed at Carthage that Baptism administered by schismatics was invalid. More than a century earlier, in the East, S. Ignatius had asserted the unlawfulness of the administration of Baptism without the authority of the bishop, from the point of view that episcopal authority gave security to all religious acts, but without entering into the question, which at later times had to be faced, whether such an unlawful act would necessarily be invalid. The North African opinion on this point was not originated by S. Cyprian; but it was strongly held and defended by him. It was affirmed, in the teeth of the opposition of Stephen, the Bishop of Rome, by the North African Councils held at Carthage. The reasons by which it was supported were that one who had become separate from the Church could not admit to the communion of the Church; that one who was himself by schism unclean could not convey the remission of sins; and that no distinction could logically be made between the minister of Baptism and the minister of Confirmation and the Eucharist. The lapse of time sufficed to bring about the abandonment of this exceptional position. As it is expressed by Archbishop Benson, 'The mischief was silently healed and perfectly. And how? By no counter-council —for later decrees merely register the reversal— but by the simple working of the Christian Society. Life corrected the error of thought.'[2]

A different, though connected, question which presented itself in the early Church was that of the value of Baptism administered by heretics. In some such cases the minister of Baptism was not only outside the communion of the Church; he also used the words of the baptismal formula in a wrong sense. The matter was one of considerable difficulty. Different opinions were held about it by teachers of acknowledged authority. Two Eastern Councils of the first half of the third century appear to have declared heretical Baptism to be invalid. The rejection of it was necessarily involved in the African rejection of all Baptism administered outside the Church. The *Apostolical Canons* and *Constitutions* assert its invalidity. Other Eastern authorities held the same opinion. On the other hand, the validity of all Baptism administered in the Name of the Father and of the Son and of the Holy Ghost was strongly affirmed, notably by the Council of Arles at the beginning of the fourth century and by S. Augustine. In the end, it came to be universally held, at any rate in the West, that Baptism administered by heretics, provided the right matter and form were used, was valid.[3]

Another problem was that of the possible case of a Baptism administered by a person himself unbaptized. S. Augustine, whose opinion on this matter was asked, refused to give an answer on the ground that the point was too difficult for an individual to decide it and must wait for a General Council.⁴ Later theologians who have discussed the subject have agreed that such a Baptism is valid.⁵

Baptism by women was forbidden by some in the early Church, though possibly rather in view of the women ministers of heretical sects than of women baptizing in cases of emergency. In later times the validity of Baptism administered by women has been recognised; and in the middle ages in the West provision was habitually made for the administration of such Baptisms when necessity should arise.⁶

The ordinary Western teaching in the middle ages on the subject of the minister of Baptism may be seen in clear statements of the famous canonist, S. Raymond of Pennafort, who teaches that when there is danger of death any person, man or woman, Catholic or Jew or Pagan, excommunicate or heretic or schismatic, may baptize; but that in all such cases a priest is to baptize in preference to one in minor orders, one in minor orders in preference to a layman, a man in preference to a woman, one of the faithful in preference to one who is not among the faithful, while the father or mother is to baptize only in the greatest emergency.

In view of emergencies, he says, women who are ordinarily present at the birth of children ought to be well instructed in the method of baptizing.[7]

Similarly, in the mediæval rubrics of the Church in England it was laid down, as one of the duties of parish priests, that they should frequently on Sundays explain to their people the right method of baptizing, so that in cases of emergency these might know what to do; and it was further directed, 'It is not lawful for a layman or a woman to baptize any one except in a case of necessity. If a man and a woman are present when a case of necessity of baptizing a child occurs and there is not present any other more fitting minister, the man, not the woman, is to baptize, unless it happen that the woman knows the sacramental words well and the man does not, or there be some other obstacle.'[8]

So great was the importance attached to the reception of Baptism that, in Hooker's words, 'Yea, "Baptism by any man in case of necessity" was the voice of the whole world heretofore.'[9]

In the sixteenth century Baptism administered by laymen, and especially by women, was fiercely attacked by the Puritans. Zwingli, indeed, allowed the validity of such Baptism. The ordinary Puritan position, however, both abroad and in England, was that the administration of Baptism by any but an ordained minister was a contravention of divine law.[10] In opposition to this teaching, the mediæval doctrine was emphatically asserted by the Council of Trent. The Council itself affirmed the validity of Baptism administered even by heretics. The Catechism of the Council, a document issued for the guidance of parish priests, teaches that the only ordinary ministers of Baptism are bishops and priests; but that deacons may baptize by the permission of a bishop or a priest; and that, in cases of necessity, any person, man, woman, Jew, infidel, or heretic, may baptize.[11]

The Church in England has adhered to historical doctrine and practice in this matter. Bishops and priests alone are recognised as the ordinary ministers of Baptism. Deacons are allowed 'in the absence of the priest to baptize infants.' The Prayer Books of 1549, 1552, and 1559 allowed the continuance of lay Baptism. In the Prayer Books of 1604 and 1662, in cases of emergency, when the 'minister of the parish' cannot be procured, Baptism by 'any other lawful minister' is contemplated. This last phrase is in itself ambiguous, since no definition of the phrase 'lawful minister' is given. In view of the traditional teaching of the Church in England and of the history of the Baptismal Offices, there is hardly room for doubt that by the words 'lawful minister' it was not intended to exclude laymen, who had been universally recognised within the Western Church as 'lawful ministers' of Baptism in cases of necessity; and where the matter has received the attention of legal experts they have decided that by this phrase lay Baptism was intended to be in emergencies allowed.[12]

Some statements of the Greek Church appear to deny the validity of Baptisms administered by deacons or laymen. When these are placed in connection with other Greek teaching in the past and in the present, and with the present practice of Greek Christians, it may be seen that their meaning is not more than that, in Western phraseology, Baptism by deacons or laymen is irregular but not invalid.[13]

The Russian Church recognises the validity of Baptism administered by laymen, by women, and by heretics. Thus, in the treatise *On the Duty of Parish Priests* it is said, 'There are some ignorant men among the clergy who would baptize Romans, as well as Lutherans and Calvinists, when they come over to the Eastern Church; while the schismatics among ourselves are not ashamed even to rebaptize those of their people who fall away from the Church, in order to go over to their errors. But the seventh canon of the second Œcumenical

Council sufficiently refutes both the ignorance of the first and the blindness of the last: for that holy Council in the canon cited forbids to re-baptize not only such as the Romans, Lutherans, and Calvinists (who all clearly confess the Holy Trinity, and admit the work of our salvation accomplished by the Incarnation of the Son of God), but even the Arians themselves, and the Macedonians or Pneumatomachi' (*i.e.* those who denied the deity of the Holy Ghost), 'with other heretics named in the same canon; and orders that they should only be made to renounce and anathematise both their own and all other heresies, and so be received by Unction with the Holy Chrism. In order to know what heretics ought to be baptized, any one may consult the eighth canon of the same Council.' 'In the case of a child being dangerously weak or sickly, if no priest be at hand, a lay person may baptize. . . . Wherefore, the priest should teach his parishioners, and not men only, but even women, who may be present at births, how to act in such circumstances: at the same time he should instruct them always in such cases to give him immediate notice.'[14]

Under exceptional circumstances a question might arise whether Baptism administered by a person to himself would be valid. An instance of such Baptism is mentioned in the *Acts of Thecla*, a work of uncertain date, possibly as old as the second century. It is there recorded that the virgin Thecla, whose Baptism the apostle S. Paul had deferred, when surrounded by wild beasts in the arena and threatened with instant death, exclaimed 'the time is come for me to wash myself,' and threw herself into a pool of water, saying, 'In the Name of Jesus Christ on my last day I baptize myself,' and subsequently, having been miraculously delivered, told S. Paul, 'I have received the washing, O Paul; for He that wrought with thee towards the Gospel hath wrought with me also that I should wash myself.' In later times the question has been deliberately considered, and the usual answer has been that Baptism thus administered would be invalid.[15]

Questions have been raised whether Baptism administered in play or in profanity, or acted on the stage, would be valid Baptism, and different answers have been given. A story, current at the end of the fourth century, that S. Athanasius when a boy baptized his companions in play and Alexander the Bishop of Alexandria declared the Baptisms valid, whatever may be the truth of the story, tends to show that at this time some Christians were disposed to affirm the validity of Baptisms administered in a religious game. In later times the usual teaching has been that rites enacted on the stage, or as a game, or in mockery, not being religious acts at all, would not be valid.[16]

In the consideration of the many difficult questions which are involved in the subject of the minister of Baptism, it is necessary to remember that our Lord Himself is the true Baptizer. When the Donatists declared that a Sacrament administered by a bad man could not confer grace, and put their opinion in practice by rebaptizing those who seceded to them from the Church, S. Augustine was never tired of affirming that the Sacraments are the Sacraments of Christ, not of the human minister who is His instrument. The force of his answer extends beyond the particular point which gave rise to it; and it is a part of the Church's traditional theology that the real Agent in Baptism, as in other Sacraments, is not man but God.[17]

Yet there is need of care lest false inferences be derived from this true doctrine. It does not support rash assertions, on the one hand, that, since Christ is the Agent in all Sacraments, therefore there is no need of an ordained minister in any Sacrament; or, on the other hand, that, since Christ is the Agent in all Sacraments, therefore an ordained minister is necessary in every Sacrament. To what extent and under what circumstances the minister is in any case restricted can only be known by an historical inquiry into the doctrine and practice of the Universal Church. Such an inquiry, while it shows clearly that the ordinary minister of Baptism is either a bishop or a priest, shows also that in the case of this Sacrament, as distinct from some other Sacraments, the administration by any minister is valid, and, when there is necessity, is both lawful and desirable. In ordinary cases which arise in this whole matter, there are three distinct though connected questions,—that of Baptism administered by heretics, that of Baptism administered by schismatics, and that of Baptism administered by laymen within the communion of the Church. In all these cases alike the judgment of the Church has been that such Baptisms are valid Sacraments. Even though they are administered in schism or heresy they are the means by which those who are baptized become the children of God and possess a claim upon the Church for other gifts which they cannot receive outside her fold.[18]

S. Augustine, with that harmony of dogmatic clearness and charitable sympathy which marks his teaching on the subject of the Church, asserts that the children who are born to God in Baptism are the fruit not of division but of union. If the religious body in which they have received Baptism has lost by separation the bond of affection and peace which should bind it to the Church, it is united to her by the one Baptism of Christians. There is only one Church which has the name Catholic; but she possesses something of her own in those who are divided from her unity; and, by virtue of this which she has in them, it is she, and not they, who is the mother of the sons. Or, to give the different presentation of a similar line of thought which Firmilian ascribes to Pope Stephen I., it is the office of the Church to nourish as her own the children whom heresy has brought into the world and then exposed. 'The Church,' says Archbishop Benson, 'has within every separated communion a something which is all her own. By that something she bears sons in them to herself. They are not born to others. When they turn homeward they are wholly hers.' [19]

From time to time a theory has been asserted in various quarters that a bad man cannot administer a valid Sacrament, and that, consequently, if the minister of Baptism is in a state of sin, the ceremony which he performs is valueless. This theory formed part of the teaching of the Novatians in the third century, and of that of the Donatists in the fourth. It was supposed, at any rate, to be included among the opinions of Wycliffe. If it were true, it would render the value of all Sacraments doubtful, since the personal character of any individual is known fully only to God. It was refuted for all time in the writings of S. Augustine against the Donatists. To quote one passage which is representative of many, ' In the case of a man, then, who does not keep the commands of heaven, who is covetous, or an extortioner, or a usurer, or envious, or who renounces the world in words and not in deeds, does he forgive sins? If the forgiveness is by the power of the Sacrament of God, as the one does, so also does the other. If the forgiveness is through his own merit, neither does the one nor the other; for the Sacrament is known to be the Sacrament of Christ, even in evil men.'[20]

Nor is any particular belief about Baptism on the part of the minister necessary to the validity of the rite. S. Thomas Aquinas asserts that there must be something to show that the application of the water is intended to be the administration of the Sacrament. He adds that what is necessary is supplied by the external saying of the sacramental words, since the minister of the Sacrament acts in the person of the whole Church.[21] The Council of Trent declares the necessity of the minister intending 'to do what the Church does.' This expression has been commonly explained by Roman Catholic theologians as asserting the need of a merely general intention of compliance with the purposes for which Baptism exists without any particular view either of the nature and limits of the Church or of the meaning and effects of the Sacrament.[22] Indeed, any assertion of the need of belief in, or intention to produce, a particular result on the part of the minister would be as fatal to the true doctrine of the Sacrament as the theory that he must be personally a good man.

CHAPTER X

THE MATTER AND FORM OF HOLY BAPTISM

THE word 'matter' is the theological term by which the *thing* employed in the administration of a Sacrament is described. The matter of the Sacrament of Baptism is water. Our Lord spoke of water when he referred to the future rite of Christian Baptism in His discourse with Nicodemus; and, as has been mentioned, it was the matter with which the Baptisms recorded in the New Testament were administered. From the time of the apostles to the present day, it has never been doubted by any qualified to speak for the Church that water is the divinely appointed matter of this Sacrament. Occasionally an heretical sect may have asserted some other means as the true method of baptizing, or a strange practice such as the baptism of the children of the rich in milk may have sprung up locally within the Church;[1] but such errors of heretics and eccentricities of Churchpeople have alike been condemned. Between the Baptism of the Ethiopian eunuch and the practice of the Church throughout the world at the present time there is no trace of any other authorised matter of Baptism than water.[2]

From the beginning of the third century at any rate, it has been customary for the water to be blessed before being used for the purposes of Baptism. Tertullian says in strong terms, 'The waters obtain the sacrament of sanctification by the invocation of God. For the Spirit immediately descends from heaven and rests upon the waters, sanctifying them by Himself, and they, being so sanctified, imbibe the power of sanctification.' S. Cyprian speaks hardly less strongly: 'The water ought first to be cleansed and sanctified by the priest that it may have power by Baptism in it to wash away the sins of the person who is baptized.' The value of these statements as witness to fact is not impaired by doctrinal peculiarities which may have existed in the Church of North Africa. In the next century, in very different quarters, the *Catechetical Lectures* of S. Cyril of Jerusalem show the existence of the practice; and S. Basil of Cæsarea expresses his opinion that it had been handed down in the Church from the time of the apostles. The prayers of Serapion of Thmuis and the *Apostolical Constitutions* include forms for the blessing of the water.[3] The Western Service Books of the middle ages made it commonly a separate rite;[4] this custom was retained in the First Prayer Book of King Edward VI.; in the present English Prayer Book it forms part of the Baptismal Office itself. In two respects references to this practice in the writings of S. Augustine are of interest. He is the earliest writer to mention the use of the sign of the cross, which became universal, in connection with the 'consecration of the font'; and he is at pains to point out that the validity of the Sacrament is independent of any such prayer or ceremony as that of the water being previously blessed.[5] On this latter subject, no serious and believing student of Christian doctrine and history is likely to think lightly of the value of the ceremony; no one who accepts the general line of Christian teaching can say that it is essential.

It has already been pointed out that the New Testament appears to contemplate the application of the water both by immersion and by other methods. It was customary in the early Church that the water should be applied three times to the person baptized; and the ordinary rule is represented in the fiftieth *Apostolical Canon*, which enacts, 'If any bishop or presbyter does not complete the three washings of the one initiation, but only one washing given into the death of the Lord, let him be deposed.' As to the method of the application of the water, language is used which at first sight appears to imply that immersion was the ordinary practice. Thus Tertullian says, 'We are immersed three times'; and S. Gregory of Nyssa explains, 'We immerse to the Father that we may be sanctified; we immerse to the Son also to the same end; we immerse also to the Holy Ghost, that we may become that which He is and is called.' Yet it has been suggested that the word 'immerse' was sometimes used to denote affusion; and, however this may have been, immersion was not regarded as essential to the Sacrament. A word meaning to 'bathe' or 'moisten' is used as if equivalent to that which may be translated 'immerse'; in the *Teaching of the Twelve Apostles* it is laid down, 'If thou hast not either' (*i.e.* either a brook or a pool), 'pour water thrice upon the head in the Name of the Father and of the Son and of the Holy Ghost'; so rigorous a writer as S. Cyprian is careful and zealous to assert the validity of Baptism administered upon a sick-bed and consequently without immersion; and the ancient representations of Baptism, whether of that which our Lord received from S. John the Baptist or of the Christian Sacrament, depict it as administered by means of affusion.[6]

Threefold immersion has continued the ordinary practice in the East. It was directed in the Western mediæval Service Books. Under the special circumstances of the Arians in Spain using the threefold immersion to support their heresy about the Holy Trinity, S. Gregory the Great advised the adoption of single immersion by the orthodox, and effect was given to this advice by the Fourth Council of Toledo in the year 633.[7]

The First Prayer Book of Edward VI., probably putting into words what had in fact previously been allowed, gave permission to the priest to pour water in certain cases instead of immersing the child, and this permission remains in the present English Prayer Book. While immersion, if it can be performed without danger to health, has some advantages; and while, failing immersion, it is greatly to be desired that the water be poured and not sprinkled; all Western theologians agree that if water is made to flow upon the head of the baptized person the baptism is valid.[8]

In words, the Greek Church restricts valid Baptism to that administered by trine immersion: in view of other teaching of that Church, and of the practice which the Greeks have now adopted of not baptizing Westerns who may join their communion, the position taken up may be rightly described in Western phraseology by calling a Baptism other than by trine immersion irregular but valid. That this explanation of the teaching of the Greeks is correct may, apart from their present practice, be illustrated by a statement made some years ago by the Archbishop of Xanthe to Mr. Athelstan Riley: 'According to our doctrine,' he said, 'the Pope of Rome himself is neither more nor less than an unbaptized layman, and if he joined our communion would have to be baptized. Still, supposing the whole Latin Church and its patriarch were to submit to us in a body, then the Church, by an exercise of the economy of the Church, would recognise Western Baptisms and Ordinations, and they would become valid by the mere act of recognition.'[9]

The word 'form' is the theological term used to denote the sacramental words. Our Lord in instituting the Sacrament of Holy Baptism commanded His apostles to administer it 'into the Name of the Father and of the Son and of the Holy Ghost.' As pointed out in an earlier chapter, there is every reason to believe that in the Baptisms which are recorded in the New Testament the words, 'into the Name of the Father and of the Son and of the Holy Ghost' were used. From that time onwards they have been the recognised form of the Sacrament.

The *Teaching of the Twelve Apostles* gives them as the ordinary formula. S. Justin Martyr records that those who are being baptized 'receive the washing in the water in the Name of God the Father and Lord of all, and of our Saviour Jesus Christ, and of the Holy Ghost,' that 'the Name of God the Father and Lord of all is named in the water over him who chooses to be regenerate and repents of his sins,' and that 'the person illuminated washes also in the Name of Jesus Christ who was crucified under Pontius Pilate, and in the Name of the Holy Ghost.' The *Acts of Xanthippe, Polyxena, and Rebecca*, which, however small their value may be doctrinally or historically, yet afford evidence of the customs of the second and third centuries, describe S. Paul as having taken Xanthippe 'into the house of Philotheus and baptized her into the Name of the Father and of the Son and of the Holy Ghost,' as having said at the Baptism of Probus, 'We baptize thee into the Name of Father, Son, and Holy Ghost.' The same work affords also a reasonable presumption that this formula was used at the Baptisms of Polyxena and Rebecca. The *Canons of Hippolytus* and the *Apostolical Constitutions* and *Canons* direct the use of the form 'into' or 'in the Name of the Father and of the Son and of the Holy Ghost.' Tertullian, S. Cyprian, and S. Basil are early witnesses to the same practice; and the importance attached to the use of these particular words may be shown by passages in S. Ambrose and S. Augustine, in which it is stated, 'The catechumen believes in the cross of Christ wherewith he himself also is signed; but unless he has been baptized in the Name of the Father and of the Son and of the Holy Ghost, he cannot receive the remission of sins or drink in the boon of spiritual grace,' and 'God is present in His own Gospel words' (that is, the words, 'In the Name of the Father and of the Son and of the Holy Ghost') 'without which the Baptism of Christ cannot be consecrated.' In the time of S. Cyprian there were some who thought that a Baptism administered 'in the Name of Jesus Christ' would be valid. At later times it has been contended as an abstract theory, or in connection with an exceptional opinion about the Baptisms recorded in the New Testament, that a valid Baptism might be administered 'in the Name of Jesus Christ,' or 'in the Name of the Trinity.'[10] It may perhaps be impossible expressly to deny the validity of such a formula. It may certainly be said, in the light of our Lord's command and of all Christian history, that no one who wishes to be loyal to the first principles of Christianity would desire to use other words than those of the recognised form, 'In the

Name of the Father and of the Son and of the Holy Ghost.'

The Western Church has shown the connection between the words and the rite by prefixing to them '*Baptizo te*,' or '*Ego baptizo te*,' 'I baptize thee.'[11] In the mediæval English Church the use of the words 'I christen thee' was contemplated in the case of private Baptisms administered by persons ignorant of Latin; and the lawfulness of the use of these words in lay Baptisms has been recognised in the Church of England since the Reformation.[12] The present custom of the Church in England follows the general Western formula, 'I baptize thee.' In the Eastern Churches, in accordance with their characteristic of emphasizing the action of the minister less than does the Western Church, the words 'The servant of God *N*. is baptized' are used.[13] No grave importance can be attached to this difference. What is of moment is that the words employed in our Lord's command be used, and that some phrase be added connecting them with the administration of the rite of Baptism. It is a matter of grave necessity that in the work of the Church abroad the greatest possible care be taken in the selection of the words used for the baptismal formula in foreign tongues.

In the event of a purely accidental deficiency in

the administration of Baptism, through the carelessness or infirmity of one seriously purposing to administer it, it can hardly be doubted that the Church by her inherent life would make good to the soul of the individual whatever may be wanting and supply the defect.

CHAPTER XI

THE TIME AND PLACE OF THE ADMINISTRATION OF HOLY BAPTISM

Tertullian is the first writer who mentions any special season for the administration of Holy Baptism. In his treatise *On Baptism* he writes thus: 'The more solemn day for Baptism is afforded by the Pasch, since then indeed the passion of the Lord into which we are baptized has been completed. Nor would it be wrong to interpret figuratively the fact that when the Lord was about to keep the last Passover He sent His disciples to make ready and said, " Ye shall find a man carrying water." From the sign of the water He showed the place for the celebration of the Passover. Further, a most wide space for the ordering of the lavers is the season of Pentecost' (*i.e.* Eastertide) 'in which the resurrection of the Lord was made known among the disciples and the grace of the Holy Spirit was bestowed and the hope of the coming of the Lord was shown, because then, when He had been received again into heaven, the angels said unto the apostles that He would so come as also He ascended into heaven, that is at the season of Pentecost. Moreover, when Jeremiah says, " I will also gather them from the ends of the earth on the festal day," he signifies "the day" of the Pasch and Pentecost which is peculiarly the " festal day." Yet every day, every hour is the Lord's; every time is suitable for Baptism: if there is a difference in the festival, it makes no difference in the grace."[1]

Easter and Pentecost came to be recognised as the appropriate times for solemn Baptisms in the early Church. In some parts of the Church there was a similar observance of other seasons also. In Jerusalem and Antioch, in Cappadocia, in Africa, in Gaul, Spain and Ireland, and in Sicily, the Epiphany was kept as a time for Baptism. Christmas, the Festivals of Apostles and Martyrs, and the Feast of S. John the Baptist, were so observed in some parts of the West. Many letters of Popes and decrees of Councils had for their object the limiting of the seasons of solemn Baptism to the Eves of Easter and Pentecost. The mediæval rubrics of the English Church directed, 'Solemn Baptism is customarily celebrated on the Holy Saturday and on the vigil of Pentecost, and therefore children born within eight days before Easter or within eight days before Pentecost ought to be reserved for Baptism on the Holy Saturday or on the vigil of Pentecost, if they can rightly and without danger be so reserved.' At the same time, the rubrics of the elaborate Holy Saturday rites apparently only contemplate Baptisms as a possibility unlikely to be realised.

'Every time,' said Tertullian, 'is suitable for Baptism.' Upon this maxim the early Church habitually acted. Regarding special seasons as of peculiar appropriateness and as rightly marked by the greater solemnities of the Baptism of adults, she yet administered Baptism at any time in cases of necessity, and apparently did not favour any long interval between an infant's birth and his Baptism. The mediæval English rubric, after the provision already quoted for Baptisms on the Eves of Easter and Pentecost, went on to say that in other cases children were to be baptized very soon after their birth. In modern times, especially in the West, the special seasons for Baptism have been little regarded. A rubric still stands in the elaborate rites of the Roman Church for Holy Saturday, to the effect that if candidates for Baptism are present they are to be baptized in the usual way; but in practice it is generally ignored. In the case of the Church in England, no provision has been made for the Eve either of Easter or of Pentecost being observed by the administration of Baptism.[2]

Yet the Church in England has in the Prayer Book laid considerable emphasis on the need of publicity and solemnity in the administration of Holy Baptism. The rubric at the beginning of the Order for the Public Baptism of Infants, while allowing that 'if necessity so require' children may be baptized on any day, directs that 'the people are to be admonished that it is most convenient that Baptism should not be administered but upon Sundays, and other Holy-days, when the most number of people come together; as well for that the congregation there present may testify the receiving of them that be newly baptized into the number of Christ's Church; as also because in the Baptism of infants every man present may be put in remembrance of his own profession made to God in his Baptism'; and the rubric at the beginning of the Order for the Baptism of 'such as are of riper years and able to answer for themselves' refers to 'the people being assembled upon the Sunday or Holy-day appointed.' Moreover, both offices contemplate the Baptisms being administered after the second lesson either at Morning or at Evening Prayer. As a matter of fact, owing to a concurrence of causes, it has become very common for

Baptism to be administered when none or very few of the general congregation are in church, sometimes at Evening Prayer on week-days in the contemplated place or at the end of the office, sometimes at a service for children on Sunday afternoons. This practice is greatly to be regretted, not only because of the disregard of the instructions of the Book of Common Prayer, but also because of its practical disadvantages. The administration of Baptism after the second lesson at Evening Prayer on some Sundays, possibly one in each month, would secure that, in a large number of churches, it was administered 'when the most number of people come together.' If it should be be undesirable to lengthen the service, this need might be met by the omission or shortening of the customary sermon, for the preaching of which at Evening Prayer no express provision is made in the Prayer Book. Any loss in the way of homiletic instruction would be well counterbalanced by the gain of the constant presentation of the Sacrament of Baptism before the eyes of the people. Very much may be learned from what is continually seen. The English Baptismal Offices are full of teaching. A due sense of the value and meaning of this Sacrament is hardly likely to be maintained among those who are never present at the administration of it.

K

As, from the course of events, there was at the first no fixed time of Baptism, so, for a similar reason, there was no fixed place. The Ethiopian eunuch was baptized in a pool of water by the wayside. The other Baptisms recorded in the Acts appear to have been administered wherever those who were baptized happened to be. The *Teaching of the Twelve Apostles* directs Baptism to be administered, if possible, in a running stream; if that cannot be, in a pool; and, failing this, by the pouring of water upon the head. S. Justin Martyr simply says that those who are to be baptized ' are led where there is water,' and are afterwards to be led back to ' the place where those who are called brethren are assembled.' The *Acts of Xanthippe* contemplate S. Paul baptizing in the house of one who had become a believer, and apparently also in a stream or pool out of doors. In the time of Tertullian, apparently, there were no fixed places; for, while in speaking of the time for Baptism he specifies Easter and Pentecost as appropriate seasons, yet saying that any time will do; in referring to the place he simply says, ' There is no difference whether one be washed in the sea or in a pool, in a river or in a spring, in a lake or in a pond; nor is there any difference between those whom John washed in the Jordan and those whom

Peter washed in the Tiber, unless indeed that eunuch whom Philip washed in water which chanced to be by the wayside obtained more or less salvation than these.'

The growth and organisation of the Church rendered necessary the provision of places for the administration of Baptism. S. Cyril of Jerusalem mentions the 'outer house,' which was the place of the renunciation and the profession of faith, and the 'inner house' where the actual Baptism was administered. The number of those baptized on the Eves of Easter and Pentecost made it necessary that the places of Baptism should be of large size. This need was increased by the customary practice of restricting the solemn Baptisms to the chief church of the diocese. When the soldiers of the Emperor Arcadius attempted to arrest S. Chrysostom on the Eve of Easter, 404, a large crowd was assembled in the place of Baptism.[3]

In the fourth century, the erection of special buildings, detached from the churches, had already been begun. The Emperor Constantine built baptisteries at Rome. That of the Lateran may have been partly his work. The circular Church of Santa Costanza, on the Via Nomentana, is by some thought to have been erected by him. Baptisteries, probably dating from the fifth and sixth centuries, still remain at Aquileia, Ravenna, Constantinople, and elsewhere. A church at Canterbury, dedicated to S. John the Baptist, built by Archbishop Cuthbert about the year 750, was partly intended for use as a baptistery.

Till at any rate the ninth century, separate buildings continued to be used for Baptism. The plan of the Church of S. Gall, which was prepared early in the ninth century, is without a detached baptistery, and there is a circular place of Baptism, of about six feet in diameter, in the middle of the nave at the west end of the church. From the ninth century it has been usual for any place of Baptism, whether a baptistery containing a font or a font placed in the nave, to form part of the church itself. In many of the fonts of the later middle ages both in England and abroad there was a leaden partition dividing the font into two compartments, or a small font by the side, so that the water actually used in the Baptism might not go back into the blessed water but might run down into consecrated ground. A similar arrangement is contemplated by the present rubrics of the Roman Church; but in practice a glass dish is frequently used as a substitute for the small font or 'font piscina,' and the water is afterwards poured from it into consecrated ground through a piscina in the wall of the church.[4]

Prayers for the dedication and blessing of the font, and instructions that the font be of a seemly character, are found in the service books of the Church. In the eighty-first canon of 1603 of the Church of England it is appointed that 'according to a former constitution, too much neglected in many places,' 'there shall be a font of stone in every church and chapel where Baptism is to be ministered; the same to be set in the ancient usual places; in which only font the minister shall baptize publicly.'[5]

The administration of Baptism in private houses was allowed in the early Church in cases of necessity. Sick persons were so baptized in the third century. Those who questioned the Christian state of any who had received Baptism in this way were severely reproved by S. Cyprian. The Synod of Laodicea, in the fourth century, directed that 'those who have received Baptism during an illness, if they recover, shall learn the Creed by heart and be made to understand that a divine gift has been vouchsafed to them.' A regulation of an earlier synod, that of Neo-Cæsarea, giving effect to what apparently had previously been customary, prohibited one who had postponed his Baptism until compelled by sickness, from being ordained priest under ordinary circumstances; and this prohibition became part of the ordinary law of the Church.

The practice of baptizing in private houses under circumstances of emergency has existed continuously till the present time. The Eastern rubrics provide for the Baptism of children immediately after birth in cases of necessity. Similar provisions have been made in the West. Yet the administration of Baptism elsewhere than in the church has always been limited to cases in which there have been exceptional circumstances. The rubrics of the English Church in the middle ages, making an exception for the 'son of a king or prince,' forbade Baptisms in private houses except when there would be danger in bringing a child to the church. The present English rubrics are explicit that unless the need is urgent, all children are to be baptized in church: 'The curates of every parish shall often admonish the people that they defer not the Baptism of their children longer than the first or second Sunday next after their birth, or other Holy-day falling between, unless upon a great and reasonable cause, to be approved by the curate. And also they shall warn them, that without like great cause and necessity they procure not their children to be baptized at home in their houses.'[6]

CHAPTER XII

PREPARATION OF CANDIDATES FOR HOLY BAPTISM

THE direct preparation in the case of those whose Baptism is recorded in the New Testament was short. No other requisites for receiving this Sacrament than that the recipients honestly desired salvation and were willing to recognise our Saviour Jesus Christ as their Lord and God are known to have been required. S. Peter's phrase, 'the interrogation of a good conscience towards God,'[1] which may possibly refer to questions and answers before the administration of Baptism, does not supply any detail. It is obvious that the needs and circumstances of the early Church differed widely from those of later times.

In the *Teaching of the Twelve Apostles* fasting before the administration or reception of Baptism is commanded. S. Justin Martyr thus described the preparation known to him: 'As many as are persuaded and believe that these things which are taught and said by us are true and promise that they are able to live thus are taught to pray and ask God with fasting for the forgiveness of their former sins, while we pray and fast with them.' Similarly, Tertullian records that those who were to be baptized were instructed in the Christian Faith, and says that it is right for them 'to pray with frequent prayers, fasts, kneeling, and watching, and with confession of all their past offences.' Fasting is directed also in the *Canons of Hippolytus* and in the *Apostolical Constitutions*.[2]

We have fuller accounts of the systematised preparation which was usual for a time in and after the fourth century. By putting together evidence from various sources much may be known about it. Those who desired to be baptized were, after careful inquiry, admitted into the number of catechumens[3] by being signed with the cross, and receiving the imposition of hands, and possibly by being anointed with oil. From the time of their admission to the catechumenate they were known as 'Christians,' although they were not reckoned among 'the faithful' until they had been baptized. For a period of two or three years or longer, in the course of which they were repeatedly exorcized, they remained under instruction and discipline. During this time they were allowed to be present at the earlier part of the Liturgy. Towards the close of the period, at the beginning of the Lenten fast, the length of which was perhaps determined by the forty days of the final catechumenate, those who wished to receive Baptism at the following Easter gave in their names. They kept the fast carefully with much prayer and watching. They received fuller instruction than before. On the second Sunday in Lent in some places, on the fourth Sunday in Lent in others, their names were written in the roll of the Church. A few days before Baptism they were taught the Creed and the Lord's Prayer, which had previously been kept from them, and learned these by heart, being forbidden to commit them to writing. As catechumens, they received the 'sacrament of the catechumens,' this being, according to some authorities, blessed salt, according to others, blessed bread.[4]

The instruction given to catechumens included the central truths of Christianity; but teaching about the Sacraments, other than what was quite elementary about Baptism itself, was withheld until after they had been baptized. The treatise of S. Augustine *On Catechising the Ignorant* contains an account of the instruction given in North Africa at the beginning of the fifth century: it refers to the history of the general dealings of God with man from the Creation to the Incarnation, and gives teaching about the resurrection of the body and the future judgment. The eighteen *Catechetical Lectures* of S. Cyril of Jerusalem supply us with the actual instruction given at Jerusalem in the middle of the fourth century. The first lecture is of an introductory character, in which S. Cyril exhorts the catechumens to sincerity, confession of sins, forgiveness of others, and the diligent seeking for grace. The next two lectures are on the subjects of repentance, remission of sins, the adversary the devil, and Baptism. The fourth lecture expounds the doctrine of God, the history of our Lord's miraculous birth, His passion, death, burial, resurrection, and ascension, the reality of future judgment, the doctrine of the Holy Spirit, truths about the soul and the body and the use of food and clothing, the general resurrection, and the authority of Holy Scripture. The fifth lecture is on faith. The remaining thirteen lectures are on the various clauses of the Creed.

The course of preparation for Baptism and the instruction of catechumens at Jerusalem some thirty years later than the *Catechetical Lectures* of S. Cyril are described in the work known as the *Pilgrimage of Silvia*. The candidates for Baptism gave in their names eight weeks before Easter;

they were then led up to the bishop, one by one, the men accompanied by their fathers, the women accompanied by their mothers. The bishop then made inquiries about their moral character. If he was satisfied on this point, he marked the name of the candidate as approved; if not satisfied, he sent the candidate away, telling him to amend and then come to the font. The accepted candidates were exorcized daily by the clergy throughout forty days. During the same period the bishop gave them a course of teaching based on the literal and spiritual meaning of Holy Scripture, beginning with the Book of Genesis, and they were instructed in the Christian Faith. At the end of five weeks they were taught the Creed and given an explanation of it. In the Holy Week they were required to repeat it individually before the bishop. The explanation of Baptism itself was not given till after Baptism, in the seven days following Easter.[5]

It was possible for the catechumenate, through the fault of the catechumen, to be much prolonged. If during the time of his probation he fell into grievous sin, the period of discipline might be extended for a few months or for years. In some cases, one who thus had fallen was not allowed to be baptized until he was on his death-bed. On the other hand, the period might be shortened if the catechumen was dangerously ill. If any catechumen, through his own neglect, should die without having been baptized, he was buried without the Service of the Church and the offering of the Eucharist customary at Christian funerals; and his name was not mentioned in the prayers which the Church offered for her departed members.

Yet prayer might be publicly offered in the early Church for a departed unbaptized catechumen who had really desired to be baptized, whose lack of Baptism was not due to his own neglect. This may be seen from the funeral oration of S. Ambrose *On the Death of Valentinian*, delivered at Milan in the year 392. The Emperor Valentinian II. had been admitted to the catechumenate; he was anxious to receive Baptism and had sent for S. Ambrose to baptize him, but before his wish could be carried out he was found dead in his bed, a victim, as some thought, of murder. In the course of the oration referred to, the following passage occurs: 'I hear that ye sorrow because he received not the Sacraments of Baptism. Tell me what else is in you but desire and request? And yet even long ago he so desired Baptism that he was made a catechumen before he had come to Italy; and quite lately he signified his wish that I should baptize him, and he thought that for this reason beyond other reasons

I might be sent for. Has he not therefore the grace which he desired? Has he not that for which he asked? Certainly, because he asked, he received. Whence are the words, "Though the righteous be prevented with death, yet shall he be in rest"? Grant, therefore, to thy servant, Holy Father, the boon which Moses received because he saw in spirit, which David obtained because he knew by means of revelation. Grant, I say, to thy servant Valentinian the boon which he desired, the boon which he asked for when he was healthy and strong and well. . . . Separate him not, Lord, I pray, from his brother' (Gratian, who had been killed in battle nine years before), 'nor suffer the bond of pious kindred to be broken. . . . What hands does he' (Gratian) 'now stretch out to Thee, O Father! What prayers does he pour forth for his brother! With what embrace does he cling to him! How does he suffer him not to be torn from him! There is too his father' (Valentinian I.) . . . 'Grant to the father his son, to the brother his own brother. . . . I will not throw flowers upon his tomb, but I will pour upon his spirit the perfume of Christ. Let others scatter lilies from their full baskets; our lily is Christ. With this will I consecrate his relics, with this will I commend his grace. Never will I divide the names of the holy brothers or separate their merits. I know that this commemoration is pleasing to the Lord and that this union delights Him.'[6]

The spread of Christianity among the nations, and with it the increasing prevalence of the practice of Infant Baptism, naturally led to the gradual abolition of the systematised catechumenate. In the missions of the mediæval Church no such elaborate machinery existed; and the haste with which Baptism was administered, sometimes to whole tribes at once, was characteristic of the work of some of the missionaries of the middle ages.[7] In modern missions the practice has greatly varied. In some cases Baptism has certainly been administered after singularly little instruction or other preparation. In some of the Anglican missions of the present century, notably in Central and South Africa, a serious attempt has been made to revive the best features of the discipline of the ancient catechumenate.

There can be no doubt that the extent and method of needed preparation must vary greatly in different cases and under different circumstances. It would be natural to baptize at once a convert from Judaism in the days of the apostles if it should appear that he was honestly accepting our Lord as the promised Messiah of the Old Testament. Gentiles of regulated habits of life might well be admitted to Baptism if there were signs that they were similarly submitting themselves to the teaching and law of Christ. The discretion and the discrimination which would accompany the miraculous gifts possessed by the apostles might often enable them to baptize without delay those in the case of whom delay would otherwise have been necessary. At the present time, delay and probation which would be necessary in the case of undisciplined savages might be out of place if a thoughtful inquirer in a civilised country should deliberately seek to be baptized. It is of great importance to endeavour to prevent apostasy or bad life among Christians by the use of due precautions in admitting to Baptism. Yet too much must not be expected from any before the grace of God bestowed in Baptism has been received. It must be left to those who are skilled in the various spheres of the Church's work to decide, with the aid of the Holy Ghost, as to the character and length of the preparation and the standard of knowledge and conduct to be required of those about to be baptized.

The English Prayer Books of the sixteenth century and that of 1604 made no provision for the Baptism of adults. In the revision of 1662 the need of such a provision was recognised. In supplying it, the revisers stated in their preface that it was 'not so necessary when the former book was compiled, yet by the growth of Anabaptism, through the licentiousness of the late times crept in among us, is now become necessary, and may always be useful for the baptizing of natives in our plantations, and others converted to the faith.' That they were fully alive to the careful preparation needed for Baptism administered to adults may be seen from the first rubric prefixed to the Office itself, which provides that 'when any such persons as are of riper years are to be baptized, timely notice shall be given to the bishop, or whom he shall appoint for that purpose, a week before at the least, by the parents, or some other discreet persons; that so due care may be taken for their examination, whether they be sufficiently instructed in the principles of the Christian Religion; and that they may be exhorted to prepare themselves with prayers and fasting for the receiving of this holy Sacrament.' In this matter, as in other matters, the Church in England has by her authorised formularies taken great pains to maintain a strong sense of the high dignity of the Sacrament of Baptism, and of the responsibility which rests upon those who are baptized, and to prevent, so far as is possible, any profanation of the Sacrament by its being unworthily received. She has done her best to protect the gifts committed to her keeping by interposing barriers to a hurried or careless approach. At the same time, she has emphasized in many ways the necessity of Baptism and the privileges to which the baptized are admitted; and the study of the preface to the Prayer Book of the revisers of 1662, and of the Office for the Baptism of Adults which they drew up, may well be commended to any who may be inclined to think that they can find justification in the system or methods of the Church in England for remaining unbaptized. The emphasis which the Prayer Book lays upon the necessity of Baptism for any who would live Christian lives is as strong and as marked as that of the undivided Church or of any other part of the Church at the present time.

CHAPTER XIII

THE CEREMONIAL OF THE ADMINISTRATION OF HOLY BAPTISM

From the necessities of the case, there was little ceremonial in the earliest Baptisms. No ceremonial details of any kind, beyond those already alluded to in connection with the matter and form, the time and the place, of Holy Baptism, are mentioned in the New Testament. The book entitled the *Teaching of the Twelve Apostles* adds little more. 'As to Baptism,' it says, ' baptize thus. When ye have recited all this' (that is, the instruction on the 'way of life' and the ' way of death ' contained in the previous chapters) ' baptize into the Name of the Father and of the Son and of the Holy Ghost in running water. But if thou hast not running water, baptize in other water; and if thou canst not do it in cold water, do it in warm water. But if thou hast not either ' (that is, either a stream of running water or a pool of standing water), ' pour water on the head three times into the Name of Father and of

Son and of Holy Ghost. And before the Baptism let him who baptizes and him who is baptized and any others who can fast; but thou art to command him who is baptized to fast for one or two days before.' The few details mentioned by S. Justin Martyr, writing in the middle of the second century with knowledge of Asia Minor and Italy, are of very much the same character. 'We will describe,' he writes, 'the way in which we dedicated ourselves to God, when we were made new through Christ, that we may not, by omitting this, seem to be unfair in what we say. As many as are convinced and believe that our teaching and words are true, and undertake to be able to live in accordance with them, are instructed to pray and to entreat God with fasting for the remission of their past sins, while we pray and fast with them. Then they are brought by us to a place where there is water and are regenerated in the way of regeneration which we ourselves underwent; for they then undergo the washing in the water in the Name of God the Father and Lord of the Universe and of our Saviour Jesus Christ and of the Holy Ghost. . . . We, after we have thus washed him who has been convinced and has assented to our teaching, bring him to the place where those who are called brethren are assembled so that we may heartily offer prayers in common on behalf of ourselves and of him who has been illuminated and of all others in every place, that we may be accounted worthy, now that we have learned the truth, by our works also to be found good citizens and keepers of the commandments in order that we may be saved with the eternal salvation. When we have ended the prayers, we salute one another with a kiss.' S. Justin then proceeds to describe the celebration of the Holy Eucharist, of which he says 'no one is allowed to partake except the man who believes that our teaching is true and has been washed with the washing which is for the remission of sins and unto regeneration and is living in such wise as Christ has commanded.'[1]

Rites used in North Africa at the end of the second century are mentioned by Tertullian. 'In the church,' he says in one treatise, 'under the hand of the bishop, we testify that we renounce the devil and his pomp and his angels. Then we are immersed three times answering something more than the Lord appointed in the Gospel. Then, being taken up from thence, we first taste a mixture of milk and honey; and from that day we abstain for a whole week from our daily washing.' 'Having come out from the bath,' he writes elsewhere, 'we are anointed with hallowed unction,' and 'the

CEREMONIAL OF ADMINISTRATION 165

hand is laid upon us, calling on and inviting the Holy Ghost by means of the blessing.' From the writings of S. Cyprian, a witness to North African practice half a century later than Tertullian, at any rate part of the profession of faith made by the baptized can be collected: 'Dost thou believe in God the Father and the Son Christ and the Holy Ghost?'—'I believe.' 'Dost thou believe in eternal life and the remission of sins through the holy Church?'—'I believe.' Like Tertullian, S. Cyprian mentions the anointing after Baptism, which may have formed part of the ceremonies either of Baptism or of Confirmation, and the imposition of hands, certainly the sign of Confirmation.[2]

We learn from the *Canons of Hippolytus* the method of the administration of Baptism at Rome at the end of the second or the beginning of the third century. The candidates are ordered to fast on the Friday before the day appointed for the rite. On the Saturday the bishop calls them together, directs them to kneel with their heads towards the east, extends his hands over them, and prays for the expulsion of the evil spirit from their whole body. At the end of the prayer the bishop breathes on their faces and makes the sign of the cross upon their breast and forehead, ears and mouth. They watch through the night and spend it in holy communing and prayer. At cockcrow they assemble at the place of the baptismal water and are divested of their clothing. The oil of exorcism and the oil of unction are blessed by the bishop. The candidates turn their faces to the west and say, 'I renounce thee, O Satan, with all thy pomp.' One of the priests in attendance on the bishop anoints them with the oil of exorcism. They then turn their faces to the east and say, 'I believe and bow myself before Thee and all Thy majesty, O Father and Son and Holy Ghost.' They go down into the water and stand in it facing towards the east. Another of the priests lays his hand upon their heads and asks, 'Dost thou believe in God the Father Almighty?' They reply, 'I believe.' Then they are immersed for the first time. After the first immersion the question is asked, 'Dost thou believe in Jesus Christ, the Son of God, Whom Mary the Virgin brought forth of the Holy Ghost, Who was crucified under Pontius Pilate, Who died and on the third day rose from the dead, and ascended into heaven, and sitteth at the right hand of the Father, and will come to judge the quick and the dead?' After replying 'I believe,' they are immersed for the second time. They are then asked, 'Dost thou believe in the Holy Ghost?' They answer 'I believe,' and are immersed for the third and last time. At each immersion the priest says, 'I baptize thee in the Name of the Father and of the Son and of the Holy Ghost.' They are then anointed with the consecrated unction known as chrism, resume their clothing, go into the church, receive from the bishop the laying on of hands, the signing of the cross on their foreheads, and the kiss of peace. Afterwards, the Eucharistic offering begins. The newly baptized make their first communion, and after it are given a taste of milk and honey from cups which are borne by priests, or, in the absence of priests, by deacons.³

S. Cyril of Jerusalem describes at some length the ceremonies of Baptism used at Jerusalem in the middle of the fourth century. The candidates for Baptism were assembled in the vestibule of the baptistery. Facing the west, they stretched out their hands and uttered the renunciation of the devil: 'I renounce thee, Satan, and all thy works, and all thy pomp, and all thy service.' Then, turning their faces from the west to the east, they made the profession of faith: 'I believe in the Father, and in the Son, and in the Holy Ghost, and in one Baptism of repentance.' After this, the candidates entered the inner chamber of the baptistery, put off their clothes and were anointed with oil which had been exorcized. They were then 'led to the holy pool of divine Baptism,' and 'asked whether' they 'believed in the Name of the Father and of the Son and of the Holy Ghost.' Having made this 'saving confession,' they 'descended three times into the water and ascended again,' this threefold immersion symbolising their dying and being buried and rising again with Christ and the three days of His sojourn in the tomb. They were next confirmed by being anointed with chrism, and, clothed in white garments and bearing lighted tapers in their hands, passed out of the baptistery into the church in readiness for their reception of the Body and Blood of Christ in the Eucharist. S. Cyril does not mention the kiss in connection with the Baptism but only at a subsequent point in the celebration of the Eucharist, and he makes no reference at all to the tasting of milk and honey by the newly baptized, which was never a Syrian custom.

The recently discovered book of liturgical prayers ascribed to Serapion, Bishop of Thmuis, implies that the rite in use in Egypt about the middle of the fourth century included, besides the blessing of the water, the renunciation of the devil, what is apparently a profession of belief, Baptism in the water, anointing with oil, and Confirmation by anointing with chrism.[4]

The blessing of the water before the use of it in Baptism, customary in the early Church both in the East and in the West, has been mentioned in a previous chapter. In connection with this it was usual in Egypt, by the end of the fifth century at any rate, to pour chrism into the water; and the fact that this custom was, in the sixth century, usual in the West, and that oil is placed in the water in the East, may perhaps point to its having been more than a merely local practice.

In Gaul and Spain and Ireland, and at Milan, the newly baptized persons underwent a ceremonial washing of the feet performed with reference to our Lord's washing of the feet of the apostles on the night before His death and as a picturesque symbol of some Christian duties. Thus, to quote a typical instance from one of the Gallican Offices, the priest was directed to say: 'Our Lord and Saviour Jesus Christ washed His apostles' feet. I wash thy feet that thou also mayest so act towards guests and strangers who may come to thee. If thou shalt have done this, thou shalt attain to eternal life for ever and ever.' [5]

It is obvious that the baptismal ritual of the early Church was largely based upon the language of Holy Scripture. The exorcism, of which the breathing upon the candidates was the outward sign, was a recognition of the power of Satan frequently referred to by our Lord and the writers of the New Testament. The unclothing was a symbol of the putting off of the 'old man' and 'his deeds.' The white garments symbolised the putting on of the 'new man,' the putting on of Christ. The lights were a sign of the enlightenment of the Christian. The reception of milk and honey would fittingly signify that those who had been baptized had been led into the promised land of which Canaan was the type, though a different explanation is given in the *Canons of Hippolytus*,[6] namely, that it showed that the baptized had become as little children and symbolised the blessings of the life to come.

The instances of rites which have been described illustrate the fact that in the early Church Baptism was immediately followed by the administration of Confirmation and First Communion. This was the case with infants as well as with adults. Certainly, so far as the Confirmation of those baptized as adults is concerned, and probably in the case of infants also, the early Church was in this matter closely following the practice of apostolic times. Those whom S. Philip the Deacon baptized in Samaria were as soon as possible confirmed by S. Peter and S. John. While it is not expressly stated that any infants who may have been baptized in this instance were confirmed, there is no indication that an exception was made in their case. The disciples who were baptized at Ephesus were immediately confirmed by S. Paul.[7]

As Infant Baptism became the ordinary custom, ceremonies originally connected with the preparation of the candidates still continued to be used. The use of the Church at Rome in the seventh and eighth centuries may be illustrated from the *Gelasian Sacramentary*, which shows the instructive and impressive ceremonies of the solemn Baptisms administered at Easter and Pentecost. In the case of the Easter Baptisms, the Mass on the third, fourth, and fifth Sundays in Lent was specially on behalf of those who were to be baptized. At the words in the Canon commemorating the living the priest was directed to say, 'Remember, O Lord, Thy servants and handmaidens who are about to be sponsors to Thy elect in the holy grace of Thy Baptism,' and to recite secretly the names of the sponsors, and later on to say, 'We implore Thee, O Lord, graciously to accept this offering which we offer unto Thee for Thy servants and handmaidens whom Thou hast deigned to number, choose, and call to eternal life and the blessed gift of Thy grace,' and after reciting the names of the candidates for Baptism to proceed, 'We beg, O Lord, that these who are to be renewed by Baptism in the font may be prepared by the gift of Thy Spirit for the fulness of Thy Sacraments.' On the third Sunday in Lent a notice was read in church announcing, 'Dearly beloved brethren, take notice that the day of the scrutiny, on which our candidates for Baptism are to receive heavenly instruction, is at hand. Therefore you are asked to assemble with due devotion on *such a day* following at noon, that, with the help of God, we may be able to perform, without reproach to our ministry, the heavenly mystery by which the devil with his pomp is overthrown and the gate of the kingdom of heaven is opened.' It is directed that the infants be brought to the church on the Monday in this week, their names written down by an acolyte, and that they be called into the church by name. The male children were then placed on the right of the priest, the female children on his left; the prayer for making a catechumen was said over them by the priest; salt was blessed by him and a particle of it placed in the mouth of each of them as a sign of sanctification and salvation; they were exorcized, and after the exorcisms the bishop said the prayer, 'I implore Thy eternal and most just loving-kindness, holy Lord, almighty Father, eternal God of light and truth, for these Thy servants and handmaidens, that Thou wouldest deign to illuminate them with the light of Thy understanding. Cleanse and sanctify them. Grant to them true knowledge that they may be made worthy to come to the grace of Thy Baptism. May they hold firm hope, right counsel, holy doctrine, that they may be fit to receive Thy grace.' On the fifth Sunday in Lent the candidates went through the ceremony of being initiated into the knowledge requisite for Baptism. During the celebration of the Mass, before the Gospel, four deacons, each carrying a book of one of the four Gospels, approached the altar, preceded by lights and incense. The four books were laid upon the altar at the four corners. The meaning of the word Gospel and the symbols of the evangelists were then explained by a priest. After the reading and explanation of a verse out of each of the four Gospels, the Creed used in the Mass, that is, the lengthened form of the Nicene Creed, was recited by an acolyte in Greek or in Latin, according to the language of those presenting the infants, and explained by the priest, as a ceremony of delivering the Creed to the catechumens. This was followed by the delivery and explanation of the Lord's Prayer. On the morning of Easter Even the catechumens were brought to the church and exorcized by a priest, who afterwards touched their nostrils and ears with saliva applied with his finger, saying, 'Ephphatha, that is, Be opened, unto the odour of sweetness. But thou, O devil, be put to flight, for the judgment of God is at hand.' They were next anointed with exorcized oil on the breast and back. Afterwards the renunciation of Satan was made, in the large majority of cases by sponsors on behalf of infants: 'Dost thou renounce Satan?'—'I renounce.' 'And all his works?'—'I renounce.' 'And all his pomps?'—'I renounce.' The priest then recited the Creed as a ceremony of the recitation of it by the candidates for Baptism. The actual Baptism took place at a later hour on the same day. After a litany in procession, the bishop came to the font and blessed the water, making upon it the sign of the cross. The catechumens were then questioned, and replies were made on their behalf. 'Dost thou believe in God the Father Almighty?'—'I believe.' 'Dost thou believe also in Jesus Christ, His only Son, our Lord, who was born and suffered?'—'I believe.' 'Dost thou believe also in the Holy Ghost, the holy Church, the remission of sins, the resurrection of the flesh?'—'I believe.' The candidates were then baptized by being immersed three times, anointed by a priest with chrism on the crown of the head, and afterwards confirmed by the bishop

CEREMONIAL OF ADMINISTRATION 175

by the laying on of hands and anointing with chrism on their foreheads. It was the custom for them to be given communion at the Mass which followed, which was reckoned as the first Mass of Easter Day. The white baptismal robes were worn throughout the octave of Easter during divine service, and to this day the liturgical name for the Sunday after Easter, as being the day of the putting off of this symbolical clothing, has continued, by a shortened form of the phrase '*Dominica in albis depositis*,' to be '*Dominica in albis*,' the 'Sunday of white robes.'[8] Among the prayers of the Easter Even Mass was one in which the celebrant said, 'O God, Who makest light this most holy night by the glory of the resurrection of the Lord, preserve in the new offspring of Thy family the spirit of adoption which Thou hast given, that they being renewed in body and mind may render pure service unto Thee.'

The Sarum Manual contains the ritual of Baptism customary in a considerable part of England from the twelfth century to the sixteenth. The general features of the Sarum rites corresponded to those used in other parts of the West. At an earlier date, in the time of S. Augustine of Canterbury, one of the differences between the British and the Roman customs was in some point connected with the administration of Baptism. What this point was is not known. It may have been that the British Church used single instead of trine immersion, or that it omitted the anointing customary elsewhere in the West after the immersion. This special custom, whatever it was, evidently ceased to be practised in consequence of the decision of the conference of Whitby in the year 664; and there was no marked difference between the continental customs in the administration of Baptism and the English practice as represented in the Sarum book.[9]

The effects of the large proportion of infants among those now baptized are seen in the Baptismal Offices of the Sarum Manual. The 'scrutinies' and the delivery of the Creed are no longer employed. The rite used is divided into distinct parts. The first part is the order for making a catechumen. The child to be baptized is brought to the door of the church. The priest signs him with the cross on the forehead and breast, lays his right hand on his head and prays for him, asking the godparents for the name and calling him by it, and again signing him with the cross on the forehead. Exorcized salt is then placed in the child's mouth; exorcisms of the devil and prayers, differing in accordance with the sex of the child to be baptized, are said; the Gospel account of our

Lord blessing little children is read as given by S. Matthew; the ears and nostrils of the child are touched with saliva; the priest, the godparents, and the bystanders repeat the Lord's Prayer, the Hail Mary, and the Apostles' Creed; the priest signs the child with the cross on his right hand and says, 'I deliver to thee the sign of our Lord Jesus Christ in thy right hand, that thou mayest sign thyself, and drive thyself away from the side of the adversary, and remain in the Catholic Faith, and have eternal life, and live for ever and ever.' Afterwards he leads the child into the church by his right hand, saying, 'Enter into the temple of God, that thou mayest have eternal life and live for ever and ever. Amen.' The second part of the service is the blessing of the font, directed to be used as often as it is necessary that fresh water should be placed in the font. A litany having been said, the priest recites a long prayer, after the form of the preface in the Eucharist, by way of blessing the water. In the course of this prayer he signs the water with the cross with his right hand, breathes upon it three times in the form of a cross, drops wax into it from a lighted candle in the form of a cross, divides it crosswise with the candle placed in the font, removes the candle, and pours holy oil and chrism in the form of a cross into the water. The third part of the service is the Baptism itself. The child is brought to the font and the name told to the priest. The renunciation is made for him by the godparents: 'Dost thou renounce Satan?'—'I renounce.' 'And all his works?'—'I renounce.' 'And all his pomps?'—'I renounce.' He is then anointed with holy oil in the form of a cross on the breast and between the shoulders. The profession of faith is made for him by the godparents: 'Dost thou believe in God the Father Almighty, Maker of heaven and earth?'—'I believe.' 'Dost thou believe also in Jesus Christ His only Son our Lord, Who was born and suffered?—'I believe.' 'Dost thou believe also in the Holy Ghost, the holy Catholic Church, the communion of saints, the remission of sins, the resurrection of the flesh, and eternal life after death?'—'I believe.' Then the priest asks further questions and the godparents reply: 'What dost thou seek?'—'Baptism.' 'Dost thou wish to be baptized?'—'I wish it.' The priest then calling the child by his name says: 'I baptize thee in the Name of the Father,' and immerses him with his head to the east and his face to the north: 'and of the Son,' and immerses him with his face to the south: 'and of the Holy Ghost. Amen,' and immerses him with his face towards the water. The godparents take the child from the hands of the priest and lift him up from the font; the priest anoints him with chrism on the crown of the head in the form of a cross, and puts on him the white robe called the chrisom, saying, 'Receive a robe, white, holy, and spotless; and mayest thou bring it safe before the judgment seat of our Lord Jesus Christ, that thou mayest have eternal life and live for ever and ever. Amen.' Finally, the priest places a lighted taper in his hand and says: 'Receive a light, burning and without reproach: guard thy Baptism, keep the commandments, that when the Lord shall come to the wedding, thou mayest be able to meet him together with the saints in the heavenly hall, that thou mayest have eternal life and live for ever and ever. Amen.' It was directed that the Baptism should be immediately followed by Confirmation if the bishop was present.[10]

The direction that Confirmation, whenever possible, should immediately follow Baptism, gradually ceased to be observed in the West. No separation between Baptism and Confirmation was ever deliberately made. But the course of events led to this separation in practice. In the later middle ages the bishops, to whom the administration of Confirmation was restricted, were often occupied in almost everything except the care of their dioceses. They were frequently men of mark, great statesmen and diplomatists. Many of them never set foot in the dioceses intrusted to them, and left their proper work to assistant bishops too few in number to perform it. The result was that it became increasingly difficult to obtain Confirmation at all; and, when it was obtained, it was very often at a long interval after Baptism.

In the Church of Rome the ceremonial has remained to the present day much as it stands in the mediæval service books. The separation of Confirmation from Baptism has become the invariable practice in the case of those baptized as infants.[11]

In the Churches of the East, which allow a priest using chrism blessed by a bishop to confirm, the custom of administering Confirmation and First Communion immediately after Baptism has been retained to the present time. They have retained, too, very much of the ceremonial of the early Church. The exorcism of the devil, accompanied by the breathing of the priest upon the person to be baptized, is followed by the renunciation of 'Satan and all his works, and all his angels, and all his service, and all his pomp,' and the profession of the Creed. The prayers for the blessing of the water are then said, the water being signed with the cross and oil poured into it. The person is anointed with oil, then baptized with three immersions, vested in a white garment, and finally confirmed by being anointed with chrism.[12]

The Church of England in the sixteenth century revised the offices of Baptism. In the First Prayer Book of King Edward VI., which came into use at Pentecost 1549, there was still a separate rite for the blessing of the font; but the two offices of the order of making a catechumen and of the Baptism itself were thrown into one. The order for the blessing of the font was new, and was modelled on the Mozarabic or Spanish rather than on the Roman or the Sarum rite. The use of it was directed before any Baptism took place when fresh water had been placed in the font; and it was ordered that the water should be changed not less often than once a month. It did not contain the ceremonies of placing wax, oil, and chrism in the font. In the actual service of Baptism some of the ceremonies formerly in use were abolished. The administration of exorcized salt and the touching of the ears and nostrils with saliva were omitted. Other ancient and mediæval ceremonies were retained. The child was still received by the priest at the church door and signed with the cross upon the forehead and breast.

The devil was exorcized in the words, 'I command thee, unclean spirit, in the Name of the Father, of the Son, and of the Holy Ghost, that thou come out and depart from these infants, whom our Lord Jesus Christ hath vouchsafed to call to His holy Baptism, to be made members of His Body and of His holy congregation. Therefore, thou cursed spirit, remember thy sentence, remember thy judgment, remember the day to be at hand wherein thou shalt burn in fire everlasting, prepared for thee and thy angels. And presume not hereafter to exercise any tyranny toward these infants, whom Christ hath bought with His precious blood, and by this His holy Baptism calleth to be of His flock.' The Gospel account of our Lord blessing little children was read as given by S. Mark. The minister, the godparents, and the people present repeated the Lord's Prayer and the Apostles' Creed. The child was led into the church to the font, the priest saying, 'The Lord vouchsafe to receive you into His holy household, and to keep and govern you alway in the same, that you may have everlasting life. Amen.' The renunciation and profession of faith remained in a slightly altered form: 'Dost thou forsake the devil and all his works?'—'I forsake them.' 'Dost thou forsake the vain pomp and glory of the world, with all the covetous desires of the same?'—'I forsake them.' 'Dost thou forsake the carnal desires of the flesh, so that thou wilt not follow nor be led by them?'—'I forsake them.' 'Dost thou believe in God the Father Almighty, Maker of heaven and earth?'—'I believe.' 'Dost thou believe in Jesus Christ His only begotten Son our Lord, and that He was conceived by the Holy Ghost, born of the Virgin Mary, that He suffered under Pontius Pilate, was crucified, dead, and buried; that He went down into hell, and also did rise again the third day; that He ascended into heaven, and sitteth on the right hand of God the Father Almighty: And from thence shall come again at the end of the world, to judge the quick and the dead: Dost thou believe this?'—'I believe.' 'Dost thou believe in the Holy Ghost, the holy Catholic Church, the communion of saints, remission of sins, resurrection of the flesh, and everlasting life after death?'—'I believe.' 'What dost thou desire?'—'Baptism.' 'Wilt thou be baptized?'—'I will.' The threefold immersion of the child, 'first dipping the right side: second, the left side: the third time dipping the face toward the font: so it be discreetly and warily done,' was ordered with an alternative 'if the child be weak, it shall suffice to pour water upon it.' The use of the baptismal form, 'N. I baptize thee in the Name of the Father and of the Son and of the Holy Ghost. Amen,' was retained. The godparents were directed to 'take and lay their hands upon the child,' and the minister to 'put upon him his white vesture commonly called the chrisom' and to say, 'Take this white vesture for a token of the innocency, which by God's grace in this holy Sacrament of Baptism is given unto thee, and for a sign whereby thou art admonished, so long as thou livest, to give thyself to innocency of living, that, after this transitory life, thou mayest be partaker of the life everlasting. Amen.' It was also ordered that the priest should 'anoint the infant upon the head' and say, 'Almighty God, the Father of our Lord Jesus Christ, who hath regenerate thee by water and the Holy Ghost, and hath given unto thee remission of all thy sins: He vouchsafe to assist thee with the unction of His Holy Spirit, and bring thee to the inheritance of everlasting life. Amen.' The older services had made provision for exhortations addressed to the godparents. The new service, following to a certain extent an ancient Gallican rite and considerably influenced by the Lutheran *Consultatio* of Archbishop Hermann of Cologne, extended this element.

In the Second Prayer Book of King Edward VI.,

published in the year 1552, further alterations were made. The prayer for the blessing of the water ceased to be used as a separate rite, and a somewhat indefinite form of it was placed in the Order of Baptism immediately before the actual administration of the Sacrament. The office was begun at the font instead of at the church door. Besides minor alterations, the exorcism, the direction for the three-fold method of the dipping of the child, the use of the chrisom, and the anointing were omitted. The signing of the child with the cross was upon the forehead only and was ordered after the act of baptizing instead of at the beginning of the service.

In the Prayer Book of 1662, the Order for the Public Baptism of Infants remained substantially the same as in 1552, with the exception that the prayer for the blessing of the water was made more definite.

The Baptismal Offices of the Church in England were thus greatly simplified in the revision of the formularies which was carried out in the sixteenth and seventeenth centuries. The essential features and the most valuable of the non-essential features were carefully retained. In a reaction from an elaboration of ceremonial, the complications of which had tended to obscure truth in the minds of many, much which was beautiful and instructive was abandoned. And the separation of Baptism from Confirmation, one of the matters in which the practice of the mediæval Church had departed most widely from the early Church, was continued and to some extent emphasized.

It may be hoped that at some future time the synods of the provinces of Canterbury and York, acting on the principles strongly affirmed by the Church in England in the sixteenth and seventeenth centuries, may restore the primitive custom of administering Confirmation and First Communion, in the case both of infants and of adults, immediately after Baptism. It is sometimes urged in defence of the existing practice of the Church in England that the value of the present preparation for Confirmation and of the renewal of the baptismal vows is very great and cannot rightly be surrendered. This argument is radically faulty. It attaches more importance to the subjective utility which is pleaded than to the objective value of the possession of Confirmation grace throughout childhood. It makes more of a utilitarian plea than of a custom of the Universal Church for many centuries. It fails to recognise the fact that this universal custom was never deliberately altered by any part of the Church but merely lapsed into disuse in the West through the course of circumstances and episcopal neglect. Further, the utility of the preparation referred to might easily be secured, in the case of persons confirmed and communicated in infancy, by a course of preparation for the first reception of the Holy Communion after attaining the age which, under existing methods, would be thought appropriate for Confirmation. A renewal of the baptismal vows corresponding to that which forms part of the introduction of the present Order of Confirmation might well be associated with the same momentous event in the child's life.

There are many good reasons which make Churchmen unwilling at the present time that steps should be taken in the direction of the revision or alteration of any part of the Book of Common Prayer. In the present circumstances of the Church in England, it is a wise course to use every effort to maintain the Prayer Book unaltered. If the years that are coming see a solid growth in the acceptance of sound Church principles, there is no good reason that a task which it would be unwise at present to undertake should not be entertained and successfully carried out.

It has been frequently laid down that the clergy are bound to administer Baptism, like other Sacraments, free of charge. To give one instance, it was enjoined at a council held at London in 1126 A.D.

that 'no charge at all be made for the Chrism or the oil or Baptism or Penance or the Visitation of the sick or Unction or the Communion of the Body of Christ or Burial.'[13]

The responsibility of seeing that gravely unsuitable names are not imposed upon infants appears to rest upon the officiating minister. In the Constitutions of Peccham, Archbishop of Canterbury towards the end of the thirteenth century, it is laid down that priests are to take care that improper names are not given to little children; and there is a similar injunction in the Church of Rome at the present day which ends with the recommendation that the names of saints are to be preferred in order that the examples of them may prove an incentive to holy life. The fifteenth century canonist, William Lyndwood, Bishop of S. David's, accurately estimates the degree of the responsibility which attaches in this matter to the clergy by saying that it is in the first instance the duty of the parents or godparents to decide the name, and that the discretion of the priest be mainly exercised in preventing names of evil import being given by the sponsors to the child.[14]

It was customary in the West in the middle ages for the priest to wear a surplice and a stole in administering Baptism. It appears to have been usual in some places for the stole to be of violet colour until after the renunciation, and then to be changed for one of white. For the services on Easter Eve, of which solemn Baptisms formed historically an important part, it was ordered in the Sarum use that the priest should wear a red cope. The present custom in the Church of Rome is for the priest to wear a surplice with stole, first of violet and then of white, at the Baptism of infants. If the Baptism is of adults, the priest may wear a violet and a white cope. If a bishop administers Baptism either to an infant or to an adult, he is directed to wear rochet, alb, girdle, stole, cope, and mitre, the colour of the stole and cope being violet for the earlier part of the office, white for the actual Baptism. The prescribed vestments in the Church of England are those ordered in the rubric which directs 'that such ornaments of the church and of the ministers thereof at all times of their ministration, shall be retained and be in use as were in this Church of England by the authority of Parliament in the second year of the reign of King Edward the Sixth.' Thus the appointed vestments for the order of Baptism are the surplice and stole in the case of ordinary Baptisms and the cope in the case of solemn Baptisms.[15]

In the Order of Holy Baptism in use in the East the rubric directs, "The priest entereth, and vesteth himself in white sacerdotal vestments and cuffs, and while all the tapers are being lighted he taketh a censer, and goeth to the font and censeth round-about."[16]

There is ground for regret that in the Church of England, and indeed throughout the West, so little regard is commonly paid to the solemnity and dignity of the administration of Holy Baptism. So much has been done of late years to restore to the Eucharistic Office and to that of Confirmation something of the beauty and outward character which they ought to possess, that the poverty of the method in which Holy Baptism is ordinarily administered is the more strongly marked. The solemn administration of this Sacrament with due dignity and ceremonial, such as is allowed by the Book of Common Prayer in this case no less than in the case of the Eucharist, at times when a congregation may reasonably be expected, would be doing honour to the ordinance of God and might be a means of removing wide-spread and deplorable ignorance. In some of the foreign missions of the English Church great pains have been taken to give greater prominence to the administration of Holy Baptism than is customary in England. This is in part the result of circumstances to some extent resembling those of the early days of Christianity; it is, at the same time, also a reproach to the Church at home.[17]

CHAPTER XIV

REASONABLE AND MORAL ASPECTS OF THE DOCTRINE OF HOLY BAPTISM

THROUGHOUT this volume the subject of Christian Baptism has been treated from the standpoint of revelation. It has been assumed that God has been pleased to reveal His truth and His will to men, that the revelation thus made is contained in the Holy Scriptures of the Old and New Testaments, that the words of our Lord are the utterances of a divine and infallible teacher, and that the authority of the apostles and of the other writers of the New Testament has the weight which is attached to the decisions and statements of those who are commissioned and inspired by God. Further, it has also been assumed that the Universal Church, as being the mystical body of Christ and as indwelt by God the Holy Ghost, is the divinely appointed instrument for teaching Christian truth and for carrying on Christian work in the world. To whatever extent the standpoint of historical Christianity thus taken up is departed from, to that extent much which has been said in this little book will naturally fail to be convincing. If this standpoint be taken, and the teaching of Holy Scripture, as interpreted and put in force by the Universal Church, be admitted as the decisive authority given by God to man in all matters of faith and morals and therefore on the subject of Holy Baptism, it will be seen that this Sacrament is not only an external sign, however vivid and picturesque and full of meaning; it must be also a covenanted means of grace whereby the baptized are admitted into the mystical body of Christ and united to Him, are brought into close relation and union with the Three Persons of the Holy Trinity, are placed in possession of new Christian life intended to issue in the joy and service of eternity, and are clothed with the righteousness of Christ; and this righteousness thus given to them is destined, when duly realized and kept and used, to find its expression in the highest holiness of which the recipient, by the grace of God, is capable. Subsidiary questions and side issues involved in difficulty and obscurity there may be: for those who are viewing the matter from the standpoint here adopted the main truth is abundantly clear.

But there are many who earnestly believe in the Bible as the Word of God, and are full of regard and affection for the Church of Christ, who wish for something more than the mere repetition of what authority has declared. Such a desire is by no means a reflection of the spirit of unbelief. In many persons it comes from a profound conviction that the revelation contained in the Old and New Testaments and the guidance of the Universal Church are the good gifts of Him Who is the author of wisdom, and that in consequence the reason of His creatures is able to trace out, at any rate to some extent, the signs of the rational purpose of all His works. To their minds it falls within the office of Christian faith to seek out the reasonableness of that which it believes, and to act on the latter no less than on the former part of S. Augustine's maxim, 'First believe, afterwards understand.'[1] Without for one moment condemning or despising or depreciating those who are content to rest in simple childlike belief in what they have been taught, they are deliberately and honestly of opinion that it is their duty to endeavour to know something about the reasons as well as about the facts. By others, again, it is felt that if so tremendous a doctrine as the Church's teaching on the subject of Baptism is true, they must not be content simply to hold it themselves for their own profit and strength and comfort, but must speak of it to others; and that, if they are to be listened to, they must be prepared to consider and discuss the matter from other points of view than that of mere authority. Themselves profoundly convinced of the claims of Christian dogma, they recognise that the ways to truth are many, and that there may be those who will approach the truth on this subject by a somewhat different road from that along which they themselves have come. And in a third group of genuine believers in the Christian religion, there may sometimes be doubts and questions which they think may be solved through the consideration of the matter from more than one point of view.

It may, therefore, rightly be expected that, even in a work on the present scale, some space should be devoted to what may be termed the consideration of the doctrine of Holy Baptism in the light of the Christian reason and conscience, or, in other words, the consideration how far this doctrine may be seen to commend itself to the mental outlook and moral principles of those who believe that Christianity is a real factor in human life.

At the outset, it is necessary to recall a truth already referred to more than once, the use of means or intermediate instrumentalities. Such instrumentalities, as has already been seen, were abundantly employed under the Jewish dispensation, and were sanctioned and used by Christ. The use of them is found throughout all nature. If science has shown us anything, it has shown us how, in the natural world, cause and effect continually succeed each other and agency after agency are ever working in succession. Christian science does not depose God from His place as creator and providential ruler; but it sees in His work the habitual use of instruments the most numerous and varied. To those whose eyes are open to the wonders of nature and the achievements of science, there should be nothing strange if in the Christian religion God uses intermediate means in what He does for the soul.

There is nothing, secondly, which need excite doubt if the work in the soul is accomplished by means of what is done to the body. It has already been noticed that similar action was provided for in the Old Testament. It is more to the point here to call attention to the close connection between the body and the soul. As we view life from the outside, the soul receives its impressions and performs its actions by means of the body. Without disregarding the possibility of divine power affecting the soul without using any bodily faculty or function, or of the soul performing acts so entirely spiritual that in them the body has no share, the impressions and actions of the soul with which we are most familiar are closely connected with the body. The soul receives its ordinary impressions through the exercise of the faculties of sight and hearing which belong to the body; the soul performs its ordinary actions by the use of the material brain. It is entirely in harmony with the principle which is here involved that in the Sacrament of Baptism the application of a material element to the human body should be the means by which a profound effect is produced in the soul.

Thirdly, it is not to be wondered at that the material means appointed to produce so great a result should be of so simple and commonplace a character. A true idea of the greatness of God sees nothing inconsistent with His dignity and majesty in His employing what some may think so poor a thing as water. Rather, any idea of such inconsistency would be incompatible with a worthy conception either of God Himself or of the natural world. A true instinct shrinks back from the thought of God despising anything which He has made; and the more we think, the more we are led to believe in the greatness even of the simplest parts of the natural world. What Christian philosophy suggests is supported by scientific research. There are very small, and to an unskilled eye seemingly very unimportant parts of the body of man which have great influence upon his reason and his life. And if God is a wise and loving ruler, is it not reasonable that the rite which all who are to become Christians need should be received by means of what is most simple and most common?

It may be asked, granting that means may rightly be used to accomplish ends, that what is material may affect what is spiritual, and that water is no inappropriate instrument for the accomplishment of a great work; is it in accordance with the fact that man is a moral being, with his own decisions to make, his own life to live, his own character to mould, and his own fate to carry out, that he should by such a way as the reception of Baptism obtain great spiritual gifts? Is there not something contrary to the highest morality in the reception of a Sacrament effecting so much? The answer to this question is really supplied by what has already been said about the meaning of regeneration. Regeneration, it has been pointed out, while it conveys priceless gifts, does not imply that they necessarily will be used well, or that they will be exercised at all; and it avails, if they are used badly, to deepen rather than to prevent the condemnation of him who has received them. Man does not cease to be treated as a moral being because privileges are bestowed upon him. Rather, the bestowing of the privileges raises him to a higher moral sphere. It gives him more for the use of which he is accountable. It does not hinder his own development of his character. On the contrary, it places him in a position by means of which he can develop it better. It would be different if the gift of regeneration were a gift of eternal life which could not be forfeited, and if those who are baptized were dispensed from the need of any effort or struggle of their own. Regeneration confers benefits which, while the sacramental character of the baptized inevitably remains, can be forfeited, and are only to be retained by real and serious effort. By it a great power is implanted in the soul, and it is of its essence that, in proportion as it is used and is beneficial, the moral character of him who uses it will be braced and enriched.

In one form or another, the fact of the existence of original sin has been acknowledged by countless thinkers who have not been Christians. The hopelessness and darkness of heathen thought have been one result of such an implicit acknowledgment. The study of human history and the experience of human life agree in their witness that somehow a distortion, a twist, a taint of evil is found in the race of man. The presence of this twist implies that if human life is to have its true development, and if man is to become what he ought to be, there is need of some new starting-point in the individual soul by which, instead of making his journey in a wrong direction, he may be enabled to begin it aright. It is in the deepest sense reasonable and moral that as the life and death and resurrection and ascension of our Lord Jesus Christ have made a new starting-point for the human race, so in the Sacrament of Baptism there is a new starting-point for the individual who is baptized.

However true a fact of human life original sin may be, Christian holiness is no less true. The history of the Church, in spite of all its dark pages, is full of records of wonderful sanctity of the most varied kinds. There have been in rich abundance the virtues that are appropriate to manhood, and womanhood, and childhood. There have been daring and purity; there have been patience and self-sacrifice; there have been the energy to work and the calmness to wait. In all sorts of positions and under all kinds of trials Christian holiness has made known its reality and its strength. It has been seen in the lives of great saints within the borders of the Church; its power has been shown by the influence which it has exercised on the ordinary level of thought and life; it has been found to produce a capacity of facing and dealing with all conditions and facts and problems of human existence.

Moreover, the character which Christianity has formed is one which possesses marked differences from characters which have existed under the highest auspices other than Christian. The distinctively Christian character has both a completeness and a refinement which is vainly sought elsewhere. To compare the strange beauty of the character of S. Paul with the highest lives we know of outside Christianity in the same period of history is to observe a difference of deep significance. Wonderful gentleness and refinement and tenderness and courtesy are seen to be joined to zeal and courage and impetuosity and stern love of truth and righteousness. It is not that single virtues are not found outside the Christian sphere. It is that this strange and beautiful combination of virtues goes to make up a temper distinctively Christian. Systems of thought and life must be tried and tested by the best they can produce as well as by their average results. The best products of Christianity are on a level altogether different from that of the best to be found elsewhere.

As the power of Christian holiness may be seen in the completeness of the Christian character, so also it has been shown in its influence on society at large, on art, and on poetry. Christian holiness has raised the whole standard of social and political and national life. It has not yet, indeed, accomplished all at which it must aim. War, for instance, still exists. But, even where, as in this instance, anti-Christian forces have been too strong to allow of its complete victory, it has done very much. Christian monarchs and governments recognise the evil of war in a way which was unknown to heathendom. No civilised statesman, in entering upon an unjust war of aggression, would now allow it to be such. He would always put forward some seemingly just pretext; and thus, while acting against the principles of Christian holiness, unconsciously acknowledge its power. The methods in which war is carried on are deeply marked by the pity which, in its highest forms, is a distinctive characteristic of Christianity. The Christian soldier affords an instance of the extraordinary power of the faith and life which have used even the horrors of war as instruments for producing a high type of singular excellence and beauty.

> 'Who, doomed to go in company with Pain,
> And Fear, and Bloodshed, miserable train!
> Turns his necessity to glorious gain;
> In face of these doth exercise a power
> Which is our human nature's highest dower;

> Controls them and subdues, transmutes, bereaves
> Of their bad influence, and their good receives:
> By objects, which might force the soul to abate
> Her feeling, rendered more compassionate;
> Is placable—because occasions rise
> So often that demand such sacrifice;
> More skilful in self-knowledge, even more pure,
> As tempted more; more able to endure,
> As more exposed to suffering and distress;
> Thence, also, more alive to tenderness.'[2]

Greek art possessed, in a supreme degree, the characteristic merit of depicting with a marvellous sense of symmetry and beauty the life and passions of this natural world: it has been left for art, under what may be called the baptism of the Christian spirit, to exhibit, so far as is possible, the life and the hope of the world to come. In like manner, the dim and fitful guesses at what was true and beautiful in the songs of the heathen poets have found a surer expression in the finest utterances of their Christian successors, who have striven to interpret the present in the light of the eternal world.

> 'Give honour unto Luke Evangelist;
>   For he it was (the aged legends say)
>   Who first taught Art to fold her hands and pray.'[3]

>   ' There seems one only worthy aim
>   For poet—that my strength were as my will!—
>   And which renounce he cannot without blame—
>   To make men feel the presence by his skill
>   Of an eternal loveliness, until

> All souls are faint with longing for their home,
> Yet the same while are strengthen'd to fulfil
> Their task on earth, that they may surely come
> Unto the land of life, who here as exiles roam.'[4]

How, in the face of the fact of the existence of original sin, are these other facts of Christian holiness and its great and far-reaching influence to be accounted for? It is at least reasonable to hear what those in whom Christian holiness has shown its reality have to say about it. They tell us that they have lived by the life of the Son of God, and that the beginnings of His life in them took their rise at the font.

Not without good reason was Baptism called the Sacrament of 'illumination' by the early Church. The whole horizon of intellectual thought has been enlarged by Christianity. The universe has a new interest and marvel for those who see in it the work of Him Who is the Word and Wisdom of God, in Whom by Baptism they are spiritually incorporated. The Christian era has been one of unexampled continuous intellectual advance and gain; and union with Christ has given enthusiasm and faith to whatever makes for the progress and enlightenment of men. The love of truth which has suggested and marked much scientific research has had new light and glory under the auspices of the Christian faith. The quickened perception which Christian pastors have loved to detect in the minds of the baptized illustrates scarcely less forcibly the same great fact.

The union with Christ which is begun in Baptism has shed light on every part of man's existence. Illuminating both his conscience and his intellect, and invigorating his moral force, it has enabled him, even in the twilight of the present life, to behold God. In doing so, it has bestowed a deep and strong joy which is without reproach from the intermixture of sin, which is independent of surroundings and circumstances and conditions. Its practical results have made it clear that the gloom of the heathen was not intended to be the lot of the creatures of God. It has shown that in the divine counsels the highest happiness and the highest holiness are inseparably joined. The true vocation of the children of the kingdom is both to walk and to rejoice in the light.

The enthusiasm of the early Christians was a great moral force. It enabled them to maintain the Christian faith and life against difficulties well-nigh insuperable. The spring of their enthusiasm lay in their union with Christ. This union they believed to have been effected by means of their Baptism. It was distinctive of the life of the baptized that they had 'put on Christ' and were 'in Christ.' By the power which was thus communicated to them, they were able to fulfil their true calling as Christians by their conquest of the world, the flesh, and the devil. From that time until the present, this power has been continuously given to Christians; and now, as then, there are known examples of its blessed results.

Baptism is only the first step in the Christian life. It is indeed a long step and one that is notable. It is the step out of darkness into light, out of wrath into divine grace, out of death into life, out of the power of Satan into the Church of God. It is the initial rite of the Gospel 'whereby,' in the splendid language of the Whitsuntide Preface of the English Church, 'we have been brought out of darkness and error into the clear light and true knowledge of' the Father 'and of' His 'Son Jesus Christ.' But it is a step which calls for many successive steps. The grace which is given by means of it needs to be drawn out into active life and work by prayer and effort and the use of other means of grace. It is never, when viewed in its true aspect, an inducement to sloth but always an incentive to work. For it is only as the Christian uses the grace which is his by virtue of his Baptism that he can realise its value. It will indeed enable him to overcome temptation, but only as he himself sets himself in opposition to temptation. It will empower him to attain to holiness, but only as he makes holiness his aim. It is a force the greatness of which no human language can adequately express, but a force which in its operation is moral and not mechanical.

A strong appeal is made to Christian reason and conscience by the Incarnation of the Son of God. But the reasonableness and moral force of the Incarnation carry with them the reasonableness and moral force of the sacramental principle and of the Sacrament of Baptism. It appeals both to the reason and to the conscience that He Who took our human nature into personal union with Himself should also unite us individually to the human nature which He made to be His own and through it to His Divine Person. This truth has found expression in the noble prayer used in the office for Holy Saturday in the Latin Church: 'God, Who didst wonderfully create man and still more wonderfully redeem him: grant us, we beseech Thee, with purpose of mind to stand fast against the allurements of sin, that we may be counted worthy to come to eternal joys.' Natural marvels yield to the wonders of supernatural grace, and of these last the Sacrament of Holy Baptism is alike the ratification and the means.

The harmony of the doctrine of Holy Baptism with the highest morality may perhaps be most clearly seen when it is remembered that, great as are the privileges and powers which Baptism conveys, the responsibilities which it imposes are no less great. The baptized are enrolled in the army of Christ, and their sins are acts of disloyalty to Him Whom they are pledged to serve. But they are far more than His soldiers and servants. They are also His members, parts of His own body, united unto Him, and living in Him. S. Paul marked the indignity done to Christ by the sin of a Christian when he used the strong words, 'Know ye not that your bodies are members of Christ? Shall I then take away the members of Christ and make them members of a harlot? God forbid.'[5] The same principle holds good with all kinds of sins. In every sin committed by a Christian there is a special act of dishonour to Christ Himself.

It has been asked, again, is there not something selfish and self-seeking in a doctrine which lays so strong stress on the privileges which Christians receive in Baptism? Does it not tend to create a class feeling of superiority through which those who have been baptized may be led to despise others? Is not the principle which underlies baptismal doctrine of a narrowing kind? It is certainly the case that it is possible for good gifts to be misused, and for great and valuable truths to be perverted. But, rightly viewed and used, the doctrine of Holy Baptism is of anything but a narrowing tendency. It creates, indeed, a strong sense of the brotherhood of Christians. It recognises that all those who have been made the sons of God and members of Christ are united together in a holy fellowship. Joined to Christ, they are joined also one to another in a unity which is not the less real because it is unseen. They have attained to that which many of the heathen have longed for and vainly struggled to reach, the true human brotherhood of a fellowship and a unity having their centre in God. But unless this thought of brotherhood be untrue to itself, it has no narrowing influence. Those who hold it see in the unbaptized something more than can be seen by any who do not believe in the doctrine of Baptism. For they look on them as beings who are capable of receiving the great gifts of regeneration and life in God; they recognise in them the elemental sonship to God which is theirs because they are His creation and share the nature taken by the Son of God in the Incarnation, an elemental sonship which pleads for the higher sonship of the baptized; they are filled with a profound pity as far as possible removed from contempt for those who are thus outside the sphere of covenanted grace; they are animated by a strong desire to communicate the good gifts which they themselves have received. The holy zeal and the self-denying labours of the great Christian missionaries may afford a sufficient answer to any who suppose that the doctrine of Baptism is of a selfish and self-seeking character and a sufficient rebuke to any Christians who are so grievously perverting it as to make it so. And, indeed, to submit to that to which we contribute nothing, so far from being selfish, is in itself a protest against any arrogance of personal character or individual claim.

Further, it may be suggested that the doctrine of Baptism and of the Sacraments generally is destructive of the true dignity of human life by making man altogether dependent upon God. Such an objection to the assertion of the sacramental principle is in reality an objection to the Christian religion itself. For the whole system of Christianity is inseparably connected with the belief that apart from God man can do nothing good. If by the use of his natural faculties he accomplishes any good result or attains to any portion of truth, he does so by using faculties which God created and can at any moment destroy. If, outside the Christian religion, he is able to perform good actions of any kind, it is because his nature still retains, in however marred a form, the image of God which makes him distinctively man. Man came from God and he goes to God, and independent of God he cannot be. To seek such independence is to place himself in rebellion against his Creator, and to risk the loss of all his powers for good. The true dignity and greatness of man are to be found, not in his independence of, but in his dependence upon, God. That in union with God he can develop his own character to its noblest height is a truth which was felt after by great heathen thinkers and is involved in the whole system of the Christian faith.

The human heart yearns to be united with God, and to find in this union the possibilities of the satisfaction of all its needs and affections and of a holiness which is not less truly its own possession because it is imparted by God. The unimpeded enjoyment of this union is not indeed to be found in the present life; and growth in it here needs recourse to many means of grace and to discipline of various kinds. But the first gift of it, which brings the soul of man into contact with the humanity of Christ and the divine life of the Holy Trinity, is bestowed in Holy Baptism; and this gift makes the distinction which exists between the baptized and the unbaptized the greatest severance that is possible between human beings, and affords a well-grounded and reasonable hope for the realisation of all the goodness and joy that man can desire.

Nor do reason and morality claim that the great gifts of Baptism be withheld until they can be consciously received. Infants enter on their natural life with tendencies of character which they themselves have not formed. They pass their earliest years amid surroundings and influences which they themselves have not chosen. As they grow up, they are placed under systems of education with the control of which they themselves have nothing to do. From the first moment of their existence they inevitably suffer from the effects of the original sin for which they have no personal responsibility. Reason and morality alike demand that they be given also the grace which may enable them to make a good beginning in their efforts to serve God, and that those who derive so much from the lives and influences and actions of others be not deprived of the highest gifts of all.

Neither, again, is it unfair to place upon the unconscious infant life the responsibilities of the baptized. This is but in accordance with what is found in daily life. The son of a peer, the child of a millionaire, the descendant of the statesman or thinker who has enriched and ennobled action and thought, has each his heavy responsibility. As the position which he inherits may be a crushing burden if it is wrongly borne or a rich blessing if it is rightly used, so the responsibilities which Baptism confers are in truth not the least of its boons.

Underlying all such considerations as those discussed in this chapter is the fact that the Christian system is a society, a kingdom, a church. It is necessary for those who are to have part in its privileges and its responsibilities to be incorporated into a body. The society which receives individuals into itself must perform some act by which they are received. That act, in the judgment of the Christian centuries, is the act of Baptism.

It is possible, then, to sum up the conclusions which may be derived from the consideration of the doctrine of Holy Baptism in the light of reason and the principles of morality. There is nothing irrational in the doctrine. If it stood alone, there might be. Standing as it does, as one harmonious part of a great system, it is in the best sense rational. The works of nature and of grace are alike accomplished by means of intermediate instrumentalities. Such an operation there is in the use of Baptism by Almighty God as a means of bestowing gifts on His creatures. The relation of body and soul is of the closest; that which is spiritual finds its expression and its help by means of what is material. In Baptism by the institution of God the material element of water together with the prescribed form of words is used to confer spiritual gifts. Sin had obtained so deep a hold in man that the strength of new life in actual union with God was needed to deliver him. This new life is given to man when he is united in Baptism to the Sacred Manhood of the Second Adam our Lord Jesus Christ. The distortion of original sin is unconsciously received by infants by reason of their descent from Adam. The grace to remedy this distortion is equally unconsciously received by them by means of Holy Baptism. If it should be urged that it is inconsistent with the dignity and majesty of Almighty God that He should employ such poor means to accomplish so great ends, it may be answered that such a view rests upon a complete misunderstanding of the greatness of God.

The doctrine of regeneration does not destroy the need of effort. Rather, it makes effort both possible and effectual. It does not impair the reality of freewill. On the contrary, it affords scope for the highest forms of the exercise of freewill. It is not a charm which acts in spite of the will of the person who receives it, but a gift of privilege and power which, if it is to produce its due effect in those who attain to the use of reason and the exercise of mental and moral freedom, requires the co-operation of the will. It does not ensure victory in the conflict, but gives power to begin and sustain it.

The doctrine, which is thus as moral as it is rational, is also true to facts. There are hardly any facts in human life which are so deeply grounded in experience as that of original sin. There is nothing that is more certain than the marvellous holiness of many Christian lives. This it would be exaggerated to refer to the grace of Baptism alone. If we are to believe the vast majority of those who have attained to this holiness in the centuries of Christian history, the source and spring of the spiritual life which was in them was the gift of God bestowed in the first instance in the Sacrament of Baptism.

When this doctrine is once accepted, the whole aspect of life is changed. It supplies an inexhaustible power of hope. It sets up a standard which is the highest. If there is real union with the life of Christ, there is special enormity in the sins of Christians, there is no limit to the righteousness at which they may aim, and there ought to be no contentment with anything short of conformity with what Christ has shown Himself to be. It places all spiritual life on a supernatural basis. It affirms that what has been sacramentally given needs to be sacramentally maintained. It emphasizes that the life of man, if it is to be in the true sense successful, must be in continual dependence upon Almighty God. It shows how, in the case of the unconscious infant, the Sacrament of Baptism sanctifies in his soul the glorious beginning of that which in the providence of God and through reliance on His grace can attain to a still more glorious end.

'O happy new-born babe, where art thou lying?
   What are these sounds that fill with healing balm
The hallowed air, of power to still thy crying
   At once, and nurse thee into heavenly calm?

'" His bosom bears me, Who on earth descended,
   Of a poor Maid vouchsafing to be born.
His saving words, with holy water blended,
   Have brought the glory to my prime of morn."

'Joy to thy nurse, more joy to her who bare thee,
   Lamb of that Shepherd's flock, whose name is Good:
As He hath won, for ever may He wear thee,
   And keep thee purified with His dear blood.

'" Amen : and therefore am I sworn His servant,
    His sacred Heart through life to be my rest,
To watch His eye with adoration fervent,
    Foe of His foes, and in His white robe drest.'

' O blest, O safe, on God's own bosom leaning !
    But passion-hours are nigh :—keep thou thy place :
And far and wide are evil watchers, gleaning
    The lambs that slight the Shepherd's fostering grace.

'" Nay, I will drink His cup ; my vow is taken ;
    With His baptizing blood mine own shall blend ;
Ne'er be that holiest charge by me forsaken,
    The dying Saviour's trust to each true friend.'

' Well hast thou sworn, and be thy warfare glorious :
    But Saints are pure, the Church is undefiled,
And Jesus welcomed from His cross victorious
    A Virgin Mother to a Virgin Child.

' " Then ask for me of the dread Son of Mary,
    Whose arms eternal are young children's home,
A loving heart, obedient eyes and wary,
    Even as I am to tarry till He come."

' Prayer shall not fail, but higher He would lead thee :
    His bosom-friend ate of that awful Bread :
So will He wait all day to bless and feed thee ;—
    Come thou adoring to be blest and fed.

' " 'Tis meet and right, and mine own bounden duty.
    Good Angels guide me with pure heart to fall
Before His Altar-step, and see His Beauty,
    And taste of Him, my first, my last, mine all."' ⁶

NOTES

CHAPTER I

[1] S. Augustine, *Quæst. in Exod.*, 73, 'Multum et solide significatur, ad vetus Testamentum timorem potius pertinere, sicut ad novum dilectionem, quamquam et in vetere novum lateat, et in novo vetus pateat.' ('There is much and solid indication that fear pertains rather to the Old Testament as love to the New, although both in the Old Testament the New Testament lies hid and in the New Testament the Old Testament is explained.')

[2] See, *e.g.*, Exodus iv. 17, vii. 15, xiv. 16, xvii. 5-6, 9, 11, 12; Numbers xxi. 8-9; 2 Kings v. 10-14; 1 Samuel xv. 23, 26, xvi. 13; 2 Samuel xii. 13; Exodus xxix.; Leviticus i.-viii.

[3] Butler, *Analogy of Religion Natural and Revealed to the Constitution and Course of Nature*, II. iv. 3. For the connection of the laws of God with His being, see S. Augustine, *C. Faustum*, xxvi. 3, 'Quid sit autem secundum naturam, quid contra naturam, homines qui sicut nos errant, nosse non possunt. Dici autem humano more contra naturam esse, quod est contra naturæ usum mortalibus notum, nec nos negamus: sicut illud est quod apostolus ait, Si tu ex naturali incisus oleastro, et contra naturam insertus es in bonam olivam: id esse contra naturam dixit, quod est

contra consuetudinem naturæ, quam notitia humana comprehendit, ut oleaster insertus in olea, non oleastri baccas, sed olivæ pinguedinem ferat. Deus autem creator et conditor omnium naturarum nihil contra naturam facit: id enim erit cuique rei naturale, quod ille fecerit, a quo est omnis modus, numerus, ordo naturæ . . . Sed contra naturam non incongrue dicimus aliquid Deum facere, quod facit contra id quod novimus in natura. Hanc enim etiam appellamus naturam, cognitum nobis cursum solitumque naturæ, contra quem Deus cum aliquid facit magnalia vel mirabilia nominantur. Contra illam vero summam naturæ legem, a notitia remotam, sive impiorum, sive adhuc infirmorum, tam Deus nullo modo facit quam contra se ipsum non facit.' ('But men who like ourselves fall into error cannot know what is in accordance with nature or contrary to nature. Yet neither do we deny that what is contrary to the custom of nature which is known to mortal men may after a human sort be said to be contrary to nature. Such is that saying of the apostle: If thou wast cut out of the natural wild olive and contrary to nature wast grafted into the good olive. He called that contrary to nature which is contrary to the custom of nature which human knowledge grasps, so that a wild olive grafted in an olive should bear not the berries of the wild olive but the fatness of the olive. But God the creator and maker of all natures does nothing contrary to nature; for whatever He may have done will be natural to each thing since He is the source of all the method and number and order of nature. . . . Yet it is not unfitting for us to say that God does contrary to nature anything which He does contrary to that which we know in nature. For we give the name nature also to the course of nature which is known to us and customary, and the things which

God does when He acts contrary to this are called great or wonderful. But contrary to that supreme law of nature which is removed from the knowledge alike of those who are irreligious and of those who are still weak, God no more does anything than He does anything contrary to Himself.')

[4] See, *e.g.*, S. Augustine, *C. litt. Petil.* ii. 87; S. Thomas Aquinas, *Summa Theologica*, III. lxi. 3; Bellarmine, *De Sacramentis in Genere*, i. 12. Cf. Council of Trent, Sess. vii., canon 2, *De Sacramentis in Genere* (Hardouin, *Concilia*, x. 52).

[5] See S. John vi. 31-5, 48-51, 58; Exodus xvi. 14, 15; Deuteronomy viii. 3; 1 S. Peter iii. 20-21; 1 Corinthians x. 2; Leviticus xiii. 34, xv. 5-13.

[6] Genesis xvii. 10-14; Colossians ii. 11-12.

[7] Galatians iii. 24, iv. 1-5.

[8] Exodus xix. 5-6; 1 S. Peter ii. 5, 9; S. Matthew v. 17.

[9] See Lightfoot, *Horæ Hebraicæ*, on S. Matthew iii. 6; Schürer, *History of the Jewish People in the Time of Jesus Christ*, II. ii. 319-24; Edersheim, *Life and Times of Jesus the Messiah*, i. 273, ii. 745-7.

[10] See S. John i. 25; and cf. Isaiah lii. 15 ('sprinkle' is the ordinary meaning of the Hiphil of נָזָה. See, *e.g.*, Leviticus iv. 6, viii. 11. In Isaiah lii. 15 some commentators interpret it 'make spring up' or 'startle.' See, *e.g.*, Orelli *in loco*, Delitzsch *in loco*, and the margin of the Revised Version); Ezekiel xxxvi. 25; Zechariah xiii. 1; Hebrews x. 22.

[11] S. Luke iii. 3.

[12] The identity of the baptism administered by S. John the Baptist with that instituted by our Lord was asserted by

some of the foreign reformers: see, *e.g.*, Calvin, *Institutes*, IV. xv. 7; and cf. Bellarmine, *De Baptismo*, i. 19-23. Anciently, the Donatist Petilian compared the two baptisms to the extent of arguing that the administration of Christian Baptism to those who had been baptized by S. John the Baptist afforded a precedent for the Donatist practice of rebaptizing those who had been baptized in the Church. See S. Augustine, *C. litt. Petil.*, ii. 85. Some orthodox writers thought that the baptism of S. John the Baptist actually conferred remission of sins. S. Cyril of Jerusalem says it 'gave redemption from the eternal fire' (ἐδίδου λύτρωσιν αἰωνίου πυρός), and that it was the means of remission, though not of adoption: see *Cat.*, iii. 7; *Cat. Myst.*, ii. 6. S. Augustine mentions but does not accept a similar view: see *De Bapt. c. Don.*, v. 12. Christian writers generally have restricted the actual baptismal remission of sins to that administered after the death of our Lord. See *e.g.*, Tertullian, *De Baptismo*, 10-11; S. Jerome, *Dial. adv. Lucif.*, 7; S. Leo., *Ep.* xvi. 3; S. Chrysostom, *In Mat. Hom.*, x. 2, xii. 1; *In Act. Apost. Hom.*, xl. 2 (καλῶς δὲ εἶπε βάπτισμα μετανοίας τὸ Ἰωάννου, καὶ οὐκ ἀφέσεως, 'Rightly did he say that the baptism of John was of repentance, not of remission'); S. John Dam., *De Fide Orth.*, iv. 9; S. Thomas Aquinas, *S. T.*, III. lxviii. 6.

[13] S. Matthew iii. 13-17. For the sanctification of water by the baptism of our Lord, see S. Ignatius, *Ad Eph.*, 18, ὅς (*i.e.* Ἰησοῦς ὁ Χριστὸς) ἐγγεννήθη καὶ ἐβαπτίσθη ἵνα τῷ πάθει τὸ ὕδωρ καθαρίσῃ ('Who was begotten and was baptized in order that He might cleanse the water by His passion'): cf. the English Baptismal Offices. On the passage in S. Ignatius, Bishop Lightfoot comments, 'The baptism of Christ might in a certain sense be said, in the language of

our liturgy, to "sanctify water to the mystical washing away of sins" (comp. Tertull., *Ad Jud.*, 8 ; *De Bapt.*, 9); but it was the death of Christ which gave their purifying effect to the baptismal waters. The baptism was only the inauguration of this sanctifying process.' See his *Apostolic Fathers*, II. ii. 75-6.

[14] S. John iii. 3, 5.

[15] S. John iii. 22, 26, iv. 1-2. This baptism by the disciples was regarded as of much the same character as that administered by S. John the Baptist by Tertullian, *De Baptismo*, 11 ; S. Chrysostom, *In Joan. Ev. Hom.*, xxix. 1. Others have regarded it as substantially identical with Christian Baptism: see, *e.g.*, S. Augustine, *In Joan. Ev. Tract.* xv. 3, *Ep.* cclxv. 5 ; Peter Lombard, *Sent.*, IV. iii. 7 : cf. S. Thom. Aq., *S. T.*, III. lxvi. 2.

[16] S. John xix. 34 ; 1 S. John v. 6 ; S. Matthew xxviii. 19-20 ; S. Luke xxiv. 49 ; Acts i. 4, ii. 1-4, 38, 41. The administration of Baptism by the apostles necessarily raises the question whether they themselves had been baptized ; and, if so, at what time. This question had evidently caused perplexity as early as the time of Tertullian : see his *De Baptismo*, 12. S. Augustine was of opinion that they were baptized by our Lord : see, *e.g.*, *Ep.*, cclxv. 3. He was followed in this by S. Thomas Aquinas : see *In Joan. Ev.*, cap. xiii. Euthymius Zigabenus mentions that some writers near the times of the apostles record that our Lord baptized His holy Mother and S. Peter, and S. Peter baptized the other apostles : see *In Joan. Ev.*, iii. 5. Nicephorus quotes Evodius as saying that our Lord baptized S. Peter, S. Peter baptized S. Andrew and the sons of Zebedee, S. Andrew and the

sons of Zebedee baptized the other apostles, and S. Peter and S. John baptized the seventy disciples: see his *H. E.*, ii. 3. There is a thoughtful statement on the subject in the late Bishop Moberly's *Bampton Lectures*: 'None can point definitely to the time at which the apostles were baptized. Perhaps the truest answer to the question when were they baptized would be to say that in the ordinary sense and regular manner they were never baptized at all. Yet in saying this, there are two or three points that should not be forgotten. First, that they surely received John's baptism, that is, they were solemnly washed with water as persons repenting of sin, and looking forward to receive forgiveness in Christ; secondly, that the Lord Himself said to Peter, "He that hath been bathed, needeth not save to wash his feet," and although the main scope of these words was no doubt referrible to the times in which the Gospel should be fully preached, and the "bath" regularly received as the outward means and pledge of the new birth, yet we can hardly suppose that they had no personal application to the apostle to whom they were spoken at the very moment when he sought to decline the washing of his feet by the Lord's hands. Indeed, S. Augustine and Thomas Aquinas conclude from this verse that the apostles had certainly received the bath of regeneration from the hands of the Lord Himself. And thirdly, that they were expressly told by the Lord immediately before the ascension that "not many days hence" they should be baptized with the Holy Ghost, and that, in terms which by the contrast with John's baptism seem unquestionably to denote Christ's baptism properly so called. Putting all these things together, it seems most in accordance with the language of Holy Scripture to conclude that either the fulness of the gift of Pentecost superseded the "bath" of water indispensable in all other cases, or more probably that, superadded to the bath of Jordan, and completing and crowning the gradual increase of that "apostolic growth" of which S. Jerome speaks, it filled up the sacrament, and completed to those who, being themselves the first, could not receive it by the agency of any other men, the administered birth of water and the Spirit': see Moberly, *The Administration of the Holy Spirit in the Body of Christ*, pp. 43-4.

[17] Butler, *Analogy of Religion Natural and Revealed to the Constitution and Course of Nature*, II. iv. 8.

CHAPTER II

[1] Acts i. 4-5 ; S. Luke xxiv. 49 ; Acts ii. 1-4 ; S. Matthew iii. 11 ; S. John xx. 22-3 ; S. Matthew xxviii. 19.

[2] See Acts ii. 37-41, viii. 12-13, 35-8, ix. 18, x. 44-8, xvi. 14-15, 30-3, xviii. 8, xix. 1-5 ; Romans vi. 3-4 ; 1 Corinthians i. 13 ; Galatians iii. 27 ; Colossians ii. 12 ; 1 S. Peter iii. 20-1 ; Hebrews vi. 1-2.

[3] See Acts ii. 41, viii. 12-13, 14-17, 38, ix. 18, x. 23, 48, xvi. 15, xviii. 8, xix. 5, xvi. 19, 23-5, 29-33 ; 1 Corinthians i. 14-17.

[4] See Acts ii. 41-2, 44, viii. 12-13, xvi. 14-15, 31, xviii. 8, xix. 2, 5, viii. 37 (the words contained in this verse are not in any of the best mss.): cf. 1 S. Peter iii. 21. For the confession of S. Peter, see S. Matthew xvi. 16.

[5] See Acts ii. 38-9, xvi. 15, 33 ; Ephesians vi. 1-4 ; Colossians iii. 20 ; 1 Corinthians vii. 14 (for a different view

as to the inferences which may be drawn from this passage, see, *e.g.*, Ellicott *in loco*), x. 1-2; Jeremiah i. 5; S. Luke i. 15; S. Matthew xix. 13-15; S. Mark x. 13-16; S. Luke xviii. 15-16.

⁶ See Acts viii. 36-9, x. 47; Ephesians v. 26; Hebrews x. 22; Acts viii. 38-9; Romans vi. 4; Colossians ii. 12; S. Luke xi. 38; Acts ii. 41, x. 44-8, xvi. 33. It has sometimes been contended that the word 'baptize' (βαπτίζειν) necessarily means to immerse. In view of this contention, an examination of the use of βαπτίζειν and the kindred words in Holy Scripture is of some importance. The verb βάπτειν is used in the Septuagint and the New Testament in the sense of 'to dip.' It occurs in Dan. iv. 30 (=iv. 33), v. 21 in Theodotion's Greek version for 'to make wet.' The intensive form of this verb, βαπτίζειν, occurs four times in the Septuagint. In 4 Reg. (=2 Kings) v. 14 it refers to Naaman's dipping of himself in the Jordan; in Isaiah xxi. 4 it is used in a metaphorical sense to denote the overwhelming force of lawlessness (ἡ ἀνομία με βαπτίζει); in Judith xii. 7 it describes the washing of herself by Judith; in Sirach (=Ecclesiasticus) xxxi. 30 (xxxiv. 25) it denotes ceremonial washing after touching a corpse (βαπτιζόμενος ἀπὸ νεκροῦ καὶ πάλιν ἁπτόμενος αὐτοῦ, τί ὠφέλησε τῷ λουτρῷ αὐτοῦ;). In the New Testament, in addition to the places where it refers to Baptism, it occurs five (or three) times. In S. Matthew xx. 22-3 (where, however, it is not in the revised text); S. Mark x. 38-9; S. Luke xii. 50, it is used metaphorically of the baptism of suffering; in S. Mark vii. 4 (where, however, the margin of the revised text has ῥαντίσωνται) it refers to the washing of hands; in S. Luke xi. 38 it similarly refers to the ceremonial washing of the hands before eating. In the last two instances it clearly does not

P

denote immersion, since, in this ceremony, the hands were not plunged into the water but were cleansed by an attendant pouring water over them. The noun βάπτισμα does not occur in the Septuagint; in the New Testament it always refers to Baptism or metaphorically to the baptism of suffering. The noun βαπτισμός does not occur in the Septuagint; in the New Testament it refers to Baptism in Hebrews vi. 2, and as a varied reading for βάπτισμα in Colossians ii. 12; elsewhere it denotes ceremonial washing: see S. Mark vii. 4, 8; Hebrews ix. 10.

[7] See Acts ii. 38, βαπτισθήτω ἕκαστος ὑμῶν ἐν (t. r. ἐπὶ) τῷ ὀνόματι Ἰησοῦ Χριστοῦ: Acts viii. 16, βεβαπτισμένοι ὑπῆρχον εἰς τὸ ὄνομα τοῦ Κυρίου Ἰησοῦ: Acts x. 48, προσέταξε δὲ (t. r. τε) αὐτοὺς ἐν τῷ ὀνόματι Ἰησοῦ Χριστοῦ (t. r. τοῦ Κυρίου) βαπτισθῆναι: Acts xix. 5, ἐβαπτίσθησαν εἰς τὸ ὄνομα τοῦ Κυρίου Ἰησοῦ: S. Matt. xxviii. 19, βαπτίζοντες αὐτοὺς εἰς τὸ ὄνομα τοῦ Πατρὸς καὶ τοῦ Υἱοῦ καὶ τοῦ Ἁγίου Πνεύματος: *Teaching of the Twelve Apostles*, ix. 5, οἱ βαπτισθέντες εἰς ὄνομα Κυρίου (as Κυρίου is without the article it probably means the Holy Trinity not our Lord specifically): *ibid.*, vii. 1, εἰς τὸ ὄνομα τοῦ Πατρὸς καὶ τοῦ Υἱοῦ καὶ τοῦ Ἁγίου Πνεύματος.

[8] See for the words 'anoint' and 'anointing' 2 Corinthians i. 21, ὁ δὲ βεβαιῶν ἡμᾶς σὺν ὑμῖν εἰς Χριστὸν, καὶ χρίσας ἡμᾶς Θεός: 1 St. John ii. 20, ὑμεῖς χρίσμα ἔχετε ἀπὸ τοῦ ἁγίου: 1 S. John ii. 27, ὑμεῖς τὸ χρίσμα ὃ ἐλάβετε ἀπ' αὐτοῦ μένει ἐν ὑμῖν καὶ οὐ χρείαν ἔχετε ἵνα τις διδάσκῃ ὑμᾶς· ἀλλ' ὡς τὸ αὐτοῦ (t. r. αὐτὸ) χρίσμα διδάσκει ὑμᾶς κ.τ.λ. On these passages it has been well said in Warren, *Liturgy and Ritual of the Ante-Nicene Church*, pp. 20-1, 'It is argued that the use of the verb "to anoint" and of the substantive "unction" or "anointing" . . . implies the existence of the practice of unction (*i.e.* at Baptism or Confirmation), 'and that the

existence of such a practice made the choice of such language natural and intelligible. But this argument may be made to cut two ways. It may, with equal probability, be argued that the existence of these metaphorical terms in the New Testament suggested, and rendered easy, the introduction of a literal rite of unction at a very early date in the history of the Church. The word "unction" ($\chi\rho\hat{\iota}\sigma\mu a$) occurs nowhere else in the New Testament, except in the two above-quoted passages of S. John. The word "anoint" ($\chi\rho\hat{\iota}\epsilon\iota\nu$) occurs in four other passages (S. Luke iv. 18; Acts iv. 27, x. 38; Hebrews i. 9), in all of which its use is metaphorical and not literal.' See also Westcott on 1 S. John ii. 20. In the cases of the anointing of the sick practised by the apostles during our Lord's ministry (S. Mark vi. 13) and enjoined by S. James in his Epistle (v. 14-15) the word used is ἀλείφειν. For the word 'seal' see 2 Corinthians i. 22, σφραγισάμενος ἡμᾶς: Ephesians i. 13, ἐσφραγίσθητε τῷ Πνεύματι τῆς ἐπαγγελίας τῷ Ἁγίῳ: Ephesians iv. 30, μὴ λυπεῖτε τὸ Πνεῦμα τὸ Ἅγιον τοῦ Θεοῦ ἐν ᾧ ἐσφραγίσθητε εἰς ἡμέραν ἀπολυτρώσεως. On these passages Mr. Warren (*ibid.*, p. 22) writes, 'If we examine the three passages in the New Testament (outside the Apocalypse) in which the word "seal" (σφραγίς) occurs, we shall see that it is used once' (*i.e.* Romans iv. 11) 'of circumcision, and in the other two passages' (*i.e.* 1 Corinthians ix. 2; 2 S. Timothy ii. 19) 'distinctly and necessarily in a metaphorical, and not in a literal sense. . . . If we examine the passages in the New Testament (outside the Apocalypse) in which the verb " to seal " (σφραγίζειν) occurs, in addition to the three passages above quoted, we shall find that they are four in number. In one passage' (*i.e.* S. Matthew xxvii. 66) 'it is used literally, but certainly with no allusion to the sign of the cross; in the other three passages' (*i.e.* S. John iii. 33, vi. 27; Romans xv. 28) 'its use is plainly metaphorical.'

⁹ The difficult passage in 1 Corinthians xv. 29 has not been referred to in the text. S. Paul there says, 'Else what shall they do which are baptized for the dead (οἱ βαπτιζόμενοι ὑπὲρ τῶν νεκρῶν)? If the dead are not raised at all, why then are they baptized for them (ὑπὲρ αὐτῶν: t.r. ὑπὲρ τῶν νεκρῶν)?' The most probable interpretation is perhaps that adopted by several Greek commentators, namely, that it means those who receive Baptism with a view to the resurrection of the dead: see, *e.g.*, S. Chrysostom, *In Ep. i. ad Cor. Hom.*, xl. 1, 2. This explanation makes the passage appropriate to the context in which it occurs. Tertullian says that S. Paul is referring to, though not necessarily approving, a custom of vicarious baptism of a living person with a view to benefiting one who died unbaptized: see *De Resur. Carn.*, 48; *Adv. Marc.*, v. 10. In this he has been followed by many. Such a practice existed among the Cerinthians and Marcionites: see, in addition to the passages in Tertullian, S. Chrysostom, *In Ep. i. ad Cor. Hom.*, xl. 1; Epiphanius, *Adv. Hær.*, xxviii. 6. Godet *in loco*, following other commentators, thinks the reference is to the 'Baptism of blood by martyrdom.' For many other interpretations, see the commentators and the *Newbery House Magazine*, January and April 1890. That the practice of vicarious baptism should have arisen illustrates the great importance attached to the rite.

CHAPTER III

¹ S. John iii. 3, 5. The unvarying patristic and mediæval treatment of this passage connects it with Holy Baptism.

See also Alford, *Greek Testament, in loco.* Calvin (*Institutes,* IV. xvi. 25) is thought to be the first interpreter who takes a different view. The word ἄνωθεν is explained by some to mean 'anew,' by others to mean 'from above.' There is probability and ancient authority in favour of both interpretations. The question does not involve any material difference. In view of the general Scriptural and patristic teaching on the subject of Baptism, to be 'begotten anew' and to be 'begotten from heaven' come to very much the same thing.

² S. Titus iii. 5, διὰ λουτροῦ παλιγγενεσίας. The evidence about the traditional interpretation of this passage is thus summarised in Pusey, *Doctrine of Holy Baptism,* pp. 57-8: 'First, then, no passage from any Father can, or has been pretended to be adduced, which should imply any other explanation; next, there is the large body of Fathers from every Church who do interpret the text, as a matter of course, of Baptism; thirdly, all the Liturgies, in all the different ways in which it is possible to apply it.'

³ See S. John i. 13, iii. 3-8; 1 Corinthians iv. 15; S. James i. 18; 1 S. Peter i. 23; Acts ii. 41; 1 Corinthians xii. 13.

⁴ The expression 'Name of God' has a special meaning in Holy Scripture to denote the revelation and attributes and being of God: see Oehler, *Theology of the Old Testament,* § 56; Pusey, *Doctrine of Holy Baptism,* pp. 69-74. Cf. Liddon, *Christmastide in S. Paul's,* p. 325, 'The Name of God is treated in Scripture as if it were a living thing; as if it were identical with His Nature, which it declares.' For the word 'into' (εἰς) cf. Romans vi. 3 (ὅσοι ἐβαπτίσθημεν εἰς Χριστὸν Ἰησοῦν, εἰς τὸν θάνατον αὐτοῦ

ἐβαπτίσθημεν); 1 Corinthians xii. 13 (ἡμεῖς πάντες εἰς ἓν σῶμα ἐβαπτίσθημεν); Galatians iii. 27 (ὅσοι γὰρ εἰς Χριστὸν ἐβαπτίσθητε, Χριστὸν ἐνεδύσασθε). In 1 Corinthians x. 2 (πάντες εἰς τὸν Μωσῆν ἐβαπτίσαντο) the preposition is differently used. S. Chrysostom (*In Ep. i. ad Cor. Hom.*, xxiii. 2) explains this by regarding the word as being used in a less exact sense in connection with the type of the Sacrament of Holy Baptism than in connection with the Sacrament itself.

[5] Galatians iii. 26-7; Romans viii. 14-19.

[6] S. John i. 12; 1 S. John iii. 1, 2, 9, 10, iv. 7, v. 2, 4, 18.

[7] Galatians iii. 27; 1 Corinthians xii. 12, 13, 27 (cf. vi. 15); Ephesians v. 26-30 (The reading 'of His flesh and of His bones'—ἐκ τῆς σαρκὸς αὐτοῦ καὶ ἐκ τῶν ὀστέων αὐτοῦ —is not in the Alexandrian and Vatican MSS. or the first hand of the Sinaitic MS. For the retention see the critical note in Alford, *The Greek Testament, in loc.* It is omitted by the revisers and by Westcott and Hort. The omission of it does not affect the general sense); Romans vi. 3-4; Colossians ii. 12-20, iii. 1. Note the significance of the tenses in, *e.g.*, Romans vi. 8, 18, 22, viii. 2, 15.

[8] See S. Matthew iii. 11; S. Mark i. 8; S. Luke iii. 16; S. John i. 26; Acts ii. 38, ix. 17-8; S. Titus iii. 5; Ephesians ii. 22; 2 Corinthians vi. 16; 1 S. Peter ii. 5; 1 Corinthians iii. 16, vi. 19, xii. 13; Galatians iv. 6; 1 S. John iii. 24; S. James iv. 5. For a fuller discussion of these passages see Chapter v.

[9] S. Mark xvi. 16; Acts ii. 41, 47, xvi. 30, 33; 1 S. Peter i. 3, 4, iii. 21; S. Titus iii. 5-7; Acts xxii. 16.

[10] Romans iv. 25. See Liddon, *Explanatory Analysis of S. Paul's Epistle to the Romans*, pp. 95-6.

[11] Romans v. 20-vi. 11.

[12] Acts xxii. 10; ix. 18, xvi. 30, 33.

[13] Acts viii. 13, 21-3; 1 Corinthians iii. 16, 17, v. 3-5; Galatians v. 2, 4, 19-21; 1 Corinthians ix. 26, 27, vi. 11-20.

[14] S. Mark iii. 29. The reading 'eternal sin' (αἰωνίου ἁμαρτήματος), adopted by the revisers and by Westcott and Hort, is found in the Sinaitic and Vatican MSS. and other authorities.

CHAPTER IV

[1] See, *e.g.*, Irenæus, *C. Hær.*, I. xxi. 3; Tertullian, *De Bapt.*, 1; Theodoret, *Hær. Fab. Comp.*, i. 10.

[2] See, *e.g.*, S. Cyril of Jerusalem, *Procat.* 16, *Cat.* i. 3, iii. 3, iv. 32, v. 5-6; S. Augustine, *De Bapt. c. Don.*, i. 5, vi. 1, *Ep.* clxxxv. 23, *De Symb. Serm. ad Cat.* 15; S. Chrysostom, *In Ep. ii. ad Cor.*, iii. 7; S. Gregory of Nazianzus, *Orat.*, xl. 3-4; S. Justin Martyr, *Apol.* i. 61, 65, *Dial. c. Tryph.* 14; S. Basil, *Hom. in Sanc. Bapt.*, 5.

[3] See on this point Pusey, *Doctrine of Holy Baptism*, pp. 31-3, 344-93. Cf., *e.g.*, S. Cyprian, *Epistola* lxiii. 8, 'Quotiescunque autem aqua sola in Scripturis sanctis nominatur, baptisma prædicatur' ('Whenever water only is named in Holy Scripture, Baptism is foretold').

[4] Hermas, *Pastor*, Sim. ix. 16, 'Ἀνάγκην, φησὶν, εἶχον δι' ὕδατος ἀναβῆναι ἵνα ζωοποιηθῶσιν· οὐκ ἠδύναντο γὰρ ἄλλως εἰσελθεῖν εἰς τὴν βασιλείαν τοῦ Θεοῦ, εἰ μὴ τὴν νέκρωσιν ἀπέθεντο τῆς ζωῆς αὐτῶν τῆς προτέρας . . . πρὶν γὰρ, φησὶ, φορέσαι τὸν

ἄνθρωπον τὸ ὄνομα τοῦ υἱοῦ τοῦ Θεοῦ νεκρός ἐστιν· ὅταν δὲ λάβῃ τὴν σφραγῖδα, ἀποτίθεται τὴν νέκρωσιν καὶ ἀναλαμβάνει τὴν ζωήν· ἡ σφραγὶς οὖν τὸ ὕδωρ ἐστίν· εἰς τὸ ὕδωρ οὖν καταβαίνουσι νεκροὶ, καὶ ἀναβαίνουσι ζῶντες ('It was necessary, said he, for them to ascend by means of water in order that they might be made to live. For they could not otherwise enter into the kingdom of God unless they put off the deadly state of their former life. . . . For, said he, before a man puts on the name of the Son of God he is dead. But when he receives the seal he puts off the condition of death and assumes life. The seal then is the water: into the water therefore men go down dead and come up living').

Epistle of Barnabas, 11, ἡμεῖς μὲν καταβαίνομεν εἰς τὸ ὕδωρ γέμοντες ἁμαρτιῶν καὶ ῥύπου, καὶ ἀναβαίνομεν καρποφοροῦντες ἐν τῇ καρδίᾳ, τὸν φόβον καὶ τὴν ἐλπίδα εἰς τὸν Ἰησοῦν ἐν τῷ πνεύματι ἔχοντες ('We go down into the water full of sins and filth, and we come up bearing fruit in our heart, having in our spirit fear and hope towards Jesus').

S. Justin Martyr, *Apol.*, i. 61 : see note 1 to chapter xiii.

S. Irenæus, *C. Hær.*, III. xvii. 1-2.

Tertullian, *De Baptismo*, l. 2, 5 ; *De Resur. Carn.*, 8.

Canons of Hippolytus, canon xix. § 138, 'to whom thou hast now given the remission of sins'; canon xxvii. § 243, 'neither after regeneration is there need of the laver, but only of the washing of the hands, nothing more, because the Holy Spirit perfumes the body of the faithful and wholly cleanses it.'

Clement of Alexandria, *Pædagogus*, i. 6, βαπτιζόμενοι, φωτιζόμεθα· φωτιζόμενοι, υἱοποιούμεθα· υἱοποιούμενοι, τελειούμεθα· τελειούμενοι, ἀπαθανατιζόμεθα. Ἐγὼ, φησὶν, εἶπα, θεοί ἐστε, καὶ υἱοὶ ὑψίστου πάντες. Καλεῖται δὲ πολλαχῶς τὸ ἔργον τοῦτο χάρισμα, καὶ φώτισμα, καὶ τέλειον, καὶ λουτρόν. Λουτρὸν μὲν, δι' οὗ τὰς ἁμαρτίας ἀπορρυπτόμεθα· χάρισμα δὲ, ᾧ τὰ ἐπὶ τοῖς ἁμαρτήμασιν ἐπιτίμια ἀνεῖται· φώτισμα δὲ, δι' οὗ τὸ ἅγιον ἐκεῖνο φῶς τὸ σωτήριον ἐποπτεύεται, τοῦτ' ἐστιν δι' οὗ τὸ θεῖον ὀξυωποῦμεν· τέλειον δὲ, τὸ ἀπροσδεὲς φαμέν· τί γὰρ ἔτι λείπεται τῷ Θεὸν ἐγνωκότι.

Origen, *In Joan.*, tom. vi. 17, παλιγγενεσίας ὀνομαζόμενον λουτρὸν; *Ibid.* ἡ χαρισμάτων θείων ἀρχὴ καὶ πηγή.

S. Cyprian, *Ep.* lxxiii.12, 'Neque enim parva res hæreticis et modica conceditur, quando a nobis baptisma eorum in acceptum refertur, cum inde incipiat omnis fidei origo et ad spem vitæ æternæ salutaris ingressio et purificandis ac vivificandis Dei servis divina dignatio. Nam si baptizari quis apud hæreticos potuit, utique et remissam peccatorum consequi potuit. Si peccatorum remissam consecutus est, et sanctificatus est. Si sanctificatus est, et templum Dei factus est' ('For it is no small and unimportant thing which is granted to heretics when their Baptism is accepted by us, since from it arises the beginning of all faith and the saving entrance into the hope of eternal life and the divine condescension for the purifying and quickening of the servants of God. For if a man has been able to be baptized among heretics, he has been able to obtain also the remission of sins. If he has obtained the remission of sins, he has also been sanctified. If he has been sanctified, he has also been made a temple of God'); *Ep.* lxxiv. 5–6, 'qua in Christo per lavacrum regenerationis nascimur' ('whereby we are born in Christ by means of the washing of regeneration'); 'Baptisma enim esse, in quo homo vetus moritur et novus nascitur, manifestat et probat beatus apostolus dicens: Servavit nos per lavacrum regenerationis. Si autem in lavacro id est in baptismo est regeneratio, quomodo generare filios Deo hæresis per Christum potest, quæ

Christi sponsa non est?' ('For that it is Baptism, in which the old man dies and the new man is born, the blessed apostle shows and proves when he says, He saved us by means of the washing of regeneration. But if regeneration is in the washing, that is, in Baptism, how can heresy, which is not the spouse of Christ, produce sons to God through Christ?'); *Ep.* lxiii. 8, 'Per baptisma enim Spiritus Sanctus accipitur' ('For by means of Baptism the Holy Spirit is received'); *Ad Donat. de Grat. Dei*, 3-4, 'Ego quum in tenebris atque in nocte cæca jacerem quumque in salo jactantis sæculi nutabundus ac dubius vestigiis oberrantibus fluctuarem vitæ meæ nescius, veritatis ac lucis alienus, difficile prorsus ac durum pro illis tunc moribus opinabar, quod in salutem mihi divina indulgentia pollicebatur, ut quis renasci denuo posset, utque in novam vitam lavacro aquæ salutaris animatus, quod prius fuerat exponeret et corporis licet manente compage hominem animo ac mente mutaret. Qui possibilis, aiebam, est tanta conversio ut repente ac perniciter exuatur, quod vel genuinum situ materiæ naturalis obduruit, vel usurpatum diu senio vetustatis inolevit? Alta hæc et profunda penitus radice sederunt. Quando parcimoniam discit, qui epularibus cœnis et largis dapibus assuevit? Et qui pretiosa veste conspicuus in auro atque in purpura fulsit, ad plebeium se ac simplicem cultum quando deponit? Fascibus ille oblectatus et honoribus esse privatus et inglorius non potest. Hic stipatus clientium cuneis, frequentiore comitatu officiosi agminis honestatus, pœnam putat esse, cum solus est. Tenacibus semper illecebris necesse est, ut solebat, vinolentia invitet, inflet superbia, iracundia inflammet, rapacitas inquietet, crudelitas stimulet, ambitio delectet, libido præcipitet. Hæc egomet sæpe mecum.

Nam ut ipse quam plurimis vitæ prioris erroribus implicitus tenebar, quibus exui me posse non crederem, sic vitiis adhærentibus obsecundans eram et desperatione meliorum malis meis veluti jam propriis ac vernaculis offavebam. Sed postquam undæ genitalis auxilio superioris ævi labe detersa in expiatum pectus serenum ac purum desuper se lumen infudit, postquam cœlitus spiritu hausto in novum me hominem nativitas secunda reparavit, mirum in modum protinus confirmare se dubia, patere clausa, lucere tenebrosa, facultatem dare, quod prius difficile videbatur, geri posse, quod impossibile putabatur, ut esset agnoscere, terrenum fuisse, quod prius carnaliter natum delictis obnoxium viveret, Dei esse cœpisse, quod jam Spiritus Sanctus animaret. Scis ipse projecto et mecum pariter recognoscis, quid detraxerit nobis quidve contulerit mors ista criminum, vita virtutum . . . Dei est, inquam, Dei est omne quod possumus. Inde vivimus, inde pollemus, inde sumto et concepto vigore hic adhuc positi futurorum indicia prænoscimus.' In the first three of these quotations S. Cyprian is arguing from the point of view that Baptism administered outside the Church is invalid. See Chapter ix.

S. Hilary of Poitiers, *Tract. in lxiv. Psalm.*, 15, 'Inebriamur autem ipsi, cum Spiritum Sanctum qui fluvius est nuncupatus accipimus . . . Est autem nobis per sacramentum baptismi renatis maximum gaudium, cum quædam in nobis Spiritus Sancti initia sentimus, cum subeat nos sacramentorum intelligentia, prophetiæ scientia, sermo sapientiæ, spei firmitas, sanationum charismata, et in dæmonia subjecta dominatus' ('But we ourselves are inebriated when we receive the Holy Spirit, who is named the river. . . . For to us who are reborn by means of the Sacrament of Baptism there is the greatest joy when we perceive certain beginnings of the

Holy Spirit in us, since there comes to us the understanding of Sacraments, the knowledge of prophecy, the word of wisdom, the firmness of hope, the gifts of healing, and the rule over the devils who are made subject').

S. Athanasius, *Ep. i. ad Serap.*, 4, τὸ πνεῦμα τὸ ἅγιον, τὸ διδόμενον τοῖς πιστεύουσι καὶ ἀναγεννωμένοις διὰ λουτροῦ παλιγγενεσίας ('the Holy Spirit who is given to those who believe and are being begotten again by means of the washing of regeneration').

S. Cyril of Jerusalem, *Procat.*, 16, αἰχμαλώτοις λύτρον· ἁμαρτημάτων ἄφεσις· θάνατος ἁμαρτίας· παλιγγενεσία ψυχῆς ('Ransom for the captives; remission of offences; death of sin; regeneration of the soul'); *Cat.* iii. 3, μέλλει τὸ πνεῦμα τὸ ἅγιον σφραγίζειν ὑμῶν τὰς ψυχάς ('the Holy Spirit is about to seal your souls'); *ibid.*, 4, τῇ τοῦ ἁγίου πνεύματος ἐνεργείᾳ τὴν σωτηρίαν ἐνδέχου ('Accept salvation by the operation of the Holy Spirit'); *Cat. Myst.*, iii. 1, εἰς Χριστὸν βεβαπτισμένοι καὶ Χριστὸν ἐνδυσάμενοι σύμμορφοι γεγόνατε τοῦ υἱοῦ τοῦ Θεοῦ . . . μέτοχοι οὖν τοῦ Χριστοῦ γενόμενοι, κ.τ.λ. ('Having been baptized into Christ, and having put on Christ, ye have become conformed to the Son of God . . . having then become partakers of Christ,' etc.); *ibid.*, ii. 4, ἐν τῷ αὐτῷ ἀπεθνήσκετε καὶ ἐγεννᾶσθε, καὶ τὸ σωτήριον ἐκεῖνο ὕδωρ καὶ τάφος ὑμῖν ἐγίνετο καὶ μήτηρ ('At the same moment ye were dying and were being begotten; and that water of salvation was to you both a grave and a mother').

S. Basil, *Adv. Eunom.*, v. (t. i. p. 303 A, Benedictine edition), διὰ λουτροῦ παλιγγενεσίας καὶ ἀνακαινώσεως πνεύματος ἁγίου υἱοθετούμεθα Θεῷ.

S. Gregory of Nazianzus, *Orat.*, xl. 4, βάπτισμα δὲ, ὡς συνθαπτομένης τῷ ὕδατι τῆς ἁμαρτίας; *Ibid.*, 3, πνεύματος ἀκολούθησις.

S. Gregory of Nyssa, *Catech. Orat.*, 33, εὐχὴ πρὸς Θεὸν, καὶ χάριτος οὐρανίας ἐπίκλησις, καὶ ὕδωρ, καὶ πίστις ἐστὶ, δι' ὧν τὸ τῆς ἀναγεννήσεως πληροῦται μυστήριον.

S. Ambrose, *De Myst.*, ix. 59, 'veritatem regenerationis operetur.'

S. Chrysostom, *In Act. Ap. Hom.*, xl. 2, τὸ κεφάλαιον ἔχομεν τῶν ἀγαθῶν διὰ τοῦ βαπτίσματος· ἄφεσιν ἁμαρτημάτων ἐλάβομεν, ἁγιασμὸν, πνεύματος μετάληψιν, υἱοθεσίαν, ζωὴν αἰώνιον.

S. Cyril of Alexandria, *In Joan. Ev.*, ii. 1 (on ii. 5), διὰ τῆς τοῦ πνεύματος ἐνεργείας τὸ αἰσθητὸν ὕδωρ πρὸς θείαν τινὰ καὶ ἄρρητον ἀναστοιχειοῦται δύναμιν, ἁγιάζει τε λοιπὸν τοὺς ἐν οἷς ἂν γένοιτο; *ibid.*, v. 2 (on vii. 39), τὸν ἄρτι βεβαπτισμένον . . . ὁ δὲ ἐκ Θεοῦ γεγένηται, κατὰ τὸ γεγραμμένον, καὶ θείας φύσεως γέγονε κοινωνός, ἐνοικοῦν ἔχων ἐν αὐτῷ τὸ ἅγιον πνεῦμα, καὶ ναὸς ἤδη χρηματίζων Θεοῦ.

S. Ephraim the Syrian, *Testamentum* (*Opera Græca*, Romæ 1743, t. ii. p. 244 F), ὁ μὴ εἰληφὼς ἀνὴρ βάπτισμα ἔοικεν οἴκῳ τινὶ ἡτοιμασμένῳ βασιλεῖ ὃν καὶ οὐδαμοῦ ᾤκησε βασιλεύς.

St. Augustine, *e.g. Serm.*, lxxi. 19, 'illa regeneratio, ubi fit omnium praeteritorum remissio peccatorum, in Spiritu Sancto fit, dicente Domino, Nisi quis renatus fuerit ex aqua et Spiritu, non potest introire in regnum Dei' ('that regeneration, wherein is accomplished the remission of all past sins, comes to pass by the operation of the Holy Spirit, as the Lord says, Except any one has been reborn of water and the Spirit, he cannot enter into the kingdom of God'); *Ep.* clxxxvii. 26, 'dicimus ergo in baptizatis parvulis, quamvis id nesciant, habitare Spiritum Sanctum' ('We say then that the Holy Spirit dwells in little children who have been baptized, although they know it not'); *De Bapt. c. Don.*, v. 28, 'Deus ergo dat etiam ipso baptizante Spiritum Sanctum' ('God then gives the Holy Spirit even when he' [*i.e.* a wicked man] 'baptizes').

S. Jerome, *Adv. Lucif.*, 6, 'Quum in Patre et Filio et Spiritu Sancto baptizatus homo templum Domini fiat, quum veteri æde destructa novum Trinitatis delubrum ædificetur, quomodo dicis sine adventu Spiritus Sancti apud Arianos peccata posse dimitti? Quomodo antiquis sordibus anima purgatur quæ Sanctum non habet Spiritum?' ('Since a man who has been baptized in the Father and the Son and the Holy Spirit becomes a temple of God and the old building being destroyed is built a new shrine of the Trinity, how do you say that sins can be remitted among the Arians without the coming of the Holy Spirit? How is a soul which has not the Holy Spirit cleansed from its old filth?')

St. Leo, *Ep.*, clxvi. 2, 'sacramentum regenerationis'; *Serm.* xxi., 3, 'cujus capitis et cujus corporis sis membrum' ('of what a head and what a body art thou a member'); 'per baptismatis sacramentum Spiritus Sancti factus es templum' ('by means of the Sacrament of Baptism thou wast made a temple of the Holy Spirit'); *Serm.*, lxvi. 2, 'fons baptismatis faciat innocentes et electio adoptionis confirmet hæredes'; *Serm.*, lxiii. 6, 'per baptismatis partum innumerabilis filiorum Dei multitudo gignatur, 'corpus regenerati fiat caro crucifixi.'

[5] S. Augustine, *Conf.*, viii. 29, 'Nec ultra volui legere nec opus erat. Statim quippe cum fine hujusce sententiæ quasi luce securitatis infusa cordi meo, omnes dubitationis tenebræ diffugerunt'; *De Bapt. c. Don.*, iv. 31, 'In baptizatis infantibus præcedit regenerationis sacramentum; et si Christianam tenuerint pietatem, sequetur etiam in corde conversio, cujus mysterium præcessit in corpore' ('In baptized infants the sacrament of regeneration goes before; and if they shall have held fast Christian holiness, conver-

sion also in the heart, of which the mystery has gone before in the body, will follow'; *ibid.* 32, 'quibus rebus omnibus ostenditur aliud esse sacramentum baptismi, aliud conversionem cordis, sed salutem hominis ex utroque compleri.'

⁶ *Apostolical Constitutions*, iii. 18, ὁ δὲ βαπτιζόμενος ὑπαρχέτω ἀλλότριος ἀσεβείας πάσης, ἀνενέργητος πρὸς ἁμαρτίαν, φίλος Θεοῦ, ἐχθρὸς διαβόλου, κληρονόμος Θεοῦ πατρὸς, συγκληρονόμος δὲ τοῦ υἱοῦ αὐτοῦ, ἀποτεταγμένος τῷ Σατανᾷ καὶ τοῖς δαίμοσι καὶ ταῖς ἀπάταις αὐτοῦ, ἁγνὸς, καθαρὸς, ὅσιος, θεοφιλὴς, υἱὸς τοῦ Θεοῦ, προσευχόμενος ὡς υἱὸς πατρί.

S. Leo, *Serm.*, xxi. 3, 'Deponamus ergo veterem hominem cum actibus suis et, adepti participationem generationis Christi, carnis renuntiemus operibus. Agnosce, O Christiane, dignitatem tuam; et divinæ consors factus naturæ, noli in veterem vilitatem degeneri conversatione redire. Memento cujus capitis et cujus corporis sis membrum. Reminiscere quia erutus de potestate tenebrarum, translatus es in Dei lumen et regnum. Per baptismatis sacramentum Spiritus Sancti factus es templum. Noli tantum habitatorem pravis de te actibus effugare, et diaboli te iterum subjicere servituti: quia pretium tuum sanguis est Christi, quia in veritate te judicabit qui in misericordia te redemit'; *Serm.*, lxx. 4, 'Huic sacramento, dilectissimi, ut inseparabiliter congruamus, magna nobis et animi et corporis intentione nitendum est, ut cum gravissimi sit piaculi festum Paschale negligere, periculosius sit ecclesiasticis quidem conventibus jungi, sed in Dominicæ passionis consortio non haberi. Nam dicente Domino "Qui non accipit crucem suam, et non sequitur me, non est me dignus," et dicente apostolo "Si compatimur, et conregnabimus," quis vere Christum passum, mortuum et resuscitatum colit, nisi qui cum ipso patitur, et moritur, et resurgit? Et haec quidem in omnibus Ecclesiæ filiis ipso jam regenerationis sunt inchoata mysterio, ubi peccati interitus vita est renascentis, et triduanam Domini mortem imitatur trina demersio, ut dimoto quodam aggere sepulturæ, quos veteres suscipit sinus fontis, eosdem novos edat unda baptismatis. Sed implendum est nihilominus opere, quod celebratum est sacramento, et natis de Spiritu Sancto quantumcumque superest mundani corporis non sine crucis susceptione ducendum est. Quamvis enim forti et crudeli tyranno per potentiam crucis Christi vasa antiquæ deprædationis erepta sint, et dominatio principis mundi a redemptorum sit ejecta corporibus: insidiari tamen etiam justificatis eadem malignitas perseverat, et multis modis eos, in quibus non regnat, impugnat, ut si quas animas negligentes imprudentesque repererit, sævioribus eas laqueis rursum innectat, et a paradiso Ecclesiæ raptas, in consortium suæ damnationis inducat. Unde cum quispiam observantiæ Christianæ se limites sentit excedere, et in id cupiditates suas tendere, quod eum a recto itinere faciat deviare: recurrat ad crucem Domini, et ligno vitae motus noxiae voluntatis adfigat, ac voce prophetica ad Dominum clamet, et dicat "Confige clavis a timore tuo carnes meas, a judiciis enim tuis timui."'

S. Augustine, *De Peccat. Meritis*, i. 25, 'Quis ignorat quod baptizatus parvulus, si ad rationales annos veniens non crediderit, nec se ab illicitis concupiscentiis abstinuerit, nihil ei proderit quod parvus accepit?'

S. Cyprian, *Ad Donat. de Grat. Dei.*, 4, 'Sit tantum timor innocentiae custos, ut qui in mentes nostras indulgentiæ coelestis allapsu clementer Dominus influxit, in animi oblectantis hospitio justa operatione teneatur, ne accepta securitas indiligentiam pariat, et vetus denuo hostis obrepat.'

[7] See, *e.g.*, S. Thomas Aquinas, *S. T.*, III. lxix. 1-8.

[8] There appear to have been different stages in the teaching of Luther about Baptism. But amid much that is confused and difficult to understand, he in many places very expressly declares the reality of the gifts in Baptism. See, *e.g.*, *The Short Catechism*, Section 4, 'It effects the remission of sins, frees us from death and the devil, and gives blessedness everlasting to those who believe what the word and the promise of God declare.' Cf. the sections on Baptism in *The Greater Catechism* and *On the Babylonish Captivity of the Church*. Cf. also the Confession of Augsburg, Article 9, where it is said that Baptism is necessary to salvation, and that by means of it the grace of God is offered.

[9] See Zwingli, *De Baptismo* and *De Peccato Originali Declaratio*.

[10] See, *e.g.*, the *Helvetic Confession*, Article 20; the *Saxon Confession*, Article 14.

[11] See Calvin, *Institutes*, IV. xv.-xvi.

[12] The Council of Trent declared that Baptism is a Sacrament, is necessary to salvation, confers grace, imparts character, differs from the baptism of S. John the Baptist; and condemned various errors: see Sess. vii., *De Sacramentis in Genere*, and *De Baptismo* (Hardouin, *Concilia*, x. 52-4).

[13] See, *e.g.*, Cardwell, *History of Conferences and other Proceedings connected with the Revision of the Book of Common Prayer*, pp. 324-5, 356. The reply of the bishops to the Puritan objections was: "'Receive remission of sins by spiritual regeneration." Most proper, for Baptism is our spiritual regeneration (S. John iii.), "Unless a man be born again of water and the Spirit," etc. And by this is received

remission of sins (Acts ii. 3), "Repent and be baptized every one of you, for the remission of sins." So the Creed: "One Baptism for the remission of sins." "We cannot in faith say that every child that is baptized is regenerate," etc. Seeing that God's sacraments have their effects where the receiver doth not "ponere obicem," put any bar against them (which children cannot do); we may say in faith of every child that is baptized, that it is regenerated by God's Holy Spirit; and the denial of it tends to anabaptism, and the contempt of this holy sacrament, as nothing worthy, nor material whether it be administered to children or no.'

[14] Synod of Bethlehem (1672 A.D.) cap. 16, ἀποτελέσματα δὲ τοῦ βαπτίσματος συνελόντι φάναι· πρῶτον, ἡ ἄφεσις τοῦ προπατορικοῦ πλημμελήματος, καὶ ὅσων ἄλλων ἁμαρτιῶν πεπραχὼς ἦν ὁ βαπτισθείς. δεύτερον, ῥύεται ἐκεῖνον τῆς ἀϊδίου ποινῆς, ᾗτινι ὑπέκειτο, εἴτε διὰ τὸ ἀρχέγονον ἁμάρτημα, εἴτε δι' ἃ ἰδικῶς ἔπραξε θανασίμως. τρίτον, δίδωσιν αὐτοῖς τὴν ἀθανασίαν· δικαιοῦν γὰρ αὐτοῖς τῶν προημαρτημένων ναοὺς Θεοῦ ἀποκαθίστησιν (Hardouin, *Concilia*, xi. 249-252); *Longer Catechism of the Russian Church* in Blackmore, *The Doctrine of the Russian Church*, pp. 84, 87.

CHAPTER V

[1] See Cranmer, *Answer to Gardiner*, book iii., p. 64, Parker Society edition: 'In Baptism we receive the Holy Ghost'; Ridley, *Disputation at Oxford*, p. 240, Parker Society edition: 'The water in Baptism hath grace promised, and by that grace the Holy Spirit is given.'

[2] Bright, *Morality in Doctrine*, pp. 91-2.

[3] Acts viii. 14-17, xix. 6.

[4] Acts ii. 38.

[5] Acts ix. 17.

[6] Romans viii. 9.

[7] 1 Corinthians xii. 13; Romans v. 5; 1 Corinthians ii. 12 S. James iv. 5; Galatians iv. 6.

[8] Cornelius, cit. Eusebius, *H. E.*, vi. 43, ὃς βοηθούμενος ὑπὸ τῶν ἐπορκιστῶν νόσῳ περιπεσὼν χαλεπῇ καὶ ἀποθανεῖσθαι ὅσον οὐδέπω νομιζόμενος ἐν αὐτῇ τῇ κλίνῃ ᾗ ἔκειτο περιχυθεὶς ἔλαβεν· εἴ γε χρὴ λέγειν τὸν τοιοῦτον εἰληφέναι. Οὐ μὴν οὐδὲ τῶν λοιπῶν ἔτυχε, διαφυγὼν τὴν νόσον, ὧν χρὴ μεταλαμβάνειν κατὰ τὸν τῆς ἐκκλησίας κανόνα, τοῦ τε σφραγισθῆναι ὑπὸ τοῦ ἐπισκόπου. Τούτου δὲ μὴ τυχών, πῶς ἂν τοῦ Ἁγίου Πνεύματος ἔτυχε; ('Who, receiving the help of the exorcists, having been taken ill of a grievous disease and being thought to be at the point of death, received it (if it be right to say such a man received it) by having water poured on him in the bed in which he was lying. However, on his recovery from the disease he never obtained the other gifts which he ought to have obtained according to the rule of the Church, namely, the sealing of the bishop. And, as he did not obtain these, how was it possible that he obtained the Holy Ghost?')

Tertullian, *De Baptismo*, 6, 'Non quod in aquis Spiritum Sanctum consequamur, sed in aqua emundati sub angelo Spiritui Sancto præparamur.'

S. Cyprian, *Epistola* lxxiv. 5, 'Qui enim peccatis in baptismo expositis sanctificatus est et in novum hominem spiritaliter reformatus ad accipiendum Spiritum Sanctum idoneus factus est' ('For he who has been sanctified by the removal of sins in Baptism and has been spiritually remade into a new man, has been made fit to receive the Holy Spirit'); *ibid.* 7, 'Porro autem non per manus impositionem quis nascitur quando accipit Spiritum Sanctum sed in baptismo ut Spiritum Sanctum jam natus accipiat, sicut in primo homine Adam factum est. Ante enim Deus eum plasmavit et tunc insufflavit in faciem ejus flatum vitæ. Nec enim potest accipi spiritus, nisi prius fuerit, qui accipiat' ('But a man is not born by means of the laying on of hands when he receives the Holy Spirit, but in Baptism, so that when he has already been born he may receive the Holy Spirit, as came to pass in the first man Adam. For God first formed him and then breathed into his face the breath of life. For neither can the Spirit be received unless there be one to receive it.')

S. Chrysostom, *In Ep. i. ad Cor. Hom.*, xxx. 2, ἐμοὶ δὲ δοκεῖ νῦν ἐκείνην λέγειν τοῦ πνεύματος τὴν ἐπιφοίτησιν τὴν ἀπὸ τοῦ βαπτίσματος καὶ πρὸ τῶν μυστηρίων ἐγγινομένην ἡμῖν ('Now it seems to me that he here means that descent of the Spirit which comes to us as a result of our Baptism and before the mysteries').

[9] S. Cyprian, *Epistola* lxix. 13-15, 'Porro autem quod quidam eos salutari aqua et fide legitima Christi gratiam consecutos non christianos, sed clinicos vocant, non invenio unde hoc nomen assumant nisi forte qui plura et secretiora legerunt apud Hippocratem vel Soranum clinicos istos deprehenderunt. Ego enim, qui clinicum de evangelio novi, scio paralytico illi et debili per longa ætatis curricula in lecto jacenti nihil infirmitatem suam obfuisse, quominus ad firmitatem cœlestem plenissime perveniret, nec tantum indulgentia dominica excitatum de grabato esse sed ipsum grabatum suum reparatis et vegetatis viribus sustulisse. Et idcirco, quantum fide concipere et sentire nobis datur, mea sententia hæc est, ut christianus judicetur legitimus quisquis

fuerit in ecclesia lege et jure divinam gratiam consecutus. Aut si aliquis existimat eos nihil consecutos eo quod aqua salutari tantum perfusi sint, sed inanes et vacui sunt, non decipiantur, ut si incommodum languoris evaserint et convaluerint, baptizentur. Si autem baptizari non possunt, qui jam baptismo ecclesiastico sanctificati sunt, cur in fide sua et Domini indulgentia scandalizantur? *An consecuti sunt quidem gratiam dominicam, sed breviore et minore mensura muneris divini ac Spiritus Sancti, ut habeantur quidem christiani, non sint tamen ceteris adæquandi? Quinimo Spiritus Sanctus non ad mensuram datur, sed super credentem totus infunditur.* Nam si dies omnibus æqualiter nascitur, et si sol super omnes pari et æquali luce diffunditur, quanto magis Christus sol et dies verus in ecclesia sua lumen vitæ æternæ pari æqualitate largitur. Cujus æqualitatis sacramentum videmus in Exodo esse celebratum cum de cœlo manna deflueret et futurorum præfiguratione alimentum panis cœlestis et cibum Christi venientis ostenderet. Illic enim sine discrimine vel sexus vel ætatis gomor a singulis æqualiter colligebatur. Unde apparebat Christi indulgentiam et cœlestem gratiam postmodum secuturam æqualiter omnibus dividi, sine sexus varietate, sine annorum discrimine, sine acceptione personæ super omnem Dei populum spiritalis gratiæ munus infundi. Plane eadem gratia spiritalis, quæ aequaliter in baptismo a credentibus sumitur, in conversatione atque actu nostro postmodum vel minuitur vel augetur, ut in evangelio dominicum semen æqualiter seminatur, sed pro varietate terræ aliud absumitur, aliud in multiformem copiam vel tricesimi vel sexagesimi vel centesimi numeri fructu exuberante cumulatur. Adhuc vero cum singuli ad denarium vocentur, quid est, ut quod a Deo æqualiter distribuitur, humana interpretatione minuatur? Quodsi aliquis in illo movetur, quod quidam de iis, qui ægri baptizantur, spiritibus adhuc immundis tentantur, sciat diaboli nequitiam pertinacem usque ad aquam salutarem valere, in baptismo vero omne nequitiæ suæ virus amittere. Quod exemplum cernimus in rege Pharaone, qui diu reluctatus et in sua perfidia demoratus tamdiu resistere potuit et prævalere, donec ad aquam veniret: quo cum venisset et victus est et exstinctus. Mare autem illud sacramentum baptismi fuisse declarat beatus apostolus Paulus dicens: Nolo enim vos ignorare, fratres, quia patres nostri omnes sub nube fuerunt et omnes per mare transierunt et omnes in Moyse baptizati sunt in nube et in mari. Et addidit dicens: Hæc autem omnia figuræ nostræ fuerunt. Quod hodie etiam geritur ut per exorcistas voce humana et potestate divina flagelletur et uratur et torqueatur diabolus et, cum exire se et homines Dei dimittere sæpe dicat, in eo tamen, quod dixerit, fallat et id, quod per Pharaonem prius gestum est, eodem mendacio obstinationis et fraudis exerceat. Cum tamen ad aquam salutarem atque ad baptismi sanctificationem venitur, scire debemus et fidere, quia illic diabolus opprimitur et homo Deo dicatus divina indulgentia liberatur. Nam sicut scorpii et serpentes, qui in sicco prævalent, in aquam præcipitati prævalere non possunt aut sua venena retinere, sic et spiritus nequam, qui scorpii et serpentes appellantur et tamen per nos data a Domino potestate calcantur, permanere ultra non possunt in hominis corpore, *in quo baptizato et sanctificato incipit Spiritus Sanctus habitare*' ('As to the fact that some call them, after they have obtained the grace of Christ by the health-giving water and lawful faith, not Christians, but clinics, I do not find whence they take this name unless perhaps those who have read much secret lore in Hippocrates and Soranus, have got hold of those clinics. For I, who know the clinic from the Gospel, know that the weakness of the man who was paralysed and for long years had been lying in sickness on his bed was no hindrance to his coming most fully to the heavenly strength, and that he was not only raised from his bed by the forgiveness of the Lord but himself took up his bed with renewed and fresh strength. And therefore, so far as it is granted to us by faith to perceive and form an opinion, my judgment is this: that whoever by law and right has obtained divine grace in the Church is to be judged a lawful Christian. Or if any one thinks that they have obtained nothing in that the health-giving water was only poured upon them, but are void and empty, let them not be deceived so as to be baptized if they shall have escaped the weakness of the disease and have recovered. But if they cannot be baptized, who have already been sanctified by the Baptism of the Church, why are stumbling-blocks put in the way of their faith and the forgiveness of the Lord? *Did they indeed obtain the grace of the Lord, but with a more scanty and smaller measure of the divine gift and the Holy Spirit, so as indeed to be considered Christians, yet not to be put on a level with the rest? Nay, the Holy Spirit is not given by measure but is poured in His fulness upon the believer.* For if the day is born to all equally, and if the sun is shed abroad upon all with like and equal light, how much more does Christ the true sun and day bestow in His Church the light of eternal life with like equality. Of which equality we see a type was set forth in the Exodus when the manna came down from heaven and prefiguring things to come showed the nourishment of the heavenly bread and the food of the coming Christ. For there without difference either of sex or of age an omer was gathered by all alike. Whence it was clear that the forgiveness of Christ and the heavenly grace which was to come is divided among all alike, and that the gift of spiritual grace is poured upon all the people of God without difference of sex, without distinction of age, without respect of persons. Certainly the same spiritual grace, which is received equally in Baptism by believers, is afterwards either diminished or increased by our life and actions, as in the Gospel the seed of the Lord is sown alike, but according to the differences of soil, some is lost, other grows with exuberant fruit into a manifold plenty of thirty-fold or sixty-fold or a hundred-fold. But again while each one is called to receive the penny, why is it that what is equally distributed by God is diminished by human interpretation? But if any one is moved by this that some of those who are baptized in sickness are still tempted by foul spirits, let him know that the persistent wickedness of the devil is strong up to the health-giving water, but in Baptism loses all the poison of its malice. An example of this we see in the case of King Pharaoh, who after long struggle and delay in his unbelief was able to resist and prevail until he came to the water: when he came to it, he was conquered and destroyed. Now the blessed apostle Paul declares that this sea was a type of Baptism when he says, For I would not have you ignorant, brethren, that all our fathers were under the cloud and all passed through the sea and all were baptized into Moses in the cloud and in the sea. And he added saying, Now all these things were figures of ourselves. And this is reproduced even nowadays, so that at the hands of exorcists by human voice and divine power the devil is scourged and burnt and tormented, and while he oftentimes says that he goes out and lets the men of God go, yet deceives in what he has said, and carries on with the same lie of obstinacy and deceit what was done before by Pharaoh. Yet when one comes to the healthgiving water and to the sanctification of Baptism, we ought to know and trust that there the devil is crushed and the man dedicated to God is set free by the divine forgiveness. For as scorpions and serpents, which are strong on dry ground, cannot be strong or retain their poisons when they are cast into water, so also the evil spirits, which are called scorpions and serpents and yet are trodden under foot by us in the power given us by the Lord, cannot remain any longer in the body of the man, *in whom, since he has been baptized and sanctified, the Holy Spirit begins to dwell*').

[10] Hutchings, *Gleanings, Spiritual, Doctrinal and Practical*, p. 201.

[11] Origen, *In Ezech. Hom.*, vi. 5, 'Qui lavatur in salutem et aquam accipit et Spiritum Sanctum' ('He who is washed unto salvation receives both the water and the Holy Spirit.')

S. Basil, *Adv. Eunom.*, v. (t. i. p. 303 A, edit. Benedic.), Τοῦτο ἡμᾶς ἀνακαινοῖ καὶ πάλιν εἰκόνας ἀναδείκνυσι Θεοῦ· διὰ λουτροῦ παλιγγενεσίας καὶ ἀνακαινώσεως Πνεύματος ἁγίου υἱοθετούμεθα Θεῷ· καινὴ πάλιν κτίσις μεταλαμβάνουσα τοῦ Πνεύματος, οὗπερ ἐστερημένη πεπαλαίωτο ('This renews us and makes us again images of God: by means of the washing of regeneration and the renewing of the Holy Spirit we are made sons of God: the creature is again new by partaking of the Spirit, by being deprived of whom it had been made old ').

S. Athanasius, *Ep. ad Scrap.*, i. 4, Ποῖον δὲ ἦσαν λαβόντες ἢ τὸ Πνεῦμα τὸ ἅγιον, τὸ διδόμενον τοῖς πιστεύουσι καὶ ἀναγεννωμένοις διὰ λουτροῦ παλιγγενεσίας ('But what had they received but the Holy Spirit, who is given to those who believe and are being begotten again by means of the washing of regeneration?')

[12] This Gallican homily was ascribed to Melchiades (Bishop of Rome 311-314 A.D.) in the forged decretals, and is quoted as his by S. Thomas Aquinas, *S. T.*, III. lxii. 1, and the *Catechism of the Council of Trent*, II. iii. 5. Cf. Peter Lombard, *Sent.*, iv. 7.

[13] See *Théologie Dogmatique Orthodoxe*, par Macaire, traduite par un Russe, Paris, 1860, § 210 (t. ii. p. 425).

[14] Synod of Bethlehem, cap. 16 (Hardouin, *Concilia*, xi. 252 A): see note 14 on Chapter iv.

[15] See Goar, *Euchologion*, p. 289, Ἐπιφάνηθι, κύριε, τούτῳ καὶ δὸς μεταποιηθῆναι τὸν ἐν αὐτῷ βαπτιζόμενον εἰς τὸ ἀποθέσθαι μὲν τὸν παλαιὸν ἄνθρωπον τὸν φθειρόμενον κατὰ τὰς ἐπιθυμίας τῆς ἀπάτης· ἐνδύσασθαι δὲ τὸν νέον τὸν ἀνακαινούμενον κατ' εἰκόνα τοῦ κτίσαντος αὐτόν, ἵνα γενόμενος σύμφυτος τῷ ὁμοιώματι τοῦ θανάτου αὐτοῦ διὰ τοῦ βαπτίσματος κοινωνὸς καὶ τῆς ἀναστάσεως γένηται, καὶ φυλάξας τὴν δωρεὰν τοῦ ἁγίου σου πνεύματος καὶ αὐξήσας τὴν παρακαταθήκην τῆς χάριτος δέξηται τὸ βραβεῖον τῆς ἄνω κλήσεως καὶ συγκαταριθμηθῇ τοῖς πρωτοτόκοις τοῖς ἀπογεγραμμένοις ἐν οὐρανῷ ('Manifest Thyself, O Lord, upon this water, and grant that he who is to be baptized in it may be remade unto putting off the old man, which waxeth corrupt according to the lusts of deceit, and unto putting on the new man, which is renewed according to the image of Him that created him; to the end that, being planted together in the likeness of His death through Baptism, he may be made partaker also of His resurrection,

and, having guarded the gift of Thy Holy Spirit and having increased the grace committed to him, he may receive the prize of the high calling and be numbered among the first-born which are enrolled in heaven'). By comparing this prayer and the words of the Synod of Bethlehem with other Eastern statements, we find teaching which can only be satisfactorily explained by saying that the Holy Spirit is received both in Baptism and in Confirmation: see the *Longer Catechism of the Russian Church* (Blackmore, *Doctrine of the Russian Church*, pp. 87-8), and the *Orthodox Confession*, part i., question 105.

[16] The opinion rejected in this chapter is advocated with skill and learning in Puller, *What is the Distinctive Grace of Confirmation?* and Mason, *The Relation of Confirmation to Baptism as taught in Holy Scripture and the Fathers*. There is an analysis of the evidence in Wirgman, *The Doctrine of Confirmation considered in Relation to Holy Baptism as a Sacramental Ordinance of the Catholic Church*. Dr. Wirgman holds that the personal indwelling of the Holy Spirit is bestowed in Baptism. The question is fully discussed from somewhat differing points of view in the *Church Quarterly Review*, April 1892 ('Primitive Teaching on Confirmation and its Relation to Holy Baptism'), and January 1898 ('The Relation of Confirmation to Baptism').

CHAPTER VI

[1] See, *e.g.*, Gaius, *Inst.*, iv. 16; Cæsar, *De Bello Civ.*, i. 23; Horace, *Carm.*, II. xvii. 10; Pliny, *Ep.*, x. 96, 'Adfirmabant autem hanc fuisse summam vel culpæ suæ vel erroris, quod essent soliti stato die ante lucem convenire carmenque

Christo quasi deo dicere secum invicem, seque sacramento non in scelus aliquod obstringere, sed ne furta, ne latrocinia, ne adulteria committerent, ne fidem fallerent, ne depositum appellati abnegarent: quibus peractis morem sibi discedendi fuisse, rursusque coeundi ad capiendum cibum, promiscuum tamen et innoxium.' On the use of 'sacramentum' in this passage see Lightfoot, *Apostolic Fathers*, II. i. 52-3.

² See, *e.g.*, S. Augustine, *Ep.* cxxxvii. 15, *Serm.* cxxviii. 3, *De Cat. Rud.* 50, *De Doct. Christ.* iii. 13, *De Bapt. c. Don.* xx. 28, c. *Faust.* xix. 17; S. Leo, *Serm.* xxi. 3, xxii. 1, liv. 1, *Ep.* xxviii. 3, 5; S. Bernard, *Serm. ii. in Purif. B. Mariæ*, 1. Cf. note 4 on chapter I. See also a note in Bright, *Select Sermons of S. Leo the Great on the Incarnation*, p. 136 (edition 2).

³ S. Thomas Aquinas, *S. T.*, III. lx. 2, 'Proprie dicitur sacramentum quod est signum alicujus rei sacræ ad homines pertinentis, ut scilicet proprie dicatur sacramentum secundum quod nunc de sacramentis loquimur quod est signum rei sacræ, in quantum est sanctificans homines' ('That is properly called a sacrament which is the sign of some sacred thing pertaining to men, so that the name sacrament is properly used in the sense in which we now speak of sacraments, that is, the sign of a sacred thing, in so far as it sanctifies men').

Catechism of the Council of Trent, II. i. 8, 'Quare, ut explicatius quid sacramentum sit declaretur, docendum erit, rem esse sensibus subjectam quæ ex Dei institutione sanctitatis et justitiæ tum significandæ tum efficiendæ vim habet' ('Wherefore that it may be more fully declared what a sacrament is, it is to be taught that it is a thing subjected to the senses which, by the institution of God, has the power at once of signifying and of effecting sanctity and righteousness').

⁴ Gregory of Bergamo, *Tractatus de Veritate Corporis Christi*, 14, 'Tria siquidem in Ecclesia gerimus sacramenta, quæ sacramentis aliis putantur non immerito digniora, scilicet baptismum, chrisma, corpus et sanguis Domini. Quorum trium primum et ultimum ex ipsius Redemptoris institutione percepimus, ex apostolica vero traditione illud quod medium posuimus. Sunt præterea quædam alia, quæ videntur velut antiquiora sacramenta, videlicet sacerdotalis ordinatio, legitimum conjugium, sacramenta quandoque dicuntur scripturarum et jusjurandi sacramentum' (' In the Church we have three sacraments, which not undeservedly are thought more worthy than the other sacraments, namely, Baptism, Chrism, the Body and Blood of the Lord. Of which three, the first and the last we have received by the institution of the Redeemer Himself, but that which we have placed between them we have received from apostolic tradition. There are besides certain others, which seem as it were more ancient sacraments, namely, priestly ordination, lawful marriage, and sometimes we speak of the sacraments of the Scriptures and the sacrament of an oath ').

Peter Lombard, *Sent.*, IV. ii. 1.

Decretum Eugenii Papæ IV. (Hardouin, *Concilia*, ix. 438–40).

Council of Paris, *Decreta fidei*, cap. 10 (Hardouin, *Concilia*, ix. 1940–42).

Council of Trent, sess. vii., *De Sacramentis in Genere*, canon 1 (Hardouin, *Concilia*, x. 52).

Council of Constantinople (1642 A.D.), cap. 15 (Hardouin, *Concilia*, xi. 174).

Synod of Bethlehem (1672 A.D.), cap. 15 (Hardouin, *Concilia*, xi. 247).

[5] See, *e.g.*, Council of Trent, sess. vii., *De Sacramentis in Genere*, canon 3 (Hardouin, *Concilia*, x. 52); Schouppe, *Elementa Theologicæ Dogmaticæ*, x. 54.

[6] See, *e.g.*, Cardwell, *History of Conferences and other Proceedings connected with the Revision of the Book of Common Prayer*, pp. 326, 357. The reason given by the bishops for not assenting to the request of the Puritans that the words 'as generally necessary to salvation' might be omitted was, 'These words are a reason of the answer that there are two only, and therefore not to be left out.'

[7] See, *e.g.*, last rubric to the English Order of the Ministration of Private Baptism of Children; *Rituale Romanum*, De Form. Bapt. For questions relating to the Baptism of unconscious persons or idiots see note 8 to Chapter x.

[8] Ephesians iv. 5-6. According to Epiphanius, *Adv. Hær.*, xlii. 3, Marcion taught that Baptism might be administered three times, and that in the second and third administration the sins committed since the previous administration were forgiven. For the Hemerobaptists, who at the end of the first and beginning of the second century taught that daily baptism was necessary, see Lightfoot, *S. Paul's Epistles to the Colossians and to Philemon*, pp. 162-7.

CHAPTER VII

[1] *Letter of the Smyrnæans on the Martyrdom of S. Polycarp*, 9, ὀγδοήκοντα καὶ ἓξ ἔτη δουλεύω [al. ἔχω δουλεύων] αὐτῷ.

S. Justin Martyr, *Apol.*, i. 15, οἱ ἐκ παίδων ἐμαθητεύθησαν τῷ Χριστῷ. The question is whether ἐμαθητεύθησαν necessarily means that they were baptized. In view of the phraseology in S. Matthew xxviii. 19, πορευθέντες οὖν μαθητεύσατε πάντα τὰ ἔθνη, it is most probable that this is the meaning.

S. Irenæus, *C. Har.*, II. xxii. 4, 'Omnes enim venit per semetipsum salvare : omnes, inquam, qui per eum renascuntur in Deum, infantes, et parvulos, et pueros, et juvenes, et seniores' ('For He came to save all by Himself : all, I say, who through Him are regenerated unto God, infants, and little children, and boys, and youths, and those who are older').

Tertullian, *De Baptismo*, 18. The terms in which Tertullian urges that caution is needed with regard to the Baptism of infants (as also of the unmarried) show that it was the ordinary custom in his time. The argument of, *e.g.*, Mr. Whitley Stokes (*Academy*, February 15, 1896, pp. 137-8) that this passage shows that the Baptism of infants was at this time being newly introduced into the Church, is forced.

Canons of Hippolytus, canon xix. § 113, 'those who make the responses for little infants.'

S. Cyprian, *Epistola* lxiv. 2.

Clement of Alexandria, *Pædag.*, iii. 11, τῶν ἐξ ὕδατος ἀνασπωμένων παιδίων.

Origen, *In Lev. Hom.*, viii. 3 ; *In S. Luc. Hom.*, xiv. ; *In Ep. ad Ro.*, v. 9.

Apostolical Constitutions, vi. 15, βαπτίζετε δὲ ὑμῶν καὶ τὰ νήπια, καὶ ἐκτρέφετε αὐτὰ ἐν παιδείᾳ καὶ νουθεσίᾳ Θεοῦ· ἄφετε γάρ, φησὶ, τὰ παιδία ἔρχεσθαι πρός με, καὶ μὴ κωλύετε αὐτά ('And baptize also your babes, and bring them up in the nurture and admonition of the Lord ; for He saith, "Suffer the little children to come unto Me, and forbid them not"').

[2] S. Gregory of Nazianzus, *Orat.*, xl. 28, τί δ' ἂν εἴποις περὶ τῶν ἔτι νηπίων, καὶ μήτε τῆς ζημίας ἐπαισθανομένων μήτε τῆς χάριτος; ἢ καὶ ταῦτα βαπτίσομεν; πάνυ γε, εἴπερ τις ἐπείγοι κίνδυνος· κρεῖττον γὰρ ἀναισθήτως ἁγιασθῆναι ἢ ἀπελθεῖν ἀσφράγιστα καὶ ἀτέλεστα . . . περὶ δὲ τῶν ἄλλων δίδωμι γνώμην, τὴν τριετίαν ἀναμείναντας, ἢ μικρὸν ἐντὸς τούτου, ἢ ὑπὲρ τοῦτο ('But what would you say about those who are still babes and do not yet perceive either the loss or the grace? Shall we baptize these also? Certainly, if some danger is pressing. For it is better to be sanctified without perceiving it than to depart without the seal and without initiation. . . . But as to the rest, I give my opinion that they should wait till they are three years old, or a little less or more, before being baptized').

[3] That the explanation given in the text of the practice of deferring Baptism is the right explanation is shown by the emphatic teaching, at the time when the practice was common, of the lawfulness and need of baptizing infants: see, *e.g.*, S. Augustine, *Serm.*, ccxciv. 8, 16, 19. Cf. *Conf.*, i. 17.

[4] For the law of King Ine see Johnson, *Collection of the Laws and Canons of the Church of England*, i. 132 (Library of Anglo-Catholic Theology). For the Church of Rome at the present time see *Rituale Romanum*, De Sacramento Baptismi, De Baptizandis Parvulis. For the East see, *e.g.*, Shann, *Book of Needs of the Holy Orthodox Church*, pp. 4, 6; Smirnoff, *The Instruction in God's Law*, p. 148 (English translation): this book has been approved by the Russian Church as a text-book for schools.

[5] Tertullian, *De Baptismo*, 18.
Canons of Hippolytus, canon xix, § 113, quoted in note 1.
Apostolical Constitutions, iii. 16, viii. 32.

⁶ S. Augustine, *Epistola* xcviii. 5, 'Offeruntur quippe parvuli ad percipiendam spiritalem gratiam, non tam ab eis quorum gestantur manibus (quamvis et ab ipsis, si et ipsi boni fideles sunt) quam ab universa societate sanctorum atque fidelium. Ab omnibus namque offerri recte intelliguntur, quibus placet quod offeruntur, et quorum sancta atque individua caritate ad communicationem Sancti Spiritus adjuvantur. Tota hoc ergo mater Ecclesia, quæ in sanctis est, facit: quia tota omnes, tota singulos parit.'

⁷ For one sponsor see, *e.g.*, *Apostolical Constitutions*, iii. 16. For the mediæval English rubric see, *e.g.*, Maskell, *Monumenta Ritualia Ecclesiæ Anglicanæ*, i. 31. The Council of Worcester (1240 A.D.), chapter 5 (Hardouin, *Concilia*, vii. 332), directed that there should be two men and one woman for each male child and one man and two women for each female child. The same regulation is in the Council of Exeter (1287 A.D.), chapter 2 (Hardouin, *Concilia*, vii. 1075). For Rome, see the Council of Trent, sess. xxiv., De Reform. Matr., cap. 2 (Hardouin, *Concilia*, x. 150), where it is ordered that there be one sponsor, or at the most one man and one woman: cf. *Rituale Romanum*, De Sacr. Bapt., De Patrinis: the *Rituale Romanum* orders that the priest is to inquire who the sponsors are previously to the Baptism so that he may reject any who are unfit. For Russia, see Blackmore, *Doctrine of the Russian Church*, p. 208.

⁸ For 'cognatio spiritualis,' held to make marriage between those so related invalid, see, *e.g.*, *Code of Justinian*, V. iv. 26, 'Ea videlicet persona omnimodo ad nuptias venire prohibenda, quam aliquis, sive alumna sit, sive non, a sacrosancto suscepit baptismate: cum nihil aliud sic

inducere potest paternam affectionem et justam nuptiarum prohibitionem quam hujusmodi nexus per quem Deo mediante animæ eorum copulatæ sunt'; S. Thomas Aquinas, *S. T.*, Suppl. lv.; Council of Trent, *ibid.* There is a clear statement on this subject in Watkins, *Holy Matrimony*, pp. 700-2. It was in consequence of the results and complications that were due to the mediæval teaching about the 'cognatio spiritualis' that the number of sponsors was reduced by the Council of Trent, which also placed some limitations on the relationship. See Council of Trent, *ibid.*

⁹ See Councils of Worcester and Exeter in note 7, *supra*.

CHAPTER VIII

¹ S. Matthew xxviii. 19; S. John iii. 5; Constitutions of Richard Poore, Bishop of Sarum (1217 A.D.), cap. 13, 'janua omnium sacramentorum, et prima tabula post naufragium, sine quo non est salus' (Hardouin, *Concilia*, vii. 92); Church Catechism. For the distinction between necessity as means and necessity because of a command, see, *e.g.*, Schouppe, *Elementa Theologiæ Dogmaticæ*, xi. 75-6.

² See, *e.g.*, S. Thomas Aquinas, *S. T.*, III. lxviii. 2, 'Sacramentum baptismi dupliciter potest alicui deesse: uno modo et re et voto, quod contingit illis qui nec baptizantur nec baptizari volunt, quod manifeste ad contemptum sacramenti pertinet, quantum ad illos qui habent usum liberi arbitrii. Et ideo hi quibus hoc modo deest baptismus salutem consequi non possunt, quia nec sacramentaliter nec mentaliter Christo incorporantur, per quem solum est salus; alio modo potest sacramentum baptismi alicui deesse re,

sed non voto; sicut cum aliquis baptizari desiderat, sed aliquo casu praevenitur morte antequam baptismum suscipiat, et talis sine baptismo actuali salutem consequi potest propter desiderium baptismi, quod procedit ex fide per dilectionem operante, per quam Deus interius hominem sanctificat, *cujus potentia sacramentis visibilibus non alligatur*' ('The Sacrament of Baptism can be lacking to any one in two ways: in one way both in fact and in wish, as happens in the case of those who neither are baptized nor wish to be baptized, which clearly pertains to contempt of the Sacrament, so far as those are concerned who have the use of free-will. And therefore those to whom Baptism is lacking in this way cannot obtain salvation, because they are not incorporated with Christ, through Whom alone is salvation, either sacramentally or mentally; in another way Baptism can be lacking to any one in fact but not in wish, as when one desires to be baptized, but through some accident is cut off by death before he receives Baptism, and such a one can obtain salvation without actual Baptism because of his desire for Baptism, which springs from faith working by love, through which God sanctifies the man within, for *His power is not tied down to visible Sacraments*'); Hooker, *Laws of Ecclesiastical Polity*, V. lvii. 4, 'Neither is it *ordinarily* His will to bestow the grace of Sacraments on any but by the Sacraments.'

³ Hooker, *Laws of Ecclesiastical Polity*, V. lx. 5. Cf., e.g., *Canons of Hippolytus*, canon xix. § 101, 'A catechumen who has been taken prisoner and brought to martyrdom and put to death before he has received Baptism is to be buried with the other martyrs, for he has been baptized in his own blood'; S. Cyril of Jerusalem, *Cat.*, iii. 10, εἴ τις μὴ λάβοι τὸ βάπτισμα σωτηρίαν οὐκ ἔχει, πλὴν μόνων μαρτύρων, οἳ καὶ χωρὶς

τοῦ ὕδατος λαμβάνουσι τὴν βασιλείαν ('If any one receive not Baptism, he has not salvation, martyrs only excepted who even without the water attain to the kingdom'); Tertullian, *De Bapt.* 16; S. Cyprian, *Ep.* lxxiii. 21; S. Thomas Aquinas, *S. T.*, III. lxvi. 11-12, lxviii. 2 (see note 2, *supra*).

[4] See S. Augustine, *De Bapt. c. Don.*, iv. 29, 'Quantum itaque valeat etiam sine visibli sacramento baptismi quod ait apostolus, Corde creditur ad justitiam, ore autem confessio fit ad salutem, in illo latrone declaratum est. Sed tunc impletur invisibiliter, quum ministerium baptismi non contemtus religionis, sed articulus necessitatis excludit'; the note 2 *supra*, and the exhortation after the Gospel in 'the Ministration of Baptism to such as are of riper years.' S. Augustine, as noted below, thought differently about infants.

[5] Last rubric to Order of Public Baptism of Infants.

[6] S. Augustine, *Ep.*, clxxxvi. 27, ccxvii. 22; *C. Jul. Pelag.*, v. 44; *Serm.* ccxciv. 3. In his earlier work, *De lib. arbit.*, iii. 66-7, S. Augustine spoke of the possibility of a future middle state. S. Gregory of Nazianzus held they will be awarded neither glory nor punishment: see *Orat.*, xl. 23. S. Gregory of Nyssa held they will attain at any rate eventually to all the bliss in heaven which they are capable of enjoying: see *Catech. Orat.*, 38, *De infantibus qui præmature abripiuntur*, *passim*. In estimating the value of this opinion of S. Gregory of Nyssa it must be remembered that in some passages in his writings he speaks of the ultimate salvation of all men and spirits, though elsewhere he teaches differently on this point. For the opinion of S. Thomas Aquinas, see *S. T.*, III. i. 4 ad 2, App. i. 1-2; 2 *Sent.*, dist. xxxiii. q. 2, a. 2, ad 5.

CHAPTER IX

[1] Tertullian, *De Baptismo*, 17, speaks of the bishop as having the right of baptizing, and of the presbyters and deacons as having it by delegation from him. The *Apostolical Canons* and *Constitutions* apparently contemplate Baptisms by bishops and presbyters only: see *Apostolical Canons*, xlix; *Apostolical Constitutions*, iii. 20, viii. 28. Tertullian, *ibid.*, says lay Baptism is valid. The Council of Elvira, canon 38, allowed it in cases of necessity (Hardouin, *Concilia*, i. 254). In ordinary cases, Baptism by a deacon or layman does not appear to have been contemplated; but it can hardly be doubted that the tradition of allowing such Baptism in cases of necessity has been continuous, at any rate in the West.

[2] The opinion referred to in the text appears to have been originated in the West by Agrippinus of Carthage: see S. Vincent of Lerins, *Commonitorium*, 16; S. Augustine, *De Bapt. c. Don.*, ii. 12, iii. 3, 17, iv. 8. For S. Cyprian's advocacy of it see *Ep.*, 69-75. The councils referred to were held in 255, 256 A.D. The subject is elaborately treated in Benson, *Cyprian, His Life, His Times, His Work*, pp. 331-436. The passage quoted in the text from this work is on pp. 425-6. Cf. note 3, *infra*. The passage in S. Ignatius referred to is *Ad Smyrn.*, 8, οὐκ ἐξόν ἐστιν χωρὶς τοῦ ἐπισκόπου οὔτε βαπτίζειν οὔτε ἀγάπην ποιεῖν· ἀλλ' ὃ ἂν δοκιμάσῃ, τοῦτο καὶ τῷ Θεῷ εὐάρεστον, ἵνα ἀσφαλὲς ᾖ καὶ βέβαιον πᾶν ὃ πράσσετε ('It is not lawful, apart from the bishop, either to baptize or to hold a love-feast; but whatever he may approve, this is well-pleasing also to God, in order that everything which ye do may be safe and secure').

³ Tertullian, *De Baptismo*, 15, regards heretical Baptism as invalid. It appears to have been rejected by councils held at Iconium and Synnada in the second quarter of the third century: see Eusebius, *H. E.*, vii. 7; Firmilian inter opera Cypriani, *Ep.*, lxxv.7. The Council of Arles, canon 8, regarded any Baptism administered in the Name of the Father and of the Son and of the Holy Ghost as valid (Hardouin, *Concilia*, i. 265). The Council of Nicæa, canon 8, recognised the validity of the Baptism of the Novatians; but in canon 19 rejected that of the Paulianists (Hardouin, *Concilia*, i. 325-32). It is doubtful what words the Paulianists used. S. Athanasius, *Orat. c. Ar.*, ii. 43, says they used the right words in an heretical sense. Innocent I., *Ep.*, xxii. 5, says 'they do not baptize in the Name of the Father and of the Son and of the Holy Ghost'; this is interpreted by some to mean that they gave the name a wrong significance, but it is more likely that Innocent thought they did not use the right words. S. Augustine taught in his controversies with the Donatists that any Baptism with the right words was valid, though the grace of it lay dormant in those outside the Church until they should join it, because of their lack of charity: see, *e.g.*, *De Bapt. c. Don.*, i. 18, iv. 23, vii. 53, and *passim*; *C. Ep. Parmen.*, ii. 29-30.

⁴ S. Augustine, *De Bapt. c. Don.* vii. 101-2, *C. Ep. Parmen.* ii. 30.

⁵ See, *e.g.*, S. Thomas Aquinas, *S. T.*, III. lxvii. 5.

⁶ Tertullian, *De Baptismo*, 17, forbids Baptism by women. Cf. *Apostolical Constitutions*, iii. 9; the so-called 'Fourth Council of Carthage,' canon 100 (Gallican, of province of Arles), (Hardouin, *Concilia*, i. 984).

⁷ Raymond of Pennafort, *Summa*, iii. 7: cf. *Sammula*.

⁸ See, *e.g.*, Maskell, *Monumenta Ritualia Ecclesiæ Anglicanæ*, i. 27-8, 30.

⁹ Hooker, *Laws of Ecclesiastical Polity*, V. lxi. 3.

¹⁰ See, *e.g.*, Zwingli, *De Bapt.*, ii. ; Helvetic Confession, 1536, cap. 20; Calvin, *Inst.*, IV. xv. 16, 20-22.

¹¹ Conc. Trid. Sess. vii. *De Baptismo*, 4 (Hardouin, *Concilia*, x. 53); Catechism of the Council of Trent, II. ii. 23-4.

¹² See Phillimore, *Ecclesiastical Law of the Church of England*, pp. 644-7. It may be noticed, in connection with this subject, that in the reign of Mary Cardinal Pole reiterated the ordinary Western teaching, and made one of his inquiries of the clergy to be whether they diligently instructed midwives in the method of baptizing: see Wilkins, *Concilia*, iv. 794-5. There is record of Archbishop Parker having licensed a midwife to baptize in 1567 : see Strype, *Annals of the Reformation*, I. ii. 243.

¹³ See Palmer, *Dissertations on Subjects relating to the 'Orthodox' or 'Eastern-Catholic' Communion*, pp. 163-9; Birkbeck, *Russia and the English Church during the Last Fifty Years*, pp. 109-110, 146-50 : on page 110 there is an important statement by Mr. Birkbeck that 'both the Patriarchate of Constantinople and the Church of the modern kingdom of Greece have now conformed to the practice of the Russian Church, and now no longer rebaptize Westerns, whether Roman Catholic, Anglican, or Protestant.' For similar teaching in the past by representative Greek theologians, see the *Confession of Dositheus*, 15 (heretical Baptism), and the *Confession of Metrophanes Critopulus*, 7

(lay Baptism), (Kimmel, *Monumenta fidei Ecclesiæ Orientalis*, i. 451, ii. 110). Cf. note 9 on Chapter x.

[14] See Blackmore, *Doctrine of the Russian Church*, pp. 209-10.

[15] For the *Acts of Thecla* see Tischendorf, *Acta Apostolorum Apocrypha*, pp. 40-63. The passages quoted are on pp. 56, 59. For the non-recognition see, *e.g.*, *Decret. Greg.*, III. xlii. 4.

[16] The story of Alexander, Bishop of Alexandria, having allowed the baptism of children baptized in play by Athanasius when a boy is in Ruffinus, *H. E.*, i. 14; Socrates, *H. E.*, i. 15; Sozomen, *H. E.*, ii. 17. Many discredit it. Whether true or not, it shows the existence of a belief that such a baptism would be valid at the time when it was current. For the rejection of such baptism see, *e.g.*, Peter Lombard, *Sent.*, IV. vi. 5; S. Thomas Aquinas, *S. T.*, III. lxiv. 8, 10.

[17] See, *e.g.*, S. Augustine, *De Bapt. c. Don.* iii. 15, *C. Litt. Petil.* iii. 59; S. Thomas Aquinas, *S. T.*, III. lxiv. 1. Cf. Bright, *Lessons from the Lives of Three Great Fathers*, pp. 154-5, 285-8.

[18] A very full and careful discussion of the subject of this chapter from a point of view different from that here adopted is in Elwin, *The Minister of Baptism*.

[19] S. Augustine, *De Bapt. c. Don.*, i. 14, 'Separata est enim a vinculo caritatis et pacis, sed juncta est in uno baptismate. Itaque est una ecclesia, quæ sola catholica nominatur; et quidquid suum habet in communionibus diversorum a sua unitate separatis, per hoc quod suum in eis habet, ipsa utique generat, non illæ. Neque enim separatio earum generat, sed quod secum de ista tenuerunt:

quod si et hoc dimittant omnino non generant. Hæc itaque in omnibus generat, cujus sacramenta retinentur, unde possit tale aliquid ubicumque generari: quamvis non omnes quos generat ad ejus pertineant unitatem, quæ usque in finem perseverantes salvabit' ('For she is separate from the bond of charity and peace but joined in the one Baptism. And so there is one Church which alone is called Catholic; and whatever of her own she has in communions of others separated from her unity, by virtue of this which she has in them of her own, it is she herself who in fact gives birth, not they. For neither does their separation give birth but that which they have kept among themselves from her; and if they let go this also, they do not give birth at all. Thus it is she whose Sacraments are kept who gives birth in the case of all, and it is for this reason that some such birth can take place everywhere; although not all of those to whom she gives birth pertain to her unity which is to save those who hold fast even to the end').

Letter of Firmilian, inter opera Cypriani, *Ep.*, lxxv. 14, 'Unde nec potest filios Dei parere, nisi si, secundum quod Stephano videtur, hæresis quidem parit et exponit, expositos autem ecclesia suscipit et quos non ipsa pepererit pro suis nutrit, cum filiorum alienorum mater esse non possit' ('Whence neither can heresy bring forth children to God unless indeed, as is the opinion of Stephen, she brings forth and exposes, while the Church takes up those who have been exposed and nourishes as if her own those whom she has not herself brought forth, since she cannot be the mother of alien sons').

Benson, *Cyprian, His Life, His Times, His Work*, p. 420.

[19] S. Augustine, *De Bapt. c. Don.*, iv. 5, 'Ergo qui

cælestia mandata non servat, avarus, raptor, fœnerator, invidus, verbis non factis sæculo renuntians, dimittit peccata? Si per vim sacramenti Dei, sicut ille, ita et ille: si per meritum suum, nec ille, nec ille. Illud enim sacramentum et in malis hominibus Christi esse cognoscitur.' The one 'ille' is a heretic; the other 'ille' is a bad man. The context is that S. Augustine is pressing the validity of Baptism administered by a heretic.

[20] S. Thomas Aquinas, *S. T.*, III. lxiv. 8. Cf. *ibid.*, 10.

[21] Council of Trent, session vii., *De sacramentis in genere*, canon 11 (Hardouin, *Concilia*, x. 53).

For the explanations of the canon referred to see, *e.g.*, Schouppe, *Elementa Theologicæ Dogmaticæ*, x. 113; Gury, *Theologia Moralis*, ii. 203.

CHAPTER X

[1] For the sect of the Seleuciani or Hermiani which rejected Baptism administered with water, see S. Augustine, *De Hær.*, 59.

For the baptism of the children of the rich in milk in Ireland in the twelfth century, see Warren, *Liturgy and Ritual of the Celtic Church*, p. 67, quoting the Synod of Cashel (1172 A.D.), 'Si divitis filius esset, ter mergeret in lacte' ('If he be the son of a rich man, let him immerse three times in milk'). Possibly this practice may have sprung out of some such mystical interpretation as that in S. Ambrose, *In Psalm. cxviii. Expos.*, xvi. 21, where, referring to the Song of Solomon, v. 12, he says, 'Baptizat in lacte Dominus, id est, in sinceritate. Et isti sunt qui vere baptizantur in lacte, qui sine dolo credunt, et puram fidem deferunt; ut immaculatam induant gratiam. Ideo candida sponsa ascendit ad Christum; quia in lacte baptizata est' ('The Lord baptizes in milk, that is, in sincerity. And those who are truly baptized in milk are those who believe without guile and hold the pure faith, so that they may put on immaculate grace. Therefore the spouse ascends white to Christ, because she has been baptized in milk').

² There has been much discussion at various times as to what might, in cases of extreme necessity, be allowed as valid matter. It has been thought by some that Siricius or Stephen II. or Stephen III. declared that in the last necessity wine might be used: see Smith and Cheetham's *Dictionary of Christian Antiquities*, i. 168. There is a story of a Jew who was baptized in sand in the third century, whose baptism was allowed by Dionysius, the Bishop of Alexandria, on water being subsequently poured over him: see Nicephorus, *H. E.*, iii. 37. Statements as to what came to be laid down in the West as to certainly valid, or certainly invalid, or doubtful matter may be found in books on moral theology: see, *e.g.*, Lehmkuhl, *Theologia Moralis*, ii. 58-9. The gist of such statements is that actual water from any source or from melted snow or ice is certainly valid; that anything clearly not water, as, for example, wine or milk or blood, is certainly invalid; and that various thin liquids, or the juice of plants, or rose-water, or unmelted snow or ice, are of doubtful validity.

A practice of mixing wine with the water was condemned in the *Excerptions of Egbert* (740 A.D.), 42: see Johnson, *Collection of the Laws and Canons of the Church of England*, i. 193 (Library of Anglo-Catholic Theology).

³ Tertullian, *De Baptismo*, 4, 'Igitur omnes aquae de

pristina originis prærogativa sacramentum sanctificationis consequuntur invocato Deo. Supervenit enim statim Spiritus de cælis et aquis superest, sanctificans eas de semetipso, et ita sanctificatæ vim sanctificandi combibunt.'

S. Cyprian, *Epistola* lxx. 1, 'Oportet ergo mundari et sanctificari aquam prius a sacerdote, ut possit baptismo suo peccata hominis, qui baptizatur, abluere ; quia per Ezechielem prophetam Dominus dicit : Et aspergam super vos aquam mundam, et mundabimini ab omnibus immunditiis vestris, et ab omnibus simulacris vestris emundabo vos et dabo vobis cor novum et spiritum novum dabo in vobis. Quomodo autem mundare et sanctificare aquam potest, qui ipse immundus est et apud quem Spiritus Sanctus non est, cum Dominus dicat in Numeris : Et omnia, quæcunque tetigerit immundus, immunda erunt?' ('The water ought first to be cleansed and sanctified by the priest that it may have power by Baptism in it to wash away the sins of the person who is baptized ; for the Lord says by Ezechiel the prophet : And I will sprinkle clean water upon you and ye shall be cleansed from all your uncleannesses, and I will cleanse you from all your idols and I will give you a new heart and a new spirit will I give in you. But how can he cleanse and sanctify the water who is himself unclean and in whom the Holy Spirit is not, since the Lord says in Numbers : And all things whatsoever an unclean person shall have touched, will be unclean?'). This passage occurs in a letter in which S. Cyprian is defending his view of the minister in Baptism : cf. note 4 on Chapter iv., and see Chapter ix.

S. Cyril of Jerusalem, *Cat.*, iii. 3, τὸ λιτὸν ὕδωρ Πνεύματος ἁγίου καὶ Χριστοῦ καὶ Πατρὸς τὴν ἐπίκλησιν λαβὸν, δύναμιν ἁγιότητος ἐπικτᾶται ('The simple water receiving the invocation of the Holy Spirit and Christ and the Father acquires the power of sanctity').

S. Basil of Cæsarea, *De Spiritu Sancto*, xxvii. 16, places among τὰ ἐκ τῆς τῶν ἀποστόλων παραδόσεως διαδοθέντα ἡμῖν ('the things delivered to us from the tradition of the apostles') that εὐλογοῦμεν τὸ ὕδωρ τοῦ βαπτίσματος ('we bless the water of Baptism').

Serapion, 7, ἔφιδε νῦν ἐκ τοῦ οὐρανοῦ καὶ ἐπίβλεψον ἐπὶ τὰ ὕδατα ταῦτα και πλήρωσον αὐτὰ πνεύματος ἁγίου. ὁ ἄρρητός σου λόγος ἐν αὐτοῖς γενέσθω καὶ μεταποιησάτω αὐτῶν τὴν ἐνέργειαν καὶ γεννητικὰ αὐτὰ κατασκευασάτω πληρούμενα τῆς σῆς χάριτος ('Look down now from heaven and behold these waters and fill them with the Holy Spirit. May Thy unspeakable Word come to be in them and transform their operation and make them generative being filled with Thy grace'): see Wobbermin in Gebhardt and Harnack's *Texte und Untersuchungen zur Geschichte der Altchristlichen Literatur*, neue Folge, Band ii. Heft 3 b.

Const. Apost., vii. 43, κάτιδε ἐξ οὐρανοῦ καὶ ἁγίασον τὸ ὕδωρ τοῦτο, δὸς δὲ χάριν καὶ δύναμιν ὥστε τὸν βαπτιζόμενον κατ' ἐντολὴν τοῦ Χριστοῦ σου αὐτῷ συσταυρωθῆναι καὶ συναποθανεῖν καὶ συνταφῆναι καὶ συναναστῆναι εἰς υἱοθεσίαν τὴν ἐν αὐτῷ, τῷ νεκρωθῆναι μὲν τῇ ἁμαρτίᾳ, ζῆσαι δὲ τῇ δικαιοσύνῃ ('Look down from heaven, and sanctify this water, and grant grace and power, so that he that is baptized according to the commandment of thy Christ may be crucified with Him and die with Him and be buried with Him and rise again with Him unto the adoption which is in Him, by being made dead unto sin and alive unto righteousness').

[4] For the Sarum Service of the 'benedictio fontis' see, *e.g.*, Maskell, *Monumenta Ritualia Ecclesiæ Anglicanæ*, i. 13-21.

[5] S. Augustine, *In Joan. Ev. Tract.*, cxviii. 5, says that the sign of the cross is made on the forehead of believers, on the water with which they are baptized, on the oil of chrism, and on the Eucharist: 'Quod signum nisi adhibeatur, sive frontibus credentium, sive ipsi aquae ex qua regenerantur, sive oleo quo chrismate unguuntur, sive sacrificio quo aluntur, nihil eorum rite perficitur.'

Id., *De Bapt. c. Don.*, vi. 46-7. In this passage S. Augustine strongly insists on the validity of any Baptism in which the formula of Baptism is used in connection with water: cf. note 10, *infra*.

[6] *Can. Apost.*, l. (al. xlii.), εἴ τις ἐπίσκοπος ἢ πρεσβύτερος μὴ τρία βαπτίσματα μιᾶς μυήσεως ἐπιτελέσῃ, ἀλλὰ ἓν βάπτισμα εἰς τὸν θάνατον τοῦ Κυρίου διδόμενον, καθαιρείσθω.

Tertullian, *De Cor. Mil.*, 3, 'ter mergitamur.'

S. Gregory of Nyssa, *In Bapt. Christi* (t. iii. p. 372 D, edit. Paris 1638), ὑποκύπτομεν οὖν τῷ πατρὶ, ἵνα ἁγιασθῶμεν· ὑποκύπτομεν καὶ υἱῷ, ἵνα αὐτὸ τοῦτο γένηται· ὑποκύπτομεν καὶ ἁγίῳ πνεύματι, ἵνα τοῦτο γενώμεθα ὅπερ ἐστὶ καὶ λέγεται.

Tertullian, *Adv. Prax.*, 26, 'Nam nec semel, sed ter, ad singula nomina in personas singulas tinguimus' ('We wet not once but three times, that is, into each of the Persons, at the mention of each name.'

Teaching of the Twelve Apostles, vii. 1-3, βαπτίσατε ... ἐν ὕδατι ζῶντι. ἐὰν δὲ μὴ ἔχῃς ὕδωρ ζῶν, εἰς ἄλλο ὕδωρ βάπτισον· εἰ δ' οὐ δύνασαι ἐν ψυχρῷ, ἐν θερμῷ. Ἐὰν δὲ ἀμφότερα μὴ ἔχῃς, ἔκχεον εἰς τὴν κεφαλὴν τρὶς ὕδωρ ('Baptize ... in living water. But if thou hast not living water, baptize in other water; and if thou canst not in cold, then in warm. But if thou hast not either, pour water three times upon the head').

S. Cyprian, *Epistola* lxix. 13-15, quoted in note 9 to Chapter v.

See also Smith and Cheetham, *Dictionary of Christian Antiquities*, i. 168-9; Duchesne, *Églises Séparées*, pp. 89-96.

[7] For the Sarum rubric see, *e.g.*, Maskell, *Monumenta Ritualia Ecclesiæ Anglicanæ*, i. 23. This rubric is quoted in note 11, *infra*. Cf. the Synod of Chelsea of 816 A.D., canon 11 (Haddan and Stubbs, *Councils and Ecclesiastical Documents*, iii. 584), 'Sciant etiam presbyterii, quando sacrum baptismum ministrant, ut non effundant aquam sanctam super capita infantuum, sed semper mergantur in acria: sicut exemplum præbuit per semetipsum Dei Filius omni credenti, quando esset ter mergatus in undis Jordanis' ('Let the priests also know, when they administer Holy Baptism, that they are not to pour the blessed water upon the heads of the infants, but these are always to be plunged in the font: as the Son of God gave an example in Himself to every one who believes, when He was three times plunged in the waters of Jordan'). On the word 'acria' Haddan and Stubbs note, 'This word stands for *aqua* or possibly for *lavacro*'; see *ibid.* p. 585.

For the introduction of single immersion by one or other of the heretics Eunomius, Theophronius, Eutychius, see Sozomen, *H. E.*, vi. 26; Theodoret, *Hæret. Fab.*, iv. 3. For the recommendation of single immersion for special local reasons in Spain in the sixth and seventh centuries, see S. Gregory the Great, *Epistola*, i. 43; Fourth Council of Toledo (633 A.D.), cap. 6 (Hardouin, *Concilia*, iii. 580-1).

[8] See, *e.g.*, Lyndwood, *Provinciale*, iii. 25, 'Sufficit quod modica stilla aquæ projecta a baptizante tangat baptizandum.

... Sufficit quod aqua aspersa tangat aliquam partem corporis' ('It is sufficient that a small drop of water thrown by the baptizer touch him who is to be baptized. ... It is sufficient that water which has been sprinkled touch some part of the body'). On questions which have been raised as to the validity of Baptisms in which the hair only or some other part of the body than the head has been touched by the water, or in which the water does not run upon the flesh, and on some connected questions, and on the Baptism of persons in a state of unconsciousness, if they have previously expressed a wish for baptism, and on the Baptism of those who have never possessed reason, see, *e.g.*, *Rituale Romanum*, De Sacramento Baptismi, De Baptizandis Parvulis; Lehmkuhl, *Theologia Moralis*, ii. 61-2, 73-8. Cf. also S. Augustine, *Ep.*, clxxxvii. 32-3; S. Thomas Aquinas, *S. T.*, III. lxviii. 11-12.

[9] See Palmer, *Dissertations on Subjects relating to the 'Orthodox' or 'Eastern-Catholic' Communion*, pp. 107-13, 163-77, 184-203. Cf. note 13 on Chapter ix. The words of the Archbishop of Xanthe are quoted from Riley, *Athos, or the Mountain of the Monks*, p. 109.

[10] *Teaching of the Twelve Apostles*, vii. 1, quoted in note 7 to Chapter ii.

S. Justin Martyr, *Apol.*, i. 61: see note 1 on Chapter xiii.

Acts of Xanthippe, Polyxena, and Rebecca, 14, εὐθέως οὖν λαβόμενος ὁ μέγας Παῦλος τῆς χειρὸς αὐτῆς, ἦλθεν ἐν τῇ οἰκίᾳ Φιλοθέου, καὶ ἐβάπτισεν αὐτὴν εἰς τὸ ὄνομα τοῦ πατρὸς καὶ τοῦ υἱοῦ καὶ τοῦ ἁγίου πνεύματος. 21, ὁ δὲ Παῦλος εἶπεν· βαπτίζομέν σε εἰς ὄνομα πατρὸς καὶ υἱοῦ καὶ ἁγίου πνεύματος. Cf. these passages and 21, ἦλθεν πρὸς τὸν Παῦλον, καὶ εὑρὼν αὐτὸν βαπτίζοντα πολλοὺς εἰς τὸ τῆς ζωαρχικῆς τριάδος ὄνομα, κ.τ.λ., with 28, σφράγισόν με καθάπερ Παῦλος σφραγίζει διὰ λουτρὸν παλιγγενεσίας, κ.τ.λ., and 29.

Canons of Hippolytus, canon xix. § 133, 'In each case he says: I baptize thee in the Name of the Father and of the Son and of the Holy Ghost.'

Apostolical Constitutions, vii. 43, καὶ μετὰ τοῦτο βαπτίσας αὐτὸν ἐν τῷ ὀνόματι τοῦ Πατρὸς καὶ τοῦ Υἱοῦ καὶ τοῦ ἁγίου Πνεύματος, κ.τ.λ. ('And after this baptizing him in the Name of the Father and of the Son and of the Holy Ghost').

Apostolical Canons, xlix. (al. xl.), εἴ τις ἐπίσκοπος ἢ πρεσβύτερος κατὰ τὴν τοῦ Κυρίου διάταξιν μὴ βαπτίσῃ εἰς Πατέρα καὶ Υἱὸν καὶ ἅγιον Πνεῦμα ... καθαιρείσθω ('If any bishop or presbyter baptize not in accordance with the appointment of the Lord into the Father and the Son and the Holy Ghost ... let him be deposed').

Tertullian, *De Baptismo*, 13, 'Lex enim tinguendi imposita est et forma praescripta. Ite, inquit, docete nationes, tinguentes eas in nomen Patris et Filii et Spiritus Sancti' ('For the law of baptizing was laid down and the form appointed. Go, He said, teach all nations, baptizing them into the Name of the Father and of the Son and of the Holy Ghost'). Cf. *Adv. Prax.*, 26.

S. Cyprian, *Epistola* lxxiii. 5, 'Dominus enim post resurrectionem discipulos suos mittens, quemadmodum baptizare deberent, instruxit et docuit dicens: Data est mihi omnis potestas in coelo et in terra. Ite ergo et docete gentes omnes baptizantes eos in nomine Patris et Filii et Spiritus Sancti. Insinuat Trinitatem, cujus sacramento gentes baptizarentur' ('For the Lord after the resurrection, when sending His disciples, instructed and taught them how they ought to baptize, saying: All power has been given unto Me in heaven and in earth. Therefore go and teach all nations baptizing them in the Name of the Father and of the Son and of the Holy Ghost. He makes known the Trinity, by whose Sacrament the nations were to be baptized').

S. Basil, *De Spiritu Sancto*, xii. 28, says it would be wrong to base upon S. Paul's words in Romans vi. 3 and Galatians iii. 27 an omission of the name either of the Father or of the Holy Spirit, and adds ὡς γὰρ πιστεύομεν εἰς Πατέρα καὶ Υἱὸν καὶ ἅγιον Πνεῦμα, οὕτω καὶ βαπτιζόμεθα εἰς τὸ ὄνομα τοῦ Πατρὸς καὶ τοῦ Υἱοῦ καὶ τοῦ ἁγίου Πνεύματος ('For as we believe in the Father and the Son and the Holy Ghost, so also are we baptized into the Name of the Father and of the Son and of the Holy Ghost ').

S. Ambrose, *De Mysteriis*, iv. 20, 'Credit autem etiam catechumenus in crucem Domini Jesu, qua et ipse signatur: sed nisi baptizatus fuerit in nomine Patris et Filii et Spiritus Sancti, remissionem non potest accipere peccatorum, nec spiritualis gratiae munus haurire.' The emphasis in this passage is, no doubt, on the words 'baptizatus fuerit,' but the structure of the sentence shows that S. Ambrose's idea of Baptism was that it was administered 'in the Name of the Father and of the Son and of the Holy Ghost.'

S. Augustine, *De Bapt. c. Don.*, vi. 47, 'Deus adest evangelicis verbis suis, sine quibus baptismus Christi consecrari non potest.' For the explanation of the 'evangelica verba' as 'in nomine Patris et Filii et Spiritus Sancti,' see *ibid.*, iii. 20.

S. Cyprian, *Ep.*, lxxiii. 17-18, says it is wrong to infer from S. Peter's words in Acts ii. 38 that Baptism may be administered in the Name of Jesus Christ, and refers to our Lord's command as given in S. Matthew xxviii. 19-20 as supplying the right formula.

On the subject of Baptisms administered 'In the Name of Christ' or 'In the Name of the Trinity,' see, *e.g.*, S. Thomas Aquinas, *S. T.*, III. lxvi. 6, and the note of the Benedictine editors on S. Ambrose, *De Spiritu Sancto*, i. 42 (t. iv. col. 11-12).

[11] For the Sarum form see, *e.g.*, Maskell, *Monumenta Ritualia Ecclesiæ Anglicanæ*, i. 23. The direction is as follows: 'Deinde accipiat sacerdos infantem . . . et . . . baptizet eum sub trina mersione tantum, sanctam Trinitatem invocando, ita dicens : N. Et ego baptizo te in nomine Patris. Et mergat eum semel facie ad aquilonem, et capite versus orientem : et Filii : et iterum mergat semel versa facie ad meridiem : et Spiritus Sancti. Amen. Et mergat tertio recta facie versus aquam ' ('Then let the priest take the infant . . . and . . . baptize him with three immersions only, invoking the Holy Trinity, saying thus : N. And I baptize thee in the Name of the Father : And let him plunge him once with his face to the north and his head to the east : And of the Son : And again let him plunge him once with his face turned to the south : And of the Holy Spirit. Amen. And let him plunge him the third time with his face straight to the water ').

[12] See, *e.g.*, Archbishop Peccham's Lambeth Constitutions (1281 A.D.), (Lyndwood, *Provinciale*, iii. 24), ' Dicatur ergo a sic baptizantibus, "I Christen thee in the Name of the Father, and of the Son, and of the Holy Ghost " : vel alias in lingua materna secundum consuetudinem patriæ, vel in Gallico sic : "Je te baptize au nom du Pere et du Filz et du Sainct Esperit."' Cf. the mediæval English rubric in, *e.g.*, Maskell, *Monumenta Ritualia Ecclesiæ Anglicanæ*, i. 28. The oath taken by the midwife Eleanor Pead in

receiving a licence from Archbishop Parker in 1567 contained the promise to use 'these words following, or the like in effect: I christen thee in the Name of the Father, the Son, and the Holy Ghost': see Strype, *Annals of the Reformation*, I. ii. 243.

[13] See, *e.g.*, Goar, *Euchologion*, p. 290, βαπτίζεται ὁ δοῦλος τοῦ Θεοῦ ὁ δεῖνα εἰς τὸ ὄνομα τοῦ Πατρὸς καὶ τοῦ Υἱοῦ καὶ τοῦ Ἁγίου Πνεύματος ('The servant of God N. is baptized into the Name of the Father and of the Son and of the Holy Ghost').

CHAPTER XI

[1] Tertullian, *De Baptismo*, 19, 'Diem baptismo sollemniorem Pascha praestat, cum et passio Domini, in quam tinguimur, adimpleta est. Nec incongruenter quis ad figuram interpretabitur, quod cum ultimum Pascha Dominus esset acturus, missis discipulis ad praeparandum: Invenietis, inquit, hominem aquam bajulantem. Paschae celebrandae locum de signo aquae ostendit. Exinde Pentecoste ordinandis lavacris latissimum spatium est, quo et Domini resurrectio inter discipulos frequentata est, et gratia Spiritus Sancti dedicata, et spes adventus Domini subostensa, quod tunc, in caelos recuperato eo, angeli ad apostolos dixerunt sic venturum, quemadmodum et in caelos conscendit, utique in Pentecoste. Sed enim Hieremias cum dicit: Et congregabo illos ab extremis terrae in die festo, Paschae diem significat et Pentecostes, qui est proprie dies festus. Ceterum omnis dies Domini est, omnis hora, omne tempus habile baptismo: si de solemnitate interest, de gratia nihil refert.'

[2] For many references on details about seasons, see

Smith and Cheetham's *Dictionary of Christian Antiquities*, i. 164-6. For the mediæval English rubrics see, *e.g.*, Maskell, *Monumenta Ritualia Ecclesiæ Anglicanæ*, i. 29-30; *Missale ad usum insignis et præclaræ ecclesiæ Sarum*, p. 354 (Burntisland Press), 'Consecratis fontibus non infundetur oleum neque chrisma, nisi fuerit aliquis baptizandus' ('When the fonts have been blessed, no oil or chrism is to be poured in, unless there is some one to be baptized'). For the present Roman rubric see *Missale Romanum* in Sabbato Sancto. The rubric in the First Prayer Book of King Edward VI. was, 'It appeareth by ancient writers that the Sacrament of Baptism in the old time was not commonly ministered but at two times in the year, at Easter and Whitsuntide, at which times it was openly ministered in the presence of all the congregation: which custom (now being grown out of use), although it cannot for many considerations be well restored again, yet it is thought good to follow the same as near as conveniently may be: wherefore the people are to be admonished,' etc.

[3] *Teaching of the Twelve Apostles*, vii. 1-3.

S. Justin Martyr, *Apol.*, i. 61, 65.

Acts of Xanthippe, Polyxena, and Rebecca, 14, Παῦλος ... ἦλθεν ἐν τῇ οἰκίᾳ Φιλοθέου (cf. 12, ἐχάρη δὲ ἡ Ξανθίππη πάνυ ὅτι καὶ Φιλόθεος ἐπίστευσεν), καὶ ἐβάπτισεν αὐτήν: ('Paul ... came unto the house of Philotheos' (cf. 12, 'Xanthippe rejoiced greatly because Philotheos also believed') 'and baptized her'); 21, ἦλθεν πρὸς τὸν Παῦλον, καὶ εὑρὼν αὐτὸν βαπτίζοντα πολλούς ... ἀποδυσάμενος τὰ ἱμάτια αὐτοῦ ... εἰσεπήδησεν εἰς τὸ ὕδωρ ('He came unto Paul and finding him baptizing many ... having put off his clothes ... he leaped into the water').

Tertullian, *De Baptismo*, 4, 'Ideoque nulla distinctio est, mari quis an stagno, flumine an fonte, lacu an alveo diluatur; nec quicquam refert inter eos, quos Joannes in Jordane et quos Petrus in Tiberi tinxit, nisi et ille spado, quem Philippus inter vias fortuita aqua tinxit, plus salutis aut minus retulit.'

S. Cyril of Jerusalem, *Cat. Myst.*, i. 2, describes the renunciation and profession as taking place in the 'antechamber of the baptistery' (ὁ προαύλιος τοῦ βαπτιστηρίου οἶκος), in i. 11 calls this 'the outer house' (ὁ ἐξώτερος οἶκος), and in ii. 1 speaks of the Baptism taking place in 'the inner house' (ὁ ἐσώτερος οἶκος).

S. Chrysostom, *Ep. ad Innoc.*, i. 3.

[4] For further details about these and other baptisteries see Smith and Cheetham's *Dictionary of Christian Antiquities*, i. 173-8. For the plan of the Church of S. Gall, see *ibid.*, i. 383. For the division of the font, or the provision of a second small font, see a paper by Miss Swann published in the *Proceedings and Excursions of the Oxford Architectural Society for the year* 1887, pp. 68-81. For the rubric of the Church of Rome see *Rituale Romanum*.

[5] For the dedication and blessing of the font see, *e.g.*, Wilson, *The Gelasian Sacramentary*, pp. 142-3. For the instructions as to the font see, *e.g.*, Maskell, *Monumenta Ritualia Ecclesiæ Anglicanæ*, i. 29, 'Presbyter autem si poterit semper habeat fontem lapideum, integrum, et honestum, ad baptizandum: si autem nequiverit, habeat vas conveniens ad baptismum, quod aliis usibus nullatenus deputetur, nec extra ecclesiam deportetur' ("The presbyter is always, if possible, to have a font of stone, unbroken, and seemly, for baptizing: but if this is not

possible, he is to have for Baptism a convenient vessel which is under no circumstances to be used for other purposes, and is not to be taken out of the church').

⁶ For the third century see, *e.g.*, S. Cyprian, *Ep.*, lxix. 13-15, quoted in note 9 on Chapter v. For the fourth century, see Synod of Laodicea, canon 47 (Hardouin, *Concilia*, i. 789); Synod of Neo-Cæsarea, canon 12 (*ibid.*, i. 283-6). Cf. Eusebius, *H. E.*, vi. 43. The canon of Neo-Cæsarea passed into the canon law: see *Decretum Gratiani*, I. lvii. For the East see, *e.g.*, Shann, *Book of Needs of the Holy Orthodox Church*, pp. 5-6. For the mediæval English rubric see, *e.g.*, Maskell, *Monumenta Ritualia Ecclesiæ Anglicanæ*, i. 29. For the present English rule, see the rubrics at the beginning of the Order for Private Baptism.

CHAPTER XII

¹ 1 S. Peter iii. 21.

² *Teaching of the Twelve Apostles*, vii. 4, πρὸ δὲ βαπτίσματος προνηστευσάτω ὁ βαπτίζων καὶ ὁ βαπτιζόμενος καὶ εἴ τινες ἄλλοι δύνανται· κελεύεις [al. κελεύσεις] δὲ νηστεῦσαι τὸν βαπτιζόμενον πρὸ μιᾶς ἢ δύο ('Before Baptism let him who baptizes fast and him who is to be baptized and any others who are able, and thou art to order him who is to be baptized to fast one or two days before').

S. Justin Martyr, *Apol.*, i. 61, ὅσοι ἂν πεισθῶσι καὶ πιστεύωσιν ἀληθῆ ταῦτα τὰ ὑφ' ἡμῶν διδασκόμενα καὶ λεγόμενα εἶναι καὶ βιοῦν οὕτως δύνασθαι ὑπισχνῶνται, εὔχεσθαί τε καὶ αἰτεῖν νηστεύοντες παρὰ τοῦ Θεοῦ τῶν προημαρτημένων ἄφεσιν διδάσκονται, ἡμῶν συνευχομένων καὶ συννηστευόντων αὐτοῖς.

Tertullian, *De Baptismo*, 20, 'Ingressuros baptismum orationibus crebris, jejuniis et geniculationibus et pervigiliis orare oportet et cum confessione omnium retro delictorum, ut exponant etiam baptismum Joannis. Tinguebantur, inquit, confitentes delicta sua. Nobis gratulandum est, si non publice confitemur iniquitates aut turpitudines nostras.'

Canons of Hippolytus, canon xix. § 106, 'Let those who are to be baptized . . . fast on the Friday.'

Apostolical Constitutions, vii. 22, πρὸ δὲ τοῦ βαπτίσματος νηστευσάτω ὁ βαπτιζόμενος ('Before the Baptism let him who is to be baptized fast').

[3] The most usually given division of the catechumens is into four classes, namely, ἐξωθούμενοι, those altogether outside and therefore instructed outside the church; ἀκροώμενοι, or hearers; γονυκλίνοντες, or kneelers; and συναιτοῦντες, the candidates for Baptism, also called φωτιζόμενοι or βαπτιζόμενοι or τελειώτεροι, as they approached Baptism. Some authorities are of opinion that there were only two classes: the ἐξωθούμενοι, the existence of whom was inferred from the word ἐξωθείσθω applied to a catechumen in the Council of Neo-Cæsarea (c. 315 A.D.), canon 5 (Hardouin, *Concilia*, i. 283-4), not being in the catechumenate, and the γονυκλίνοντες and the συναιτοῦντες being the same. See, *e.g.*, Hefele, *History of the Christian Councils*, i. 421 (English translation). For the care taken in the admission of catechumens see, *e.g.*, *Canons of Hippolytus*, canon x. §§ 60-4; *Apostolical Constitutions*, viii. 32.

[4] For admission by the sign of the cross, see S. Augustine, *Confes.* i. 17, *De Pecc. Mer.* ii. 42; for imposition of hands, see Council of Elvira (305 A.D.), canon 39 (Hardouin, *Concilia*, i. 254); Council of Arles (314 A.D.), canon 6 (Har-

douin, *Concilia*, i. 264) (for a different interpretation of these canons see Hefele, *History of the Christian Councils*, i. 152-4, 187, English translation); Serapion, 28; for anointing see, *e.g.*, S. Augustine, *In Joan Ev. Tract.*, xliv. 2; Council of Rome (402 A.D.), canon 8 (Hard., *Conc.*, i. 1036). For name 'Christiani' as distinct from 'fideles,' see, *e.g.*, the so-called canon 7 of the Council of Constantinople (381 A.D.) (Hard., *Conc.*, i. 813): cf. S. Cyril of Jerusalem, *Procatechesis ad fin.*, *Cat.*, i. 4. For two years' catechumenate see, *e.g.*, Council of Elvira (305 A.D.), canon 42 (Hard., *Conc.*, i. 254); for three years' see, *e.g.*, *Apostolical Constitutions*, viii. 32. For the exorcisms see, *e.g.*, S. Cyril of Jerusalem, *Procatechesis*, 9. For exclusion from the latter part of the Liturgy by dismissal see, *e.g.*, *Apostolical Constitutions*, viii. 12. For fast, prayer, watching, and fuller instruction on approaching Baptism see, *e.g.*, Tertullian, *De Baptismo*, 20; S. Cyril of Jerusalem, *Cat.*, i. 5; S. Augustine, *De Fid. et Oper.*, 8-9; *Apostolical Constitutions*, viii. 6. For enrolment see, *e.g.*, S. Cyril of Jerusalem, *Procat.* 1, *Cat.* iii. 2; S. Augustine, *De Fid. et Oper.*, 8; *De cura ger. pro mort.*, 15. For teaching immediately before Baptism see, *e.g.*, S. Augustine, *Serm. ad Catechumenos*. For the 'sacrament of the catechumens' see S. Augustine, *De Pecc. Mer.*, ii. 42, 'Catechumenos secundum quemdam modum suum per signum Christi et orationem manus impositionis puto sanctificari: et quod accipiunt, quamvis non sit corpus Christi, sanctum est tamen et sanctius quam cibi quibus alimur, quoniam sacramentum est' ('I consider that the catechumens in a sort of way special to them are sanctified by means of the sign of Christ and the prayer of the imposition of the hand: and that which they receive, though it is not the body of Christ, is yet holy and more holy than the food by which we are nourished, since it is a sacrament.'

[5] See S. Augustine, *De Catechizandis Rudibus*; S. Cyril of Jerusalem, *Catechetical Lectures*. For the course of preparation and instruction at Jerusalem, about 385 A.D., see *S. Silviæ Aquitanæ Peregrinatio ad loca sancta*, printed by J. F. Gamurrini in *Studi e documenti di storia e diritto*, 1888, pp. 99-174: the passage referred to is on pp. 168-71.

[6] For extension of catechumenate see, *e.g.*, Council of Elvira, canon 11 (Hard., *Conc.*, i. 251); Council of Nicæa, canon 14 (Hard., *Conc.*, i. 329). For death in catechumenate see, *e.g.* S. Chrysostom, *In Ep. ad Phil. Hom.*, iii. 4; S. Ambrose, *De obitu Valentiniani consolatio*, 51-56, 'Sed audio vos dolere quod non acceperit sacramenta baptismatis. Dicite mihi quid aliud in nobis est, nisi voluntas, nisi petitio? Atqui etiam dudum hoc voti habuit, ut et antequam in Italiam venisset, initiaretur, et proxime baptizari se a me velle significavit; et ideo præ ceteris causis me accersendum putavit. Non habet ergo gratiam quam desideravit, non habet quam poposcit? Certe quia poposcit, accepit. Et unde illud est: "Justus quacumque morte præventus fuerit, anima ejus in requie erit." Solve igitur, Pater Sancte, munus servo tuo quod Moyses quia in spiritu vidit, accepit, quod David, quia ex revelatione cognovit, emeruit. Solve, inquam, servo tuo Valentiniano munus quod concupivit, munus quod poposcit sanus, robustus, incolumis ... Ne quæso eum, Domine, a fratre sejungas, nec jugum hoc piæ germanitatis patiaris abrumpi ... Quas ille nunc manus ad te, Pater, erigit! quas pro fratre preces fundit! quo ei inhæret amplexu!

quem ad modum sibi eum non patitur avelli ! Adest etiam pater... Dona patri filium, fratri germanum suum... Non ego floribus tumulum ejus adspergam, sed spiritum ejus Christi odore perfundam. Spargant alii plenis lilia calathis, nobis lilium est Christus. Hoc reliquias ejus sacrabo, hoc ejus commendabo gratiam. Nunquam ego piorum fratrum separabo nomina, merita discernam. Scio quod Dominum commemoratio ista conciliet, et copula ista delectet.' The quotation is from *Wisdom* iv. 7.

[7] See, *e.g.*, Robertson, *History of the Christian Church*, v. 278-89 : cf. Maclear, *History of Christian Missions during the Middle Ages*, pp. 421-3.

CHAPTER XIII

[1] *Teaching of the Twelve Apostles*, vii., περὶ δὲ τοῦ βαπτίσματος, οὕτω βαπτίσατε· ταῦτα πάντα προειπόντες, βαπτίσατε εἰς τὸ ὄνομα τοῦ Πατρὸς καὶ τοῦ Υἱοῦ καὶ τοῦ ἁγίου Πνεύματος ἐν ὕδατι ζῶντι. ἐὰν δὲ μὴ ἔχῃς ὕδωρ ζῶν, εἰς ἄλλο ὕδωρ βάπτισον· εἰ δ' οὐ δύνασαι ἐν ψυχρῷ, ἐν θερμῷ. ἐὰν δὲ ἀμφότερα μὴ ἔχῃς, ἔκχεον εἰς τὴν κεφαλὴν τρὶς ὕδωρ εἰς ὄνομα Πατρὸς καὶ Υἱοῦ καὶ ἁγίου Πνεύματος. πρὸ δὲ τοῦ βαπτίσματος προνηστευσάτω ὁ βαπτίζων καὶ ὁ βαπτιζόμενος καὶ εἴ τινες ἄλλοι δύνανται. κελεύεις [al. κελεύσεις] δὲ νηστεῦσαι τὸν βαπτιζόμενον πρὸ μιᾶς ἢ δύο.

S. Justin Martyr, *Apol.*, i. 61, 65, 66, ὃν τρόπον δὲ καὶ ἀνεθήκαμεν ἑαυτοὺς τῷ Θεῷ, καινοποιηθέντες διὰ τοῦ Χριστοῦ, ἐξηγησόμεθα, ὅπως μὴ τοῦτο παραλιπόντες δόξωμεν πονηρεύειν τι ἐν τῇ ἐξηγήσει. ὅσοι ἂν πεισθῶσι καὶ πιστεύωσιν ἀληθῆ ταῦτα τὰ ὑφ' ἡμῶν διδασκόμενα καὶ λεγόμενα εἶναι, καὶ βιοῦν οὕτως δύνασθαι ὑπισχνῶνται, εὔχεσθαί τε καὶ αἰτεῖν νηστεύοντες παρὰ τοῦ Θεοῦ τῶν προημαρτημένων ἄφεσιν διδάσκονται, ἡμῶν συνευχομένων καὶ συννηστευόντων αὐτοῖς. ἔπειτα ἄγονται ὑφ' ἡμῶν ἔνθα ὕδωρ ἐστὶ, καὶ τρόπον ἀναγεννήσεως ὃν καὶ ἡμεῖς αὐτοὶ ἀνεγεννήθημεν, ἀναγεννῶνται. ἐπ' ὀνόματος γὰρ τοῦ πατρὸς τῶν ὅλων καὶ δεσπότου Θεοῦ, καὶ τοῦ σωτῆρος ἡμῶν Ἰησοῦ Χριστοῦ, καὶ Πνεύματος ἁγίου, τὸ ἐν τῷ ὕδατι τότε λουτρὸν ποιοῦνται . . . ἡμεῖς δὲ, μετὰ τὸ οὕτως λοῦσαι τὸν πεπεισμένον καὶ συγκατατεθεμένον, ἐπὶ τοὺς λεγομένους ἀδελφοὺς ἄγομεν ἔνθα συνηγμένοι εἰσὶ, κοινὰς εὐχὰς ποιησόμενοι ὑπέρ τε ἑαυτῶν καὶ τοῦ φωτισθέντος, καὶ ἄλλων πανταχοῦ πάντων εὐτόνως, ὅπως καταξιωθῶμεν τὰ ἀληθῆ μαθόντες, καὶ δι' ἔργων ἀγαθοὶ πολιτευταὶ, καὶ φύλακες τῶν ἐντεταλμένων εὑρεθῆναι, ὅπως τὴν αἰώνιον σωτηρίαν σωθῶμεν. ἀλλήλους φιλήματι ἀσπαζόμεθα παυσάμενοι τῶν εὐχῶν . . . ἧς (i.e. the Holy Eucharist) οὐδενὶ ἄλλῳ μετασχεῖν ἐξόν ἐστιν ἢ τῷ πιστεύοντι ἀληθῆ εἶναι τὰ δεδιδαγμένα ὑφ' ἡμῶν, καὶ λουσαμένῳ τὸ ὑπὲρ ἀφέσεως ἁμαρτιῶν καὶ εἰς ἀναγέννησιν λουτρὸν καὶ οὕτως βιοῦντι ὡς ὁ Χριστὸς παρέδωκεν.

For the custom of the officiant being fasting in the fourth century see S. Chrysostom, *Serm. antequam iret in exsilium*, 4.

² Tertullian, *De Cor. Mil.*, 3, 'In ecclesia sub antistitis manu contestamur, nos renuntiare diabolo et pompæ et angelis ejus. Dehinc ter mergitamur amplius aliquid respondentes quam dominus in evangelio determinavit. Inde suscepti, lactis et mellis concordiam prægustamus, exque ea die lavacro quotidiano per totam hebdomadem abstinemus'; *Ibid., De Bapt.*, 7-8, 'Egressi de lavacro perungimur benedicta unctione . . . Dehinc manus imponitur, per benedictionem advocans et invitans Spiritum Sanctum.' S. Cyprian, *Ep.*, lxix. 7, 'Quodsi aliquis illud opponit, ut dicat, eandem Novatianum legem tenere, quam catholica ecclesia teneat, eodem symbolo, quo et nos, baptizare, eundem nosse Deum patrem, eundem filium Christum,

eundem Spiritum Sanctum . . . cum dicunt, Credis remissionem peccatorum et vitam æternam per sanctam ecclesiam?'; lxx. 2, 'Cum dicimus, Credis in vitam æternam et remissionem peccatorum per sanctam ecclesiam?'

For the anointing and the imposition of hands, see S. Cyprian, *Ep.*, lxx. 2, lxxiii. 9.

[3] *Canons of Hippolytus,* canons xix. §§ 106-148, 'The candidates for Baptism may wash themselves and eat on the fifth day of the week. On the sixth day they are to fast. . . . On the Sabbath' (Saturday) 'the bishop is to assemble the candidates for Baptism, and admonish them that they kneel with their heads turned to the east, and to spread his hands over them and pray so as to drive the evil spirit out from all their members. . . . After he has finished the exorcisms, he is to breathe upon their faces and sign their breasts and foreheads, ears, and mouths. They are to spend all this night watching, occupied with sacred words and prayers. At cock-crow they are to take their stand near flowing water of the sea pure, prepared, sacred. Those who make the answers for little infants are to strip them of their clothing. Those who have attained to strength are to perform this part of the preparation for themselves. All the women are to have other women with them who are to help them to undress. The women are to put off their golden and other ornaments, to unbind their hair, so that there may not go down with them into the water of regeneration anything alien which comes from the alien spirits. The bishop is to pray over the oil of exorcism and to hand it to a presbyter. Then he is to pray over the oil of unction, which is the oil of thanksgiving, and to hand it to another presbyter. He who holds

the oil of exorcism in his hand is to stand on the left of the bishop, and he who holds the oil of unction is to stand on the right of the bishop. The candidate for Baptism is to turn his face to the west and say, "I renounce thee, O Satan, with all thy pomp." When he has said this, the presbyter is to anoint him with the oil of exorcism over which he' (*i.e.* the bishop) 'had prayed that every evil spirit might depart from it. Then he hands it to the presbyter who stands above the water, and the presbyter who performs the office of deacon takes hold of his right hand and turns his face towards the east as he stands in the water. Before he goes down into the water, standing above the water with his face turned towards the east, he says after he has received the oil of exorcism, "I believe and bow myself before Thee and all Thy majesty, O Father and Son and Holy Spirit." Then he is to go down into the water, and the presbyter is to place his own hand upon his head and to ask him this question, " Dost thou believe in God, the Father Almighty?" The candidate for Baptism answers, "I believe." Then he is immersed in the water for the first time, while he' (*i.e.* the presbyter) 'leaves his hand upon his head. The second time he asks him this question, " Dost thou believe in Jesus Christ, the Son of God, Whom Mary the Virgin brought forth of the Holy Ghost [Who came to save the human race], Who was crucified [for us] under Pontius Pilate, Who died and rose from the dead on the third day, and ascended into heaven, and sitteth at the right hand of the Father and will come to judge the quick and the dead?" He answers, "I believe," and is immersed in the water a second time. He is asked, thirdly, " Dost thou believe in the Holy Ghost [the Paraclete, proceeding from the Father and the Son]?"

He answers, "I believe," and is immersed in the water a third time. On each occasion he' (*i.e.* the presbyter) 'says, "I baptize thee in the Name of the Father and of the Son and of the Holy Ghost [Who is equal]." When he comes up out of the water, the presbyter takes hold of the chrism of thanksgiving and signs his forehead and mouth and breast with the sign of the cross and anoints his whole body and his head and face, saying, "I anoint thee in the Name of the Father and of the Son and of the Holy Ghost." Then he wipes him with a cloth, and when he has put on his clothing brings him into the church. There the bishop lays his hand on all those who have been baptized and prays in these words, "We bless Thee, O Lord God Almighty, because Thou hast made these to be worthy to be born again and dost pour upon them Thy Holy Spirit that they may now be united to the body of the Church and may never be separated by alien works. Grant rather unto those to whom Thou hast now given the remission of their sins also the earnest of Thy kingdom, through our Lord Jesus Christ, through Whom to Thee with Himself and with the Holy Ghost be glory for ever and ever. Amen." Then he signs their foreheads with the sign of love and kisses them saying, "The Lord be with you." And the baptized answer, "And with Thy spirit." Thus he does in the case of each of those who have been baptized. Now they pray together with all the people, who kiss them, rejoicing with them in exultation. . . . The presbyters carry other' (*i.e.* other than the chalice for the Communion) 'cups of milk and honey, that they may teach those who communicate that they have been born again as little children because little children receive milk and honey. . . . Afterwards' (*i.e.* after Communion) 'they are to receive milk and honey as a reminder of the future life and the sweetness of good things which are the desire of him who does not return to bitterness.'

The above is translated from the Latin translation of the canons given by Achelis in his edition in Gebhardt and Harnack's *Texte und Untersuchungen zur Geschichte der Altchristlichen Literatur*, Band vi. Heft 4. The words in square brackets are marked by Achelis as later additions.

[4] S. Cyril of Jerusalem, *Cat. Myst.*, i.-iv.; *Procat.*, 15; Serapion, 7-11, 15-16.

[5] For the pouring of chrism into the water, see Dionysius the Areopagite, *De Eccl. Hier.*, ii. 7, αὐτὸς ἐπὶ τὴν μητέρα τῆς υἱοθεσίας ἔρχεται, καὶ τὸ ταύτης ὕδωρ ταῖς ἱεραῖς ἐπικλήσεσι καθαγιάσας, καὶ τρισὶ τοῦ παναγεστάτου μύρου σταυροειδέσι χύσεσι τελειώσας αὐτὸ, κ.τ.λ. ('He' [*i.e.* the bishop] 'comes to the mother of the adoption' [*i.e.* the font] 'and sanctifies the water in it with the sacred invocations, and completes it by pouring three times into it the all-holy chrism'); iv. 10; S. Gregory the Great, *Liber Sacramentorum* (t. iii. col. 73 B, Benedictine edition), 'Inde accipiens vas aureum cum chrismate fundit chrisma in fonte in modum crucis' ('Then taking the golden vessel containing chrism, he pours the chrism in the font after the manner of a cross'; *Missale Romanum*, Sabbato Sancto (both oil and chrism). For the East see, *e.g.*, Goar, *Euchologion*, p. 290; Shann, *Book of Needs of the Holy Orthodox Church*, p. 32. For the washing of the feet in Gaul see the Gothic and Gallican Missals printed in Neale and Forbes, *Ancient Liturgies of the Gallican Church*, pp. 97, 191, 270 (parts ii. and iii.); Cæsarius of Arles, *Serm.* clxviii. 3, cclvii. 2 in Appendix to S. Augustine, t. v. Cf. the sermon in Appendix to S. Augustine, t. vi.

col. 291-2: in Spain see Council of Elvira, canon 48 (Hardouin, *Concilia*, i. 225): in Ireland, see Warren, *Liturgy and Ritual of the Celtic Church*, pp. 66, 217-8: at Milan, see S. Ambrose, *De Myst.*, 31-3; Pseudo-Ambrose, *De Sacr.*, iii. 1-7. It was forbidden by the Council of Elvira, *u. s.* S. Ambrose and Pseudo-Ambrose, like the Gothic and Gallican Missals, connect this washing of the feet with the incident of our Lord washing the feet of the apostles. Pseudo-Ambrose mentions that the custom did not exist at Rome.

[6] See S. John xii. 31, xiv. 30, xvi. 11; Ephesians ii. 2, vi. 12; Colossians i. 13; Hebrews ii. 14; Revelation ii. 13; Ephesians iv. 22; Colossians iii. 9; Ephesians iv. 24; Galatians iii. 27; Hebrews vi. 4, x. 22; Exodus iii. 8. For the explanation of the milk and honey in the *Canons of Hippolytus*, see note 3, *supra*.

[7] Acts viii. 14-17, xix. 1-6.

[8] See, *e.g.*, Wilson, *The Gelasian Sacramentary*, pp. 34-89. Cf. the *Liber Sacramentorum* in the works of S. Gregory the Great.

[9] Bede, *H. E.*, ii. 2, 'Ut ministerium baptizandi, quo Deo renascimur, juxta morem Sanctæ Romanæ et Apostolicæ Ecclesiæ compleatis' ('That ye fully perform the ministry of baptizing, whereby we are reborn to God, according to the custom of the holy Roman and Apostolic Church'). Cf. Haddan and Stubbs, *Councils and Ecclesiastical Documents*, i. 153-4; Bright, *Chapters of Early English Church History*, pp. 79-80.

[10] See Maskell, *Monumenta Ritualia Ecclesiæ Anglicanæ*, i. 3-32.

[11] See *Rituale Romanum.*

[12] See, *e.g.*, Goar, *Euchologion,* pp. 273-305; Shann, *Book of Needs of the Holy Orthodox Church,* pp. 13-36.

[13] For the prohibition of any charge see, *e.g.*, Council of London (1126 A.D.), cap. 2 (Hardouin, *Concilia,* vi. [2], 1125); Lyndwood, *Provinciale,* v. 2.

[14] For the matter of names, see Peccham in Lyndwood, *ibid.*, iii. 24; *Rituale Romanum,* De Sacramento Baptismi, De sacris oleis et aliis requisitis. The commonness of the names Thomas and Mary in England may be noticed as due to children being called by the names of S. Thomas of Canterbury and the Blessed Virgin Mary.

[15] See, *e.g.*, Maskell, *Monumenta Ritualia Ecclesiæ Anglicanæ,* i. 3, note 1; a Bangor MS. quoted in Lee, *Directorium Anglicanum,* p. 153 (second edition); *Missale ad usum insignis et præclaræ ecclesiæ Sarum,* p. 348 (Burntisland Press); *Rituale Romanum,* De Sacramento Baptismi; rubric prefixed to the Order for Morning Prayer.

[16] See, *e.g.*, Goar, *Euchologion,* p. 287; Shann, *Book of Needs of the Holy Orthodox Church,* p. 24.

[17] To mention a recent instance, the *Report of the Universities' Mission to Central Africa for* 1897 (p. 26) quotes a letter in which the following passage occurs:

'It was a wonderful service. The people fasted all day, as the Church orders in the Prayer Book. At the service all the forty folks stood around the west end, wearing dark blue garments. It took an hour to question them alone, as each one has to be asked the questions separately. After they were baptized they went just outside the church and changed their clothes for white ones, and each one was given a lighted candle to hold. When they were all baptized you can fancy how different the west end of the church looked with all the forty clothed in white and holding tapers. It was a striking sight.

'When the service was over we had a kind of solemn evensong, during which the newly baptized sat in front. They had never sat in the front of the church before, for the unbaptized are not allowed to go beyond a certain portion at the back, neither are they allowed to stay during the whole of the Holy Communion service: they have to go out before the Creed. The morning after their Baptism they came to church in their white garments, and stayed to the whole of the service for the first time. We are so used to seeing little ones baptized in England that we hardly realize what a great thing Holy Baptism is. But when one sees forty people, all grown up, and when one sees how different they look, *outwardly*, after they have changed their dark clothes for white ones, one feels how true it is that, *inwardly*, Baptism brings us out of darkness into light.'

Parts of the ceremonial used in the case of adult Baptisms could not, of course, be used in the case of infant Baptisms. There is very much, however, both in the way of ceremonial and in the way of the solemnity of the service, which is applicable to both.

CHAPTER XIV

[1] S. Augustine, *De Symb. ad Catech.*, 4, 'Prius credite, postea intelligite.' Cf. *id.*, *De Lib. Arbit.*, i. 4, 'Aderit enim Deus, et nos intelligere quod credidimus faciet'

('God will be with us and will make us understand that which we have believed'); S. Anselm, *Cur Deus Homo*, i. 2 (Boso), 'negligentia mihi videtur, si postquam confirmati sumus in fide, non studemus quod credimus intelligere' ('It seems to me negligence, if after we have been made strong in the faith, we do not take pains to understand what we believe').

[2] Wordsworth, *Character of the Happy Warrior*.

[3] Rossetti, *The House of Life*, lxxiv., 'S. Luke the Painter.'

[4] Trench, *To Poetry*.

[5] 1 Corinthians vi. 15.

[6] Keble, *Lyra Innocentium*, i. 4, 'Baptismal Vows.'

INDEX OF SUBJECTS

ADOPTION in Baptism, 26-7, 41, 44-5, 48, 49, 59.
Affusion, 22, 133-6, 271-2.
Alexander, Bishop of Alexandria, d. 326, 125, 264.
Anointing, 23-4, 164-8, 174-9, 181, 184-5, 285-7.
Apostles, whether they were baptized, 11-12, 222-4.
Arcadius, Emperor, d. 408, 147.
Arians in Spain and threefold immersion, 135, 271.
Aspersion, 135.
Athanasius, d. 373, 125, 264.
Augustine of Canterbury, d. 604, 175, 289.

BAPTISTERIES, 147-8, 278.
Blessing of water, 132-3, 168-9, 177, 180-1, 185.
Blood, Baptism of, 112, 114, 259-60.
British Church, 175-6, 289.

CANTERBURY, Convocation of, 105.
Catechumens, 152-8.
Character imprinted at Baptism, 94.
Christ, baptism of S. John Baptist received by, 9-10, 221-2.
Christ the Agent in the Sacraments, 126.

Chrysostom, attempt to arrest, in 404 A.D., 147.
Church, admission to, by Baptism, 14-18, 24, 26, 41, 213.
Clothing of the baptized, 167-8, 170, 175, 179, 181, 184, 185.
Conditional Baptism, 95, 254.
Conditions of Baptism, 100-9.
Confirmation, separation of from Baptism, 179-80, 186-7.
Constantine, Emperor, d. 337, 147.
Conversion, 35, 51-2.
Cross, sign of, 23-4, 133, 152, 165, 167, 174, 176, 177, 178, 179, 181, 185, 270, 285, 287.

DEAD, Baptism for the, 228.
Disciples, Baptism administered by, during Christ's ministry, 10, 222.
Donatists, century iv., 126, 128-9.

ENGLAND, Church in, 58-63, 66, 67-9, 82, 90-3, 98-9, 102, 104-9, 111, 113, 115, 121, 122-3, 135, 139, 143-5, 148-50, 159-61, 175-91, 206.

FACTS, doctrine of Baptism true to, 38, 195-206, 215.

Fasting before Baptism, 152, 153, 160, 163, 165, 281, 283-5, 290.
Forgiveness in Baptism, 31, 41, 43-50, 57, 59-60.
Form of Baptism, 22-3, 24, 136-9, 162-3, 167, 178, 184.
Free Will, 38, 39, 214-15.

GREEK CHURCH, 64, 83, 89, 123, 135-6, 180-1, 250-1, 263-4, 276, 288, 290.

HEMEROBAPTISTS, 254.
Heretical Baptism, 119-24, 127.
Holy Ghost, The, descent of, at Pentecost, making Baptism possible, 7, 11-14.
Holy Ghost, The, received in Baptism, 28-30, 44, 45, 47-9, 59, 67-85.

IMAGE of God, 31.
Immersion, 22, 24, 133-6, 176, 225-6, 270-2.
Immersion, trine, 133-6, 164, 166, 168, 174, 176, 178, 181, 183, 270-1.
Immersion, single, 135, 176, 271.
Indwelling of the Holy Ghost, 67-85.
Infants, Baptism of, 19-21, 96-109, 212-3, 214, 216, 254-7.

JOHN THE BAPTIST, baptism of, 8-9, 220-1.

KISS in Baptism, 164, 167, 168, 287.

LAY Baptism, 18-19, 24, 117, 120-4.
Lights in Baptism, 168, 170, 179, 291.
Likeness of God, 31-2.

MATTER of Baptism, 21, 131-2, 266-7.
Means, use of, in the Incarnation, 3, 196.
Means, use of in Old Testament, 1-3, 196.
Messiah, expectation that he would baptize, 8, 220.
Milk used as matter of Baptism, 131, 266-7.
Milk and honey in Baptism, 164, 167, 168, 170, 284, 287-8.
Minister of Baptism, 18-19, 24, 117-30, 261-6.
Missions in the middle ages, 158.
Missions, modern, 139, 158, 190-1.
Moral character of doctrine of Baptism, 198-9, 208-15.

NAMES applied to Baptism, 42, 204.
Necessity of Baptism, 10, 110-6, 258-60.
Nicodemus, discourse of Christ with, 10, 110, 131.
Novatians, century iii., 128.

OLD TESTAMENT, Baptism prefigured in, 4-5.
Old Testament, sacramental principle prefigured in, 1-3, 6, 196.
Old Testament, use of means in, 1-3, 196.

PAULIANISTS, centuries iii.-v., 262.
Places of Baptism, 22, 146-50.
Practical aspect of doctrine of Baptism, 206-7.
Preparation for Baptism, 151-61.
Priestly character of Christianity, 6-7.

INDEX OF SUBJECTS

Priestly character of Jewish religion, 6-7.
Privileges of the baptized, 25-31, 38-9.
Profession of belief in Baptism, 19, 24, 151, 155, 165-8, 174, 178, 180, 183, 286-7.
Proselytes, Baptism of, 7-8.

RATIONAL character of doctrine of Baptism, 195-216.
Regeneration in Baptism, 25-6, 41, 43-64, 66, 73-4, 184, 214.
Regeneration, how different from conversion, 35, 51-2.
Regeneration, how different from perseverance, 36-8, 51-7, 61-3, 206-7, 215.
Regeneration, how different from ultimate salvation, 36-8, 51-7, 215.
Renunciations in Baptism, 164, 166, 167, 168, 174, 178, 180, 182-3, 286.
Responsibilities of the baptized, 39, 53-7, 61-3, 106-9, 208, 212-3, 215-6.
Russian Church, 83, 102-3, 123-4, 139, 150, 180-1, 242, 250-1, 257, 263-4, 276, 288, 290.

SACRAMENT, meaning of word, 86-8, 251-3.
Sacrament of the catechumens, 153, 281-2.
Sacramental principle prefigured in Old Testament, 1-3, 6, 196.

Sacramental principle implied in the Incarnation, 3.
Sacraments, number of, 88-93.
Salvation, connection of, with Baptism, 29-31, 43-50, 57, 59, 62, 64.
Self-administered Baptism, 124-5.
Sponsors, 100-109, 257-8.
Sport, Baptism administered in, 125-6, 264.

TIMES of Baptism, 141-5.

UNBAPTIZED, Baptism administered by, 119-20.
Unbaptized, infants dying, 115-6, 260.
Unclothing before Baptism, 166, 167, 170.
Union with Christ in Baptism, 27-8, 30, 39, 43, 48, 49, 53-4, 57, 59, 60, 62, 204-5, 207-12, 214.

VALENTINIAN II., death of, in 392 A.D., when a catechumen, 156-8.

WASHING of feet, 169, 288-9.
Wine, whether valid matter of Baptism, 267.
Wine, mixing of, with water for use in Baptism condemned, 267.
Women, Baptism by, 120-2, 124, 262-3.

YORK, Convocation of, 105.

INDEX OF PASSAGES IN HOLY SCRIPTURE REFERRED TO

I. OLD TESTAMENT

	PAGE
Genesis xvii. 10-14,	5
Exodus iii. 8,	170
iv. 17,	2
vii. 15,	2
xiv. 16,	2
xvi. 14-15,	4
xvii. 5, 6, 9, 11-12,	2
xix. 5-6,	6
xxix.	2
Leviticus i.-viii.	2
xiii. 34,	4-5
xv. 5-13,	4-5
Numbers xxi. 8-9,	2
Deuteronomy viii. 3,	4
1 Samuel xv. 23, 26,	2
xvi. 13,	2
2 Samuel xii. 13,	2
2 Kings v. 10-14,	2
14,	225
Song of Solomon v. 12,	266
Isaiah xxi. 4,	225
lii. 15,	8
Jeremiah i. 5,	20
Ezekiel xxxvi. 25,	8
Daniel iv. 33, v. 21,	225
Zechariah xiii. 1,	8

II. DEUTERO-CANONICAL BOOKS

	PAGE
Judith xii. 7,	225
Ecclesiasticus xxxi. 30 (xxxiv. 25),	225

III. NEW TESTAMENT

S. Matthew iii. 13-17,	9-10
v. 17,	7
xvi. 16,	19
xix. 13-15,	20-1
xx. 22-3,	225
xxvii. 66,	227
xxviii. 19-20,	11, 23, 26-7, 99, 136, 274.
S. Mark i. 8,	29
vi. 13,	227
vii. 4,	225
x. 13-16,	20-1
38-9,	225
S. Luke i. 15,	20
iii. 3,	8
16,	9, 13
iv. 18,	227
xi. 38,	22, 225
xii. 50,	225

INDEX OF PASSAGES REFERRED TO

	PAGE
S. Luke xviii. 15-16,	20-1
xxiv. 49,	13
S. John i. 12-13,	27
25,	8
iii. 3-8, 10, 25, 110,	228-9
22,	10
26,	10
33,	228
iv. 1-2,	10
vi. 27,	228
31-5, 48-51, 58,	4
xii. 31,	170
xiii. 5,	169
xiv. 30,	170
xvii. 11,	26-7
xix. 34-35,	11
Acts i. 4,	13
ii. 1-4,	13
37-41, 14-15, 18, 19, 29, 30, 75-6, 274.	
47,	30
iv. 27,	227
viii. 12-13,	15, 18
15-17,	74-5
21-23,	36
35-8, 15, 18, 19, 21, 131-2, 146.	
ix. 17-18,	15, 18, 35, 76
x. 23,	18
38,	227
44-8,	16, 18, 21, 22
xvi. 14-15,	16, 18
22-33,	16, 18, 19, 21, 22
xviii. 8,	16, 18, 19-20
xix. 1-5,	16-17, 18, 22-3
6	75
xxii. 10,	35
16,	31
Romans iv. 11,	227
25,	33
v. 20-vi. 11,	34-5

	PAGE
Romans vi. 3-4, 21-2, 28,	274
8, 18, 22,	230
viii. 2,	230
9,	77
15,	27, 230
19,	27
xv. 28,	228
1 Corinthians i. 14-17,	18-19
iii. 16-17,	27, 36
iv. 15,	27
v. 3-5,	36-7
vi. 11-20,	37, 208
vii. 14,	20, 224-5
ix. 2,	227
x. 1-2,	20
xii. 12-13,	27-8, 29, 77, 79.
xv. 29,	228
2 Corinthians i. 21,	226
22,	227
Galatians iii. 24, iv. 1-5,	5
iii. 26-7,	27, 274
6,	29, 77
v. 2, 4, 19-21,	37
Ephesians i. 13,	227
ii. 2,	170
22,	29
iv. 5-6,	95
30,	227
v. 25-32,	21, 28
vi. 1-4,	20
Colossians i. 13,	170
ii. 11-12,	28
iii. 20-1,	20
2 S. Timothy ii. 19,	227
S. Titus iii. 5-7,	26, 29, 229
Hebrews i. 9,	227
ii. 14,	170
vi. 1-2,	17
x. 22,	21
S. James i. 18,	27

	PAGE		PAGE
S. James iv. 5,	29, 77	1 S. John iii. 1-2, 9, 10,	27
v. 14-15,	227	24,	29, 77
1 S. Peter i. 3,	27	iv. 7,	27
23,	27, 30	v. 2, 4,	27
ii. 5-9,	6-7	6,	11
iii. 20-1,	4	18,	27
21,	30, 151	Revelation ii. 13,	170
1 S. John ii. 20, 27,	226-7		

INDEX OF AUTHORS AND BOOKS REFERRED TO

Academy, 255.
Agrippinus, Bishop of Carthage, end of century ii. or beginning of century iii., 261.
Alford, Dr. H., Dean of Canterbury, d. 1871, 229, 230.
Ambrose, Bishop of Milan, d. 397, 48, 138, 156-8, 266-7, 274, 282-3, 289.
Apostolical Canons, probably of the latter part of the fourth century, 133-4, 137, 261, 270, 273.
Apostolical Constitutions, probably of the latter part of the fourth century, embodying older material, 53, 132, 137, 152, 239, 261, 269, 273, 280.
Aquinas. *See* Thomas Aquinas.
Arles, Council of (314), 119, 262, 280.
Athanasius, Bishop of Alexandria, d. 373, 47-8, 81, 236, 249-50, 262.
Augsburg, Confession of (1531, 1540), 241.
Augustine, Bishop of Hippo, d. 430, 1, 3, 49, 51-2, 55-6, 101, 115, 119-20, 126, 127-8, 129, 133, 138, 153-4, 194, 218-20, 221, 222, 237, 238-9, 240, 252, 256, 257, 260, 261, 264-6, 270, 274, 281-2, 291-2.

Barnabas, Epistle of, probably early in century ii., possibly earlier, 43, 232.
Basil, Bishop of Cæsarea, d. 379, 48, 81, 132, 137, 236, 249, 269, 274.
Bede, the Venerable, d. 735, 289.
Benson, Dr. E. W., Archbishop of Canterbury, d. 1896, 118, 128, 261, 265.
Bethlehem, Synod of (1672), 64, 83, 89, 242.
Birkbeck, W. J., 263.
Bright, Dr. W., Regius Professor of Ecclesiastical History, Oxford, 73-4, 242, 252, 289.
Butler, Dr. J., Bishop of Durham, d. 1752, 4, 12.

CÆSARIUS of Arles, Bishop of Arles, d. 542, 288.
Calvin, d. 1564, 25, 58, 229, 241, 263.
Carthage, Councils of (255-6), 118, 261.

Carthage, so-called 'Fourth Council of' (probably century vi.), 262.
Cashel, Council of (1172), 266.
Chalcedon, Council of (451), 40.
Cheetham. *See* Smith and Cheetham.
Chelsea, Council of (816), 271.
Chrysostom, Bishop of Constantinople, d. 407, 48-9, 79, 237, 244.
Church Quarterly Review, 251.
Clement of Alexandria, d. early in century iii., 44-5, 97, 232-3, 255.
Constantinople, Council of (381), 40.
Constantinople, Council of (1642), 89.
Cornelius, Bishop of Rome (251-2), d. 252, 78, 79.
Cyprian, Bishop of Carthage, d. 258, 45-7, 56, 78-81, 97, 98, 118, 132, 134, 138, 149, 165, 233-5, 240, 243-9, 255, 261, 268, 273-4, 284-5.
Cyril of Alexandria, Bishop of Alexandria, d. 444, 49, 237.
Cyril of Jerusalem, Bishop of Jerusalem, d. 386, 48, 132, 147, 154, 167-8, 236, 268-9, 278, 281-2.

DIONYSIUS THE AREOPAGITE, so-called, probably end of century v., 288.
Dositheus, Patriarch of Jerusalem, century xvii., 263.
Duchesne, L'abbé L., 271.

EDERSHEIM, Dr. A., d. 1889, 220.
Egbert, Excerptions of (740), 267.

Elvira, Council of (305), 280-1, 289.
Elwin, W., 264.
Ephraim the Syrian, d. about 373, 49, 237.
Epiphanius, Bishop of Salamis, d. 403, 228, 254.
Eugenius IV., Bishop of Rome (1431-47), d. 1447, 89.
Eunomius, Bishop of Cyzicus, extreme Arian, d. about 392, 271.
Euthymius Zigabenus, century xii., 222.
Eutychius, extreme Arian, century iv., 271.
Evodius, Bishop of Antioch, century i., 222.
Exeter, Council of (1287), 257.

FIRMILIAN, Bishop of Cæsarea in Cappadocia, d. 272, 128.

Gallican Missal, 169, 288.
Gelasian Sacramentary, 171-5.
Gothic Missal, 288.
Gratian, Benedictine, canonist, century xii., 279.
Gregory of Bergamo, Bishop of Bergamo, d. 1146, 88-9, 253.
Gregory the Great, Bishop of Rome (590-604), d. 604, 135, 271, 288.
Gregory of Nazianzus, Bishop of Constantinople, d. about 392, 48, 97-8, 236, 256, 260.
Gregory of Nyssa, Bishop of Nyssa, d. about 395, 48, 134, 237, 260, 270.
Gury, J. P., S.J., 266.

HADDAN (A. W., d. 1873) and

INDEX OF AUTHORS AND BOOKS 301

Stubbs (Dr. W., Bishop of Oxford), 271, 289.
Hefele, Dr. C. J., Bishop of Rottenburg, 280, 281.
Helvetic Confession, (1536), 241.
Hermann, Archbishop of Cologne, d. 1552, 184.
Hermas, probably middle of century ii., 43, 231-2.
Hilary of Poitiers, Bishop of Poitiers, d. 368, 47, 235-6.
Hippolytus, Canons of, probably late in century ii. or early in century iii., 44, 97, 101, 137, 152, 165-7, 170, 232, 255, 273, 280, 285-8.
Hooker, Richard, d. 1600, 112, 121.
Hutchings, W. H., Archdeacon of Cleveland, 81.

IGNATIUS, Bishop of Antioch, d. about 117, 118, 261.
Ine, Laws of (693), 98, 256.
Innocent I., Bishop of Rome (398-402), d. 402, 262.
Irenæus, Bishop of Lyons, d. 202, 43, 96-7, 255.

JEROME, d. 420, 49, 238.
Justin Martyr, d. middle of century ii., 43, 96, 137, 151-2, 163-4, 254-5, 277, 279, 283-4.
Justinian, Emperor, d. 565, 103, 257-8.

KEBLE, JOHN, d. 1866, 216-7.

LAODICEA, Synod of (date doubtful: probably between 343 and 381), 149, 279.
Lee, Dr. F. G., 290.

Lehmkuhl, Augustine, S.J., 267, 272.
Leo I., Bishop of Rome (440-461), d. 461, 49, 53-5, 238, 239-40.
Liddon, Dr. H. P., Canon of S. Paul's, d. 1890, 229, 231.
Lightfoot, Dr. John, d. 1675, 220.
Lightfoot, Dr. J. B., Bishop of Durham, d. 1889, 252, 254.
London, Council of (1126) 187-8.
Luther, Martin, d. 1546, 58.
Lyndwood, Bishop of S. David's, d. 1446, 188, 271-2, 275, 290.

MACLEAR, Dr. G. F., Warden of S. Augustine's College, Canterbury, 283.
Macarius, Bishop of Vinitza, 83.
Marcion, Gnostic, century ii., 228, 254.
Maskell, W., d. 1890, 263, 269, 271, 275, 277, 278-9, 289, 290.
Mason, Dr. A. J., Lady Margaret Professor of Divinity, Cambridge, 251.
Metrophanes Critopulus, Patriarch of Constantinople, century xvii., 263-4.
Missale Romanum, 277, 288.
Moberly, Dr. G., Bishop of Salisbury, d. 1885, 223-4.

NEO-CÆSAREA, Synod of (date doubtful: between 314 and 325), 149, 279, 280.
Nicæa, Council of (325), 40, 262.
Nicephorus, century xv., 222, 267.
Novatian, schismatic Bishop of Rome, century iii., 78.

ORIGEN, d. 253, 45, 81, 97, 233, 249, 255.

PALMER, W., d. 1885, 263, 272.
Paris, Council of (1528), 89.
Parker, M., Archbishop of Canterbury, d. 1575, 263, 276.
Peccham, J., Archbishop of Canterbury, d. 1292, 188, 275, 290.
Peter Lombard, Bishop of Paris, d. 1164, 82, 89, 250, 253.
Pliny the younger, Governor of Bithynia about 110, 86-7, 251-2.
Pole, R., Archbishop of Canterbury, d. 1558, 263.
Polycarp, Bishop of Smyrna (d. 155), *Letter of the Smyrnæans on Death of*, 96, 254.
Poore, Bishop of Sarum, *Constitutions of* (1217), 111, 258.
Pseudo-Ambrose, author of *De Sacramentis*, 289.
Puller, F. W., S.S.J.E., 251.
Pusey, Dr. E. B., Regius Professor of Hebrew, Oxford, d. 1882, 229.

RAYMOND OF PENNAFORT, General of the Dominican Order, canonist, d. 1275, 120-1, 262.
Reformed Confessions, 58, 241.
Riley, A., 136, 272.
Rituale Romanum, 257, 272, 290.
Robertson, Dr. J. C., Canon of Canterbury, d. 1882, 283.
Rossetti, D. G., d. 1882, 203.
Rufinus, d. 401, 264.

Sarum Manual, 176-9, 275, 278-9, 289-90.
Sarum Missal, 277, 290.
Saxon Confession (1551), 241.
Schouppe, F. X., S.J., 258, 266.
Schürer, Dr. E., Professor of Theology at Giessen, 220.

Serapion, Bishop of Thmuis in Egypt, d. about 365, 132, 168, 269, 288.
Silvia, Pilgrimage of, century iv., 154-5.
Siricius, Bishop of Rome (384-398), d. 398, 267.
Smirnoff, Archpriest, Dean of S. Isaac's Cathedral, S. Petersburg, 99, 256.
Smith (Dr. W.) and Cheetham (Professor S., Archdeacon of Rochester), 267, 271, 276-7.
Socrates, century v., 264.
Sozomen, century v., 264.
Stephen I., Bishop of Rome (254-257), d. 257, 118.
Stephen II., otherwise Stephen III., Bishop of Rome (752-757), d. 757, 267.
Stephen III., otherwise Stephen IV., Bishop of Rome (768-772), d. 772, 267.
Stokes, Whitley, 255.
Stubbs. *See* Haddan and Stubbs.
Strype, J., d. 1737, 263, 276.

Teaching of the Twelve Apostles, probably latter part of century i., 23, 134, 137, 146, 151, 162-3, 226, 270, 279, 283.
Tertullian, d. first half of century iii., 43-4, 78-81, 97, 100, 132, 134, 141-2, 143, 146-7, 152, 164-5, 243, 255, 261-2, 267-8, 270, 273, 276, 278, 280, 284.
Thecla, Acts of, possibly of century ii., 124-5.
Theodoret, d. about 458, 231.
Theophronius, extreme Arian, century iv., 271.
Thomas Aquinas, Dominican, d.

INDEX OF AUTHORS AND BOOKS

1274, 57, 115-6, 129, 220, 222, 241, 250, 252, 258-9, 260, 262, 264, 266, 275.
Toledo, Council of (633), 135, 271.
Trench, Dr. R. C., Archbishop of Dublin, d. 1886, 203-4.
Trent, Council of (1545-63), 58, 89, 103, 122, 129-30, 241, 252-3, 257, 263, 266.

VINCENT OF LERINS, d. about 450, 261.

WARREN, F. E., 226-8, 266, 289.
Watkins, O. D., 258.

Westcott, Dr. B. F., Bishop of Durham, 227.
Whitby, Conference of (664), 176.
Wirgman, A. T., 251.
Worcester, Council of (1240), 257.
Wordsworth, W., d. 1850, 202-3.
Wycliffe, John, d. 1384, 129.

Xanthippe, Polyxena, and Rebecca, Acts of, probably middle of century iii., 137, 146, 272-3, 277.

ZWINGLI, d. 1531, 58, 121, 241, 263.

Printed by T. and A. CONSTABLE, Printers to Her Majesty
at the Edinburgh University Press

THE
Orford Library of Practical Theology

PRODUCED UNDER THE EDITORSHIP OF THE

REV. W. C. E. NEWBOLT, M.A.
CANON AND CHANCELLOR OF S. PAUL'S

AND THE

REV. F. E. BRIGHTMAN, M.A.
LIBRARIAN OF THE PUSEY HOUSE, OXFORD

THE FOLLOWING IS A LIST OF VOLUMES AS AT PRESENT PROPOSED.

The Price of each Volume is 5s.

1. **RELIGION.**
   By the Rev. W. C. E. NEWBOLT, M.A., Canon and Chancellor of S. Paul's.
2. **BAPTISM.**
   By the Rev. DARWELL STONE, M.A., Principal of the Missionary College, Dorchester.
3. **CONFIRMATION.**
   By the Right Rev. A. C. A. HALL, D.D., Bishop of Vermont.
4. **HOLY MATRIMONY.**
   By the Rev. W. J. KNOX LITTLE, M.A., Canon of Worcester.
5. **THE HOLY COMMUNION.**
   By the Rev. F. W. PULLER, M.A., Mission Priest of S. John Evangelist, Cowley.
6. **THE PRAYER BOOK.**
   By the Rev. LEIGHTON PULLAN, M.A., Fellow of S. John's College, Oxford.
7. **RELIGIOUS CEREMONIAL.**
   By the Rev. F. E. BRIGHTMAN, M.A., Librarian of the Pusey House, Oxford.
8. **PRAYER.**
   By the Rev. ARTHUR JOHN WORLLEDGE, M.A., Canon of Truro.
9. **VISITATION OF THE SICK.**
   By the Rev. E. F. RUSSELL, M.A., S. Alban's, Holborn.

CONFESSION AND ABSOLUTION.
FASTING AND ALMSGIVING.
RETREATS, MISSIONS, Etc.
CHURCH WORK.

DEVOTIONAL BOOKS AND READING.
ORDINATION.
FOREIGN MISSIONS.
THE BIBLE.

LONGMANS, GREEN, AND CO.
LONDON, NEW YORK, AND BOMBAY

April 1899.

A Selection of Works

IN

THEOLOGICAL LITERATURE

PUBLISHED BY

Messrs. LONGMANS, GREEN, & CO.

London : 39 Paternoster Row, E.C.
New York : 91 and 93 Fifth Avenue.
Bombay : 32 Hornby Road.

Abbey and Overton.—THE ENGLISH CHURCH IN THE EIGHTEENTH CENTURY. By Charles J. Abbey, M.A., Rector of Checkendon, Reading, and John H. Overton, D.D., Canon of Lincoln. *Crown 8vo. 7s. 6d.*

Adams.—SACRED ALLEGORIES. The Shadow of the Cross—The Distant Hills—The Old Man's Home—The King's Messengers. By the Rev. William Adams, M.A. *Crown 8vo. 3s. 6d.*
The four Allegories may be had separately, with Illustrations. 16mo. 1s. each.

Aids to the Inner Life.
Edited by the Venble. W. H. Hutchings, M.A., Archdeacon of Cleveland, Canon of York, Rector of Kirby Misperton, and Rural Dean of Malton. *Five Vols. 32mo, cloth limp, 6d. each; or cloth extra, 1s. each.*
OF THE IMITATION OF CHRIST. By Thomas à Kempis.
THE CHRISTIAN YEAR
THE DEVOUT LIFE. By St. Francis de Sales.
THE HIDDEN LIFE OF THE SOUL.
THE SPIRITUAL COMBAT. By Laurence Scupoli.

Alexander.—THE CHRISTIANITY OF ST. PAUL. By the Rev. S. A. Alexander, M.A., Reader of the Temple Church.

Barnett.—THE SERVICE OF GOD : Sermons, Essays, and Addresses. By Samuel A. Barnett, Warden of Toynbee Hall, Whitechapel ; Canon of Bristol Cathedral ; Select Preacher before Oxford University. *Crown 8vo. 6s.*

Bathe.—Works by the Rev. Anthony Bathe, M.A.
A LENT WITH JESUS. A Plain Guide for Churchmen. Containing Readings for Lent and Easter Week, and on the Holy Eucharist. *32mo, 1s.; or in paper cover, 6d.*
AN ADVENT WITH JESUS. *32mo, 1s.; or in paper cover, 6d.*
WHAT I SHOULD BELIEVE. A Simple Manual of Self-Instruction for Church People. *Small 8vo, limp, 1s. ; cloth gilt, 2s.*

Bathe and Buckham.—THE CHRISTIAN'S ROAD BOOK. 2 Parts. By the Rev. Anthony Bathe and Rev. F. H. Buckham.
Part I. DEVOTIONS. *Sewed, 6d. ; limp cloth, 1s. ; cloth extra, 1s. 6d.*
Part II. READINGS. *Sewed, 1s. ; limp cloth, 2s. ; cloth extra, 3s. ; or complete in one volume, sewed, 1s. 6d. ; limp cloth, 2s. 6d. ; cloth extra, 3s. 6d.*

Benson.—Works by the Rev. R. M. BENSON, M.A., Student of Christ Church, Oxford.

THE FINAL PASSOVER: A Series of Meditations upon the Passion of our Lord Jesus Christ. *Small 8vo.*

Vol. I.—THE REJECTION. 5s.
Vol. II.—THE UPPER CHAMBER.
Part I. 5s.
Part II. 5s.
Vol. III.—THE DIVINE EXODUS. Parts I. and II. 5s. each.
Vol. IV.—THE LIFE BEYOND THE GRAVE. 5s.

THE MAGNIFICAT; a Series of Meditations upon the Song of the Blessed Virgin Mary. *Small 8vo.* 2s.

SPIRITUAL READINGS FOR EVERY DAY. 3 vols. *Small 8vo.* 3s. 6d. each.

I. ADVENT.   II. CHRISTMAS.   III. EPIPHANY.

BENEDICTUS DOMINUS: A Course of Meditations for Every Day of the Year Vol. I.—ADVENT TO TRINITY. Vol. II.—TRINITY, SAINTS' DAYS, e. *Small 8vo.* 3s. 6d. each; *or in One Volume*, 7s.

BIBLE TEACHINGS: The Discourse at Capernaum.—St. John vi. *Small 8vo.* 3s. 6d.

THE WISDOM OF THE SON OF DAVID: An Exposition of the First Nine Chapters of the Book of Proverbs. *Small 8vo.* 3s. 6d.

THE MANUAL OF INTERCESSORY PRAYER. *Royal 32mo.*; *cloth boards*, 1s. 3d.; *cloth limp*, 9d.

THE EVANGELIST LIBRARY CATECHISM. Part I. *Small 8vo.* 3s.

PAROCHIAL MISSIONS. *Small 8vo.* 2s. 6d.

Bickersteth.—YESTERDAY, TO-DAY, AND FOR EVER: a Poem in Twelve Books. By EDWARD HENRY BICKERSTETH, D.D., Lord Bishop of Exeter. *One Shilling Edition*, 18mo. *With red borders*, 16mo, 2s. 6d.

The Crown 8vo Edition (5s.) may still be had.

Blunt.—Works by the Rev. JOHN HENRY BLUNT, D.D.

THE ANNOTATED BOOK OF COMMON PRAYER: Being an Historical, Ritual, and Theological Commentary on the Devotional System of the Church of England. *4to.* 21s.

THE COMPENDIOUS EDITION OF THE ANNOTATED BOOK OF COMMON PRAYER: Forming a concise Commentary on the Devotional System of the Church of England. *Crown 8vo.* 10s. 6d.

DICTIONARY OF DOCTRINAL AND HISTORICAL THEOLOGY. By various Writers. *Imperial 8vo.* 21s.

DICTIONARY OF SECTS, HERESIES, ECCLESIASTICAL PARTIES AND SCHOOLS OF RELIGIOUS THOUGHT. By various Writers. *Imperial 8vo.* 21s.

THE REFORMATION OF THE CHURCH OF ENGLAND: its History, Principles, and Results. 1574-1662. *Two Vols.* 8vo. 34s.

IN THEOLOGICAL LITERATURE. 3

Blunt.—Works by the Rev. JOHN HENRY BLUNT, D.D.—*contd.*
THE BOOK OF CHURCH LAW. Being an Exposition of the Legal Rights and Duties of the Parochial Clergy and the Laity of the Church of England. Revised by the Right Hon. Sir WALTER G. F. PHILLIMORE, Bart., D.C.L., and G. EDWARDES JONES, Barrister-at-Law. *Crown 8vo.* 9s.
A COMPANION TO THE BIBLE: Being a Plain Commentary on Scripture History, to the end of the Apostolic Age. *Two Vols. small 8vo. Sold separately.* OLD TEST. 3s. 6d. NEW TEST. 3s. 6d.
HOUSEHOLD THEOLOGY: a Handbook of Religious Information respecting the Holy Bible, the Prayer Book, the Church, etc., etc. *Paper cover,* 16mo. 1s. *Also the Larger Edition,* 3s. 6d.

Body.—Works by the Rev. GEORGE BODY, D.D., Canon of Durham.
THE LIFE OF LOVE. A Course of Lent Lectures. 16mo. 2s. 6d.
THE SCHOOL OF CALVARY; or, Laws of Christian Life revealed from the Cross. 16mo. 2s. 6d.
THE LIFE OF JUSTIFICATION. 16mo. 2s. 6d.
THE LIFE OF TEMPTATION. 16mo. 2s. 6d.
THE PRESENT STATE OF THE FAITHFUL DEPARTED. *Small 8vo. sewed,* 6d. 32mo. *cloth,* 1s.

Boultbee.—A COMMENTARY ON THE THIRTY-NINE ARTICLES OF THE CHURCH OF ENGLAND. By the Rev. T. P. BOULTBEE, formerly Principal of the London College of Divinity, St. John's Hall, Highbury. *Crown 8vo.* 6s.

Bright.—Works by WILLIAM BRIGHT, D.D., Regius Professor of Ecclesiastical History in the University of Oxford, and Canon of Christ Church, Oxford.
SOME ASPECTS OF PRIMITIVE CHURCH LIFE. *Crown 8vo.* 6s.
THE ROMAN SEE IN THE EARLY CHURCH: And other Studies in Church History. *Crown 8vo.* 7s. 6d.
WAYMARKS IN CHURCH HISTORY. *Crown 8vo.* 7s. 6d.
LESSONS FROM THE LIVES OF THREE GREAT FATHERS. St. Athanasius, St. Chrysostom, and St. Augustine. *Crown 8vo.* 6s.
THE INCARNATION AS A MOTIVE POWER. *Crown 8vo.* 6s.

Bright and Medd.—LIBER PRECUM PUBLICARUM ECCLESIÆ ANGLICANÆ. A GULIELMO BRIGHT, S.T.P., et PETRO GOLDSMITH MEDD, A.M., Latine redditus. *Small 8vo.* 7s. 6d.

Browne.—WEARIED WITH THE BURDEN: A Book of Daily Readings for Lent. By ARTHUR HEBER BROWNE, M.A., LL.D., late Rector of St. John's, Newfoundland. *Crown 8vo.* 4s. 6d.

Browne.—AN EXPOSITION OF THE THIRTY-NINE ARTICLES, Historical and Doctrinal. By E. H. BROWNE, D.D., sometime Bishop of Winchester. 8vo. 16s.

Campion and Beamont.—THE PRAYER BOOK INTERLEAVED. With Historical Illustrations and Explanatory Notes arranged parallel to the Text. By W. M. CAMPION, D.D., and W. J. BEAMONT, M.A. *Small 8vo.* 7s. 6d.

Carter.—Works by, and edited by the Rev. T. T. CARTER, M.A., Hon. Canon of Christ Church, Oxford.

THE SPIRIT OF WATCHFULNESS AND OTHER SERMONS. *Crown 8vo.* 5s.

THE TREASURY OF DEVOTION: a Manual of Prayer for General and Daily Use. Compiled by a Priest.
18mo. 2s. 6d.; *cloth limp,* 2s. Bound with the Book of Common Prayer, 3s. 6d. Red-Line Edition. *Cloth extra, gilt top.* 18mo, 2s. 6d. *net.* Large-Type Edition. *Crown 8vo.* 3s. 6d.

THE WAY OF LIFE: A Book of Prayers and Instruction for the Young at School, with a Preparation for Confirmation. Compiled by a Priest, 18mo. 1s. 6d.

THE PATH OF HOLINESS: a First Book of Prayers, with the Service of the Holy Communion, for the Young. Compiled by a Priest. With Illustrations. 16mo. 1s. 6d.; *cloth limp,* 1s.

THE GUIDE TO HEAVEN: a Book of Prayers for every Want. (For the Working Classes.) Compiled by a Priest. 18mo. 1s. 6d.; *cloth limp,* 1s. *Large-Type Edition. Crown 8vo.* 1s. 6d.; *cloth limp,* 1s.

THE STAR OF CHILDHOOD: a First Book of Prayers and Instruction for Children. Compiled by a Priest. With Illustrations. 16mo. 2s. 6d.

SIMPLE LESSONS; or, Words Easy to be Understood. A Manual of Teaching. I. On the Creed. II. The Ten Commandments. III. The Sacrament. 18mo. 3s.

A BOOK OF PRIVATE PRAYER FOR MORNING, MID-DAY, AND OTHER TIMES. 18mo. *limp cloth,* 1s.; *cloth, red edges,* 1s. 3d.

NICHOLAS FERRAR: his Household and his Friends. With Portrait engraved after a Picture by CORNELIUS JANSSEN at Magdalene College, Cambridge. *Crown 8vo.* 6s.

MANUAL OF DEVOTION FOR SISTERS OF MERCY. 8 parts in 2 vols. 32mo. 10s. Or separately:—Part I. 1s. 6d. Part II. 1s. Part III. 1s. Part IV. 2s. Part V. 1s. Part VI. 1s. Part VII. Part VIII. 1s. 6d.

HARRIET MONSELL: A Memoir of the First Mother Superior of the Clewer Community. With Portrait. *Crown 8vo.* 2s. 6d.

PARISH TEACHINGS. First and Second Series. *Crown 8vo.* 4s. 6d. *each sold separately.*

SPIRITUAL INSTRUCTIONS. *Crown 8vo.*

THE HOLY EUCHARIST. 3s. 6d.	OUR LORD'S EARLY LIFE. 3s. 6d.
THE DIVINE DISPENSATIONS. 3s. 6d.	OUR LORD'S ENTRANCE ON HIS
THE LIFE OF GRACE. 3s. 6d.	MINISTRY. 3s. 6d.

THE RELIGIOUS LIFE. 3s. 6d.

THE DOCTRINE OF THE PRIESTHOOD IN THE CHURCH OF ENGLAND. *Crown 8vo.* 4s.

THE DOCTRINE OF CONFESSION IN THE CHURCH OF ENGLAND. *Crown 8vo.* 5s.

THE DOCTRINE OF THE HOLY EUCHARIST, drawn from the Holy Scriptures and the Records of the Church of England. *Fcp. 8vo.* 9d.

VOWS AND THE RELIGIOUS STATE. *Crown 8vo.* 2s.

Coles.—LENTEN MEDITATIONS. By the Rev. V. S. S. COLES, M.A., Principal of the Pusey House, Oxford. 18mo. 2s. 6d.

Congreve.—CHRISTIAN LIFE A RESPONSE. With other Retreat Addresses and Sermons. By GEORGE CONGREVE, Mission Priest of the Society of St. John the Evangelist, Cowley St. John, Oxford. Crown 8vo. 5s.

Conybeare and Howson.—THE LIFE AND EPISTLES OF ST. PAUL. By the Rev. W. J. CONYBEARE, M.A., and the Very Rev. J. S. HOWSON, D.D. With numerous Maps and Illustrations.
LIBRARY EDITION. Two Vols. 8vo. 21s. STUDENTS' EDITION. One Vol. Crown 8vo. 6s. POPULAR EDITION. One Vol. Crown 8vo. 3s. 6d.

Creighton.—A HISTORY OF THE PAPACY FROM THE GREAT SCHISM TO THE SACK OF ROME (1378-1527). By Right Hon. and Right Rev. MANDELL CREIGHTON, D.D., Lord Bishop of London. Six volumes. Crown 8vo. 6s. each.

DAY-HOURS OF THE CHURCH OF ENGLAND, THE. Newly Revised according to the Prayer Book and the Authorised Translation of the Bible. Crown 8vo. sewed, 3s. ; cloth, 3s. 6d.
SUPPLEMENT TO THE DAY-HOURS OF THE CHURCH OF ENGLAND, being the Service for certain Holy Days. Crown 8vo. sewed, 3s. ; cloth, 3s. 6d.

Devotional Series, 16mo, Red Borders. *Each 2s. 6d.*

BICKERSTETH'S YESTERDAY, TO-DAY, AND FOR EVER.
CHILCOT'S TREATISE ON EVIL THOUGHTS.
THE CHRISTIAN YEAR.
HERBERT'S POEMS AND PROVERBS.
KEMPIS' (à) OF THE IMITATION OF CHRIST.
LEAR'S (H. L. SIDNEY) FOR DAYS AND YEARS.
FRANCIS DE SALES' (ST.) THE DEVOUT LIFE.
WILSON'S THE LORD'S SUPPER. *Large type.*
*TAYLOR'S (JEREMY) HOLY LIVING.
*——— ——— HOLY DYING.

* *These two in one Volume. 5s.*

Devotional Series, 18mo, without Red Borders. *Each 1s.*

BICKERSTETH'S YESTERDAY, TO-DAY, AND FOR EVER.
THE CHRISTIAN YEAR.
KEMPIS' (à) OF THE IMITATION OF CHRIST.
HERBERT'S POEMS AND PROVERBS.
WILSON'S THE LORD'S SUPPER. *Large type.*
FRANCIS DE SALES' (ST.) THE DEVOUT LIFE.
*TAYLOR'S (JEREMY) HOLY LIVING.
*——— ——— HOLY DYING.

* *These two in one Volume. 2s. 6d.*

Edersheim.—Works by ALFRED EDERSHEIM, M.A., D.D., Ph.D.
THE LIFE AND TIMES OF JESUS THE MESSIAH. Two Vols. 8vo. 24s.
JESUS THE MESSIAH : being an Abridged Edition of 'The Life and Times of Jesus the Messiah.' Crown 8vo. 7s. 6d.
HISTORY OF THE JEWISH NATION AFTER THE DESTRUCTION OF JERUSALEM UNDER TITUS. 8vo. 18s.

Ellicott.—Works by C. J. ELLICOTT, D.D., Bishop of Gloucester.

A CRITICAL AND GRAMMATICAL COMMENTARY ON ST. PAUL'S EPISTLES. Greek Text, with a Critical and Grammatical Commentary, and a Revised English Translation. 8vo.

GALATIANS. 8s. 6d.
EPHESIANS. 8s. 6d.
PHILIPPIANS, COLOSSIANS, AND PHILEMON. 10s. 6d.
THESSALONIANS. 7s. 6d.
PASTORAL EPISTLES. 10s. 6d.

HISTORICAL LECTURES ON THE LIFE OF OUR LORD JESUS CHRIST. 8vo. 12s.

ENGLISH (THE) CATHOLIC'S VADE MECUM: a Short Manual of General Devotion. Compiled by a PRIEST. 32mo. limp, 1s.; cloth, 2s.

PRIEST'S Edition. 32mo. 1s. 6d.

Epochs of Church History.—Edited by Right Hon. and Right Rev. MANDELL CREIGHTON, D.D., Lord Bishop of London. Small 8vo. 2s. 6d. each.

THE ENGLISH CHURCH IN OTHER LANDS. By the Rev. H. W. TUCKER, M.A.

THE HISTORY OF THE REFORMATION IN ENGLAND. By the Rev. GEO. G. PERRY, M.A.

THE CHURCH OF THE EARLY FATHERS. By the Rev. ALFRED PLUMMER, D.D.

THE EVANGELICAL REVIVAL IN THE EIGHTEENTH CENTURY. By the Rev. J. H. OVERTON, D.D.

THE UNIVERSITY OF OXFORD. By the Hon. G. C. BRODRICK, D.C.L.

THE UNIVERSITY OF CAMBRIDGE. By J. BASS MULLINGER, M.A.

THE ENGLISH CHURCH IN THE MIDDLE AGES. By the Rev. W. HUNT, M.A.

THE CHURCH AND THE EASTERN EMPIRE. By the Rev. H. F. TOZER, M.A.

THE CHURCH AND THE ROMAN EMPIRE. By the Rev. A. CARR, M.A.

THE CHURCH AND THE PURITANS, 1570-1660. By HENRY OFFLEY WAKEMAN M.A.

HILDEBRAND AND HIS TIMES. By the Rev. W. R. W. STEPHENS, M.A.

THE POPES AND THE HOHENSTAUFEN. By UGO BALZANI.

THE COUNTER REFORMATION. By ADOLPHUS WILLIAM WARD, Litt. D.

WYCLIFFE AND MOVEMENTS FOR REFORM. By REGINALD L. POOLE, M.A.

THE ARIAN CONTROVERSY. By the Rev. H. M. GWATKIN, M.A.

EUCHARISTIC MANUAL (THE). Consisting of Instructions and Devotions for the Holy Sacrament of the Altar. From various sources. 32mo. cloth gilt, red edges. 1s. Cheap Edition, limp cloth. 9d.

Farrar.—Works by FREDERICK W. FARRAR, D.D., Dean of Canterbury.

THE BIBLE: Its Meaning and Supremacy. 8vo. 15s.

TEXTS EXPLAINED; or, Helps to Understand the New Testament. Crown 8vo. [In the press.

ALLEGORIES. With 25 Illustrations by AMELIA BAUERLE. Crown 8vo. 6s.

CONTENTS.—The Life Story of Aner—The Choice—The Fortunes of a Royal House—The Basilisk and the Leopard.

IN THEOLOGICAL LITERATURE. 7

Fosbery.—Works edited by the Rev. THOMAS VINCENT FOSBERY, M.A., sometime Vicar of St. Giles's, Reading.
VOICES OF COMFORT. *Cheap Edition. Small 8vo.* 3s. 6d.
The Larger Edition (7s. 6d.) may still be had.
HYMNS AND POEMS FOR THE SICK AND SUFFERING. In connection with the Service for the Visitation of the Sick. Selected from Various Authors. *Small 8vo.* 3s. 6d.

Geikie.—Works by J. CUNNINGHAM GEIKIE, D.D., LL.D., late Vicar of St. Martin-at-Palace, Norwich.
HOURS WITH THE BIBLE: the Scriptures in the Light of Modern Discovery and Knowledge. *New Edition, largely rewritten. Complete in Twelve Volumes. Crown 8vo.* 3s. 6d. *each.*

OLD TESTAMENT.
In Six Volumes. Sold separately. 3s. 6d. *each.*

CREATION TO THE PATRIARCHS. *With a Map and Illustrations.*

MOSES TO JUDGES. *With a Map and Illustrations.*

SAMSON TO SOLOMON. *With a Map and Illustrations.*

REHOBOAM TO HEZEKIAH. *With Illustrations.*

MANASSEH TO ZEDEKIAH. *With the Contemporary Prophets. With a Map and Illustrations.*

EXILE TO MALACHI. *With the Contemporary Prophets. With Illustrations.*

NEW TESTAMENT.
In Six Volumes. Sold separately. 3s. 6d. *each.*

THE GOSPELS. *With a Map and Illustrations.*

LIFE AND WORDS OF CHRIST. *With Map.* 2 vols.

LIFE AND EPISTLES OF ST. PAUL. *With Maps and Illustrations.* 2 vols.

ST. PETER TO REVELATION. *With* 29 *Illustrations.*

LIFE AND WORDS OF CHRIST.
   Cabinet Edition. *With Map.* 2 vols. *Post 8vo.* 7s.
   Cheap Edition, *without the Notes.* 1 vol. 8vo. 5s.

A SHORT LIFE OF CHRIST. *With Illustrations. Crown 8vo.* 3s. 6d. ; *gilt edges,* 4s. 6d.

OLD TESTAMENT CHARACTERS. *With Illustrations. Crown 8vo.* 3s. 6d.

LANDMARKS OF OLD TESTAMENT HISTORY. *Crown 8vo.* 3s. 6d.

THE ENGLISH REFORMATION. *Crown 8vo.* 3s. 6d.

ENTERING ON LIFE. A Book for Young Men. *Crown 8vo.* 2s. 6d.

THE PRECIOUS PROMISES. *Crown 8vo.* 2s.

GOLD DUST: a Collection of Golden Counsels for the Sanctification of Daily Life. Translated and abridged from the French by E. L. E. E. Edited by CHARLOTTE M. YONGE. Parts I. II. III. Small Pocket Volumes. *Cloth, gilt, each* 1s. Parts I. and II. in One Volume. 1s. 6d. Parts I., II., and III. in One Volume. 2s.

*** The two first parts in One Volume, *large type*, 18mo. cloth, gilt. 2s. 6d. Parts I. II. and III. are also supplied, bound in white cloth, with red edges, in box, price 3s.

Gore.—Works by the Rev. CHARLES GORE, M.A., D.D., Canon of Westminster.
THE MINISTRY OF THE CHRISTIAN CHURCH. 8vo. 10s. 6d.
ROMAN CATHOLIC CLAIMS. *Crown 8vo.* 3s. 6d.

GREAT TRUTHS OF THE CHRISTIAN RELIGION. Edited by the Rev. W. U. RICHARDS. *Small 8vo.* 2s.

Hall.—Works by the Right Rev. A. C. A. HALL, D.D., Bishop of Vermont.
THE VIRGIN MOTHER: Retreat Addresses on the Life of the Blessed Virgin Mary as told in the Gospels. With an appended Essay on the Virgin Birth of our Lord. *Crown 8vo.* 4s. 6d.
CHRIST'S TEMPTATION AND OURS. *Crown 8vo.* 3s. 6d.

Hall.—THE KENOTIC THEORY. Considered with Particular Reference to its Anglican Forms and Arguments. By the Rev. FRANCIS J. HALL, D.D., Instructor of Dogmatic Theology in the Western Theological Seminary, Chicago, Illinois. *Crown 8vo.* 5s.

HALLOWING OF SORROW, THE. By E. R. With a Preface by H. S. HOLLAND, M.A., Canon and Precentor of St. Paul's. *Small 8vo.* 2s.

Harrison.—Works by the Rev. ALEXANDER J. HARRISON, B.D., Lecturer of the Christian Evidence Society.
PROBLEMS OF CHRISTIANITY AND SCEPTICISM. *Crown 8vo.* 7s. 6d.
THE CHURCH IN RELATION TO SCEPTICS: a Conversational Guide to Evidential Work. *Crown 8vo.* 3s. 6d.
THE REPOSE OF FAITH, IN VIEW OF PRESENT DAY DIFFICULTIES. *Crown 8vo.* 7s. 6d.

Hatch.—THE ORGANIZATION OF THE EARLY CHRISTIAN CHURCHES. Being the Bampton Lectures for 1880. By EDWIN HATCH, M.A., D.D., late Reader in Ecclesiastical History in the University of Oxford. 8vo. 5s.

Heygate.—THE MANUAL: a Book of Devotion. Adapted for General Use. By the Rev. W. E. HEYGATE, M.A., Rector of Brighstone. 18mo. *cloth limp*, 1s.; *boards*, 1s. 3d. *Cheap Edition*, 6d. *Small 8vo. Large Type*, 1s. 6d.

Holland.—Works by the Rev. HENRY SCOTT HOLLAND, M.A., Canon and Precentor of St. Paul's.

GOD'S CITY AND THE COMING OF THE KINGDOM. *Cr. 8vo.* 3s. 6d.
PLEAS AND CLAIMS FOR CHRIST. *Crown 8vo.* 3s. 6d.
CREED AND CHARACTER: Sermons. *Crown 8vo.* 3s. 6d.
ON BEHALF OF BELIEF. Sermons. *Crown 8vo.* 3s. 6d.
CHRIST OR ECCLESIASTES. Sermons. *Crown 8vo.* 2s. 6d.
LOGIC AND LIFE, with other Sermons. *Crown 8vo.* 3s. 6d.

Hollings.—Works by the Rev. G. S. HOLLINGS, Mission Priest of the Society of St. John the Evangelist, Cowley, Oxford.

THE HEAVENLY STAIR; or, A Ladder of the Love of God for Sinners. *Crown 8vo.* 3s. 6d.
PORTA REGALIS; or, Considerations on Prayer. *Crown 8vo. limp cloth*, 1s. 6d. net; cloth boards, 2s. net.
MEDITATIONS ON THE DIVINE LIFE, THE BLESSED SACRAMENT, AND THE TRANSFIGURATION. *Crown 8vo.* 3s. 6d.
CONSIDERATIONS ON THE SPIRITUAL LIFE. Suggested by Passages in the Collects for the Sundays in Lent. *Crown 8vo.* 2s. 6d.
CONSIDERATIONS ON THE WISDOM OF GOD. *Crown 8vo.* 4s.
PARADOXES OF THE LOVE OF GOD, especially as they are seen in the way of the Evangelical Counsels. *Crown 8vo.* 4s.
ONE BORN OF THE SPIRIT; or, the Unification of our Life in God. *Crown 8vo.* 3s. 6d.

Hutchings.—Works by the Ven. W. H. HUTCHINGS, M.A. Archdeacon of Cleveland, Canon of York, Rector of Kirby Misperton, and Rural Dean of Malton.

SERMON SKETCHES from some of the Sunday Lessons throughout the Church's Year. *Vols. I and II. Crown 8vo.* 5s. each.
THE LIFE OF PRAYER: a Course of Lectures delivered in All Saints Church, Margaret Street, during Lent. *Crown 8vo.* 4s. 6d.
THE PERSON AND WORK OF THE HOLY GHOST: a Doctrinal and Devotional Treatise. *Crown 8vo.* 4s. 6d.
SOME ASPECTS OF THE CROSS. *Crown 8vo.* 4s. 6d.
THE MYSTERY OF THE TEMPTATION. Lent Lectures delivered a St. Mary Magdalene, Paddington. *Crown 8vo.* 4s. 6d.

Hutton.—THE CHURCH OF THE SIXTH CENTURY. Six Chapters in Ecclesiastical History. By WILLIAM HOLDEN HUTTON, B.D., Birkbeck Lecturer in Ecclesiastical History, Trinity College, Cambridge. *With* 11 *Illustrations. Crown* 8*vo.* 6*s.*

Hutton.—THE SOUL HERE AND HEREAFTER. By the Rev. R. E. HUTTON, Chaplain of St. Margaret's, East Grinstead. *Crown* 8*vo.* 6*s.*

INHERITANCE OF THE SAINTS; or, Thoughts on the Communion of Saints and the Life of the World to come. Collected chiefly from English Writers by L. P. With a Preface by the Rev. HENRY SCOTT HOLLAND, M.A. *Seventh Edition. Crown* 8*vo.* 7*s.* 6*d.*

Jameson.—Works by Mrs. JAMESON.

SACRED AND LEGENDARY ART, containing Legends of the Angels and Archangels, the Evangelists, the Apostles. With 19 Etchings and 187 Woodcuts. 2 *vols.* 8*vo.* 20*s. net.*

LEGENDS OF THE MONASTIC ORDERS, as represented in the Fine Arts. With 11 Etchings and 88 Woodcuts. 8*vo.* 10*s. net.*

LEGENDS OF THE MADONNA, OR BLESSED VIRGIN MARY. With 27 Etchings and 165 Woodcuts. 8*vo.* 10*s. net.*

THE HISTORY OF OUR LORD, as exemplified in Works of Art. Commenced by the late Mrs. JAMESON; continued and completed by LADY EASTLAKE. With 31 Etchings and 281 Woodcuts. 2 *Vols.* 8*vo.* 20*s. net.*

Jennings.—ECCLESIA ANGLICANA. A History of the Church of Christ in England from the Earliest to the Present Times. By the Rev. ARTHUR CHARLES JENNINGS, M.A. *Crown* 8*vo.* 7*s.* 6*d.*

Jukes.—Works by ANDREW JUKES.

THE NEW MAN AND THE ETERNAL LIFE. Notes on the Reiterated Amens of the Son of God. *Crown* 8*vo.* 6*s.*

THE NAMES OF GOD IN HOLY SCRIPTURE: a Revelation of His Nature and Relationships. *Crown* 8*vo.* 4*s.* 6*d.*

THE TYPES OF GENESIS. *Crown* 8*vo.* 7*s.* 6*d.*

THE SECOND DEATH AND THE RESTITUTION OF ALL THINGS. *Crown* 8*vo.* 3*s.* 6*d.*

THE ORDER AND CONNEXION OF THE CHURCH'S TEACHING, as set forth in the arrangement of the Epistles and Gospels throughout the Year. *Crown* 8*vo.* 2*s.* 6*d.*

THE CHRISTIAN HOME. *Crown* 8*vo.* 3*s.* 6*d.*

Knox Little.—Works by W. J. KNOX LITTLE, M.A., Canon Residentiary of Worcester, and Vicar of Hoar Cross.

    THE PERFECT LIFE: Sermons. *Crown 8vo.* 7s. 6d.

    CHARACTERISTICS AND MOTIVES OF THE CHRISTIAN LIFE. Ten Sermons preached in Manchester Cathedral, in Lent and Advent. *Crown 8vo.* 2s. 6d.

    SERMONS PREACHED FOR THE MOST PART IN MANCHESTER. *Crown 8vo.* 3s. 6d.

    THE MYSTERY OF THE PASSION OF OUR MOST HOLY REDEEMER. *Crown 8vo.* 2s. 6d.

    THE LIGHT OF LIFE. Sermons preached on Various Occasions. *Crown 8vo.* 3s. 6d.

    SUNLIGHT AND SHADOW IN THE CHRISTIAN LIFE. Sermons preached for the most part in America. *Crown 8vo.* 3s. 6d.

Lear.—Works by, and Edited by, H. L. SIDNEY LEAR.

    FOR DAYS AND YEARS. A book containing a Text, Short Reading, and Hymn for Every Day in the Church's Year. 16mo. 2s. 6d. *Also a Cheap Edition*, 32mo. 1s.; *or cloth gilt*, 1s. 6d.; *or with red borders*, 2s. 6d.

    FIVE MINUTES. Daily Readings of Poetry. 16mo. 3s. 6d. *Also a Cheap Edition*, 32mo. 1s.; *or cloth gilt*, 1s. 6d.

    WEARINESS. A Book for the Languid and Lonely. *Large Type. Small 8vo.* 5s.

    JOY: A FRAGMENT. With a slight sketch of the Author's life. *Small 8vo.* 2s. 6d.

    CHRISTIAN BIOGRAPHIES. *Nine Vols. Crown 8vo.* 3s. 6d. *each.*

MADAME LOUISE DE FRANCE, Daughter of Louis XV., known also as the Mother Térèse de St. Augustin.

A DOMINICAN ARTIST: a Sketch of the Life of the Rev. Père Besson, of the Order of St. Dominic.

HENRI PERREYVE. By PÈRE GRATRY.

ST. FRANCIS DE SALES, Bishop and Prince of Geneva.

THE REVIVAL OF PRIESTLY LIFE IN THE SEVENTEENTH CENTURY IN FRANCE.

A CHRISTIAN PAINTER OF THE NINETEENTH CENTURY.

BOSSUET AND HIS CONTEMPORARIES.

FÉNELON, ARCHBISHOP OF CAMBRAI.

HENRI DOMINIQUE LACORDAIRE.

[continued.

Lear. — Works by, and Edited by, H. L. SIDNEY LEAR — *continued.*

DEVOTIONAL WORKS. Edited by H. L. SIDNEY LEAR. *New and Uniform Editions. Nine Vols.* 16*mo.* 2*s.* 6*d. each.*

FÉNELON'S SPIRITUAL LETTERS TO MEN.

FÉNELON'S SPIRITUAL LETTERS TO WOMEN.

A SELECTION FROM THE SPIRITUAL LETTERS OF ST. FRANCIS DE SALES. Also *Cheap Edition*, 32*mo*, 6*d. cloth limp;* 1*s. cloth boards.*

THE SPIRIT OF ST. FRANCIS DE SALES.

THE HIDDEN LIFE OF THE SOUL.

THE LIGHT OF THE CONSCIENCE. Also *Cheap Edition*, 32*mo*, 6*d. cloth limp;* and 1*s. cloth boards.*

SELF-RENUNCIATION. From the French.

ST. FRANCIS DE SALES' OF THE LOVE OF GOD.

SELECTIONS FROM PASCAL'S 'THOUGHTS.'

Lepine. — THE MINISTERS OF JESUS CHRIST: a Biblical Study. By J. FOSTER LEPINE, Curate of St. Paul's, Maidstone. *Crown* 8*vo.* 5*s.*

Liddon. — Works by HENRY PARRY LIDDON, D.D., D.C.L., LL.D.

SERMONS ON SOME WORDS OF ST. PAUL. *Crown* 8*vo.* 5*s.*

SERMONS PREACHED ON SPECIAL OCCASIONS, 1860-1889. *Crown* 8*vo.* 5*s.*

EXPLANATORY ANALYSIS OF ST. PAUL'S FIRST EPISTLE TO TIMOTHY. 8*vo.* 7*s.* 6*d.*

CLERICAL LIFE AND WORK: Sermons. *Crown* 8*vo.* 5*s.*

ESSAYS AND ADDRESSES: Lectures on Buddhism — Lectures on the Life of St. Paul — Papers on Dante. *Crown* 8*vo.* 5*s.*

EXPLANATORY ANALYSIS OF ST. PAUL'S FIRST EPISTLE TO TIMOTHY. 8*vo.* 7*s.* 6*d.*

EXPLANATORY ANALYSIS OF PAUL'S EPISTLE TO THE ROMANS. 8*vo.* 14*s.*

SERMONS ON OLD TESTAMENT SUBJECTS. *Crown* 8*vo.* 5*s.*

SERMONS ON SOME WORDS OF CHRIST. *Crown* 8*vo.* 5*s.*

THE DIVINITY OF OUR LORD AND SAVIOUR JESUS CHRIST. Being the Bampton Lectures for 1866. *Crown* 8*vo.* 5*s.*

ADVENT IN ST. PAUL'S. *Two Vols. Crown* 8*vo.* 3*s.* 6*d. each. Cheap Edition in one Volume. Crown* 8*vo.* 5*s.*

CHRISTMASTIDE IN ST. PAUL'S. *Crown* 8*vo.* 5*s.*

PASSIONTIDE SERMONS. *Crown* 8*vo.* 5*s.*

EASTER IN ST. PAUL'S. Sermons bearing chiefly on the Resurrection of our Lord. *Two Vols. Crown* 8*vo.* 3*s.* 6*d. each. Cheap Edition in one Volume. Crown* 8*vo.* 5*s.*

SERMONS PREACHED BEFORE THE UNIVERSITY OF OXFORD. *Two Vols. Crown* 8*vo.* 3*s.* 6*d. each. Cheap Edition in one Volume. Crown* 8*vo.* 5*s.*

[*continued.*

Liddon.—Works by HENRY PARRY LIDDON, D.D., D.C.L., LL.D.—*continued.*

 THE MAGNIFICAT. Sermons in St. Paul's. *Crown 8vo.* 2s. 6d.

 SOME ELEMENTS OF RELIGION. Lent Lectures. *Small 8vo.* 2s. 6d. [*The Crown 8vo. Edition* (5s.) *may still be had.*]

 SELECTIONS FROM THE WRITINGS OF. *Crown 8vo.* 3s. 6d.

 MAXIMS AND GLEANINGS. *Crown 16mo.* 1s.

Linklater.—TRUE LIMITS OF RITUAL IN THE CHURCH. Edited by Rev. ROBERT LINKLATER, D.D., Vicar of Stroud Green. *Crown 8vo.* 5s.

 CONTENTS.—Preface—Introductory Essay, by the Rev. ROBERT LINKLATER, D.D.—The Ornaments Rubric, by J. T. MICKLETHWAITE, V.P.S.A.—The Catholic Principle of Conformity in Divine Worship, by the Rev. C. F. G. TURNER—A Plea for Reasonableness, by the Rev. JOHN WYLDE—Intelligible Ritual, by the Rev. HENRY ARNOTT—The English Liturgy, by the Rev. T. A. LACEY—Eucharistic Ritual, by the Rev. W. F. COBB, D.D.—Suggestions for a Basis of Agreement in Matters Liturgical and Ceremonial, by the Rev. H. E. HALL.

Luckock.—Works by HERBERT MORTIMER LUCKOCK, D.D., Dean of Lichfield.

 THE HISTORY OF MARRIAGE, JEWISH AND CHRISTIAN, IN RELATION TO DIVORCE AND CERTAIN FORBIDDEN DEGREES. *Second Edition. Crown 8vo.* 6s.

 AFTER DEATH. An Examination of the Testimony of Primitive Times respecting the State of the Faithful Dead, and their Relationship to the Living. *Crown 8vo.* 3s. 6d.

 THE INTERMEDIATE STATE BETWEEN DEATH AND JUDGMENT. Being a Sequel to *After Death. Crown 8vo.* 3s. 6d.

 FOOTPRINTS OF THE SON OF MAN, as traced by St. Mark. Being Eighty Portions for Private Study, Family Reading, and Instruction in Church. *Crown 8vo.* 3s. 6d.

 FOOTPRINTS OF THE APOSTLES, as traced by St. Luke in the Acts. Being Sixty Portions for Private Study, and Instruction in Church. A Sequel to 'Footprints of the Son of Man, as traced by St. Mark.' *Two Vols. Crown 8vo.* 12s.

 THE DIVINE LITURGY. Being the Order for Holy Communion, Historically, Doctrinally, and Devotionally set forth, in Fifty Portions. *Crown 8vo.* 3s. 6d.

 STUDIES IN THE HISTORY OF THE BOOK OF COMMON PRAYER. The Anglican Reform—The Puritan Innovations—The Elizabethan Reaction—The Caroline Settlement. With Appendices. *Crown 8vo.* 3s. 6d.

 THE BISHOPS IN THE TOWER. A Record of Stirring Events affecting the Church and Nonconformists from the Restoration to the Revolution. *Crown 8vo.* 3s. 6d.

MacColl.—Works by the Rev. MALCOLM MACCOLL, D.D., Canon Residentiary of Ripon.
  THE REFORMATION SETTLEMENT: Examined in the Light of History and Law. With an Introductory Letter to the Right Hon. W. V. Harcourt, M.P. *Crown 8vo.*
  CHRISTIANITY IN RELATION TO SCIENCE AND MORALS. *Crown 8vo.* 6s.
  LIFE HERE AND HEREAFTER: Sermons. *Crown 8vo.* 7s. 6d.

Mason.—Works by A. J. MASON, D.D., Lady Margaret Professor of Divinity in the University of Cambridge and Canon of Canterbury.
  THE CONDITIONS OF OUR LORD'S LIFE UPON EARTH. Being the Bishop Paddock Lectures, 1896. To which is prefixed part of a First Professorial Lecture at Cambridge. *Crown 8vo.* 5s.
  THE PRINCIPLES OF ECCLESIASTICAL UNITY. Four Lectures delivered in St. Asaph Cathedral. *Crown 8vo.* 3s. 6d.
  THE FAITH OF THE GOSPEL. A Manual of Christian Doctrine. *Crown 8vo.* 7s. 6d. *Cheap Edition. Crown 8vo.* 3s. 6d.
  THE RELATION OF CONFIRMATION TO BAPTISM. As taught in Holy Scripture and the Fathers. *Crown 8vo.* 7s. 6d.

Maturin.—Works by the Rev. B. W. MATURIN.
  SOME PRINCIPLES AND PRACTICES OF THE SPIRITUAL LIFE. *Crown 8vo.* 4s. 6d.
  PRACTICAL STUDIES ON THE PARABLES OF OUR LORD. *Crown 8vo.* 5s.

Medd.—THE PRIEST TO THE ALTAR; or, Aids to the Devout Celebration of Holy Communion, chiefly after the Ancient English Use of Sarum. By PETER GOLDSMITH MEDD, M.A., Canon of St. Alban's. Fourth Edition, revised and enlarged. *Royal 8vo.* 15s.

Meyrick.—THE DOCTRINE OF THE CHURCH OF ENGLAND ON THE HOLY COMMUNION RESTATED AS A GUIDE AT THE PRESENT TIME. By the Rev. F. MEYRICK, M.A. *Crown 8vo.* 4s. 6d.

Mortimer.—Works by the Rev. A. G. MORTIMER, D.D., Rector of St. Mark's, Philadelphia.

JESUS AND THE RESURRECTION: Thirty Addresses for Good Friday and Easter. *Crown 8vo.* 5s.

CATHOLIC FAITH AND PRACTICE: A Manual of Theology. Two Parts. *Crown 8vo.* Sold separately. Part I. 7s. 6d. Part II. 9s.

HELPS TO MEDITATION: Sketches for Every Day in the Year.
  Vol. I. ADVENT to TRINITY. 8vo. 7s. 6d.
  Vol. II. TRINITY to ADVENT. 8vo. 7s. 6d.

STORIES FROM GENESIS: Sermons for Children. *Crown 8vo.* 4s.

THE LAWS OF HAPPINESS; or, The Beatitudes as teaching our Duty to God, Self, and our Neighbour. 18mo. 2s.

THE LAWS OF PENITENCE: Addresses on the Words of our Lord from the Cross. 16mo. 1s. 6d.

SERMONS IN MINIATURE FOR EXTEMPORE PREACHERS: Sketches for Every Sunday and Holy Day of the Christian Year. *Cr. 8vo.* 6s.

NOTES ON THE SEVEN PENITENTIAL PSALMS, chiefly from Patristic Sources. *Fcp. 8vo.* 3s. 6d.

THE SEVEN LAST WORDS OF OUR MOST HOLY REDEEMER: with Meditations on some Scenes in His Passion. *Crown 8vo.* 5s.

LEARN OF JESUS CHRIST TO DIE: Addresses on the Words of our Lord from the Cross, taken as Teaching the way of Preparation for Death. 16mo. 2s.

Mozley.—Works by J. B. MOZLEY, D.D., late Canon of Christ Church, and Regius Professor of Divinity at Oxford.

ESSAYS, HISTORICAL AND THEOLOGICAL. *Two Vols. 8vo. 24s.*

EIGHT LECTURES ON MIRACLES. Being the Bampton Lectures for 1865. *Crown 8vo. 3s. 6d.*

RULING IDEAS IN EARLY AGES AND THEIR RELATION TO OLD TESTAMENT FAITH. *8vo. 6s.*

SERMONS PREACHED BEFORE THE UNIVERSITY OF OXFORD, and on Various Occasions. *Crown 8vo. 3s. 6d.*

SERMONS, PAROCHIAL AND OCCASIONAL. *Crown 8vo. 3s. 6d.*

A REVIEW OF THE BAPTISMAL CONTROVERSY. *Crown 8vo. 3s. 6d.*

Newbolt.—Works by the Rev. W. C. E. NEWBOLT, M.A., Canon and Chancellor of St. Paul's Cathedral.

RELIGION. *Crown 8vo. 5s.* (*The Oxford Library of Practical Theology.*)

PRIESTLY IDEALS; being a Course of Practical Lectures delivered in St. Paul's Cathedral to 'Our Society' and other Clergy, in Lent, 1898. *Crown 8vo. 3s. 6d.*

THE GOSPEL OF EXPERIENCE; or, the Witness of Human Life to the truth of Revelation. Being the Boyle Lectures for 1895. *Crown 8vo. 5s.*

COUNSELS OF FAITH AND PRACTICE: being Sermons preached on various occasions. *New and Enlarged Edition. Crown 8vo. 5s.*

SPECULUM SACERDOTUM; or, the Divine Model of the Priestly Life. *Crown 8vo. 7s. 6d.*

THE FRUIT OF THE SPIRIT. Being Ten Addresses bearing on the Spiritual Life. *Crown 8vo. 2s. 6d.*

THE MAN OF GOD. *Small 8vo. 1s. 6d.*

THE PRAYER BOOK: Its Voice and Teaching. *Crown 8vo. 2s. 6d.*

Newman.—Works by JOHN HENRY NEWMAN, B.D., sometime Vicar of St. Mary's, Oxford.

LETTERS AND CORRESPONDENCE OF JOHN HENRY NEWMAN DURING HIS LIFE IN THE ENGLISH CHURCH. With a brief Autobiography. Edited, at Cardinal Newman's request, by ANNE MOZLEY. *2 vols. Crown 8vo. 7s.*

PAROCHIAL AND PLAIN SERMONS. *Eight Vols. Cabinet Edition. Crown 8vo. 5s. each. Cheaper Edition. 3s. 6d. each.*

SELECTION, ADAPTED TO THE SEASONS OF THE ECCLESIASTICAL YEAR, from the 'Parochial and Plain Sermons.' *Cabinet Edition. Crown 8vo. 5s. Cheaper Edition. 3s. 6d.*

FIFTEEN SERMONS PREACHED BEFORE THE UNIVERSITY OF OXFORD *Cabinet Edition. Crown 8vo. 5s. Cheaper Edition. 3s. 6d.*

SERMONS BEARING UPON SUBJECTS OF THE DAY. *Cabinet Edition. Crown 8vo. 5s. Cheaper Edition. Crown 8vo. 3s. 6d.*

LECTURES ON THE DOCTRINE OF JUSTIFICATION. *Cabinet Edition. Crown 8vo. 5s. Cheaper Edition. 3s. 6d.*

*** *A Complete List of Cardinal Newman's Works can be had on Application.*

Osborne.—Works by EDWARD OSBORNE, Mission Priest of the Society of St. John the Evangelist, Cowley, Oxford.

THE CHILDREN'S SAVIOUR. Instructions to Children on the Life of Our Lord and Saviour Jesus Christ. *Illustrated.* 16mo. 2s. 6d.

THE SAVIOUR KING. Instructions to Children on Old Testament Types and Illustrations of the Life of Christ. *Illustrated.* 16mo. 2s. 6d.

THE CHILDREN'S FAITH. Instructions to Children on the Apostles' Creed. *Illustrated.* 16mo. 2s. 6d.

Ottley.—ASPECTS OF THE OLD TESTAMENT: being the Bampton Lectures for 1897. By ROBERT LAWRENCE OTTLEY, M.A., Vicar of Winterbourne Bassett, Wilts; sometime Principal of the Pusey House. 8vo. *New and Cheaper Edition.* 7s. 6d.

The Oxford Library of Practical Theology.

PRODUCED UNDER THE EDITORSHIP OF

The Rev. W. C. E. NEWBOLT, M.A., Canon and Chancellor of St. Paul's, and the Rev. F. E. BRIGHTMAN, M.A., Librarian of the Pusey House, Oxford.

The Price of each Volume will be Five Shillings.

The following is a list of Volumes as at present arranged :—

1. RELIGION. By the Rev. W. C. E. NEWBOLT, M.A., Canon and Chancellor of St. Paul's. *Crown 8vo.* 5s.
2. BAPTISM. By the Rev. DARWELL STONE, M.A., Principal of the Missionary College, Dorchester. *Crown 8vo.* 5s. [*In the press.*
3. CONFIRMATION. By the Right Rev. A. C. A. HALL, D.D., Bishop of Vermont.
4. HOLY MATRIMONY. By the Rev. W. J. KNOX LITTLE, M.A., Canon of Worcester.
5. THE HOLY COMMUNION. By the Rev. F. W. PULLER, M.A., Mission Priest of St. John Evangelist, Cowley.
6. THE PRAYER BOOK. By the Rev. LEIGHTON PULLAN, M.A., Fellow of St. John's College, Oxford.
7. RELIGIOUS CEREMONIAL. By the Rev. F. E. BRIGHTMAN, M.A., Librarian of the Pusey House, Oxford.
8. PRAYER. By the Rev. A. J. WORLLEDGE, M.A., Canon of Truro.
9. VISITATION OF THE SICK. By the Rev. E. F. RUSSELL, M.A., St. Alban's, Holborn.

CONFESSION and ABSOLUTION.	DEVOTIONAL BOOKS and READING.
FASTING and ALMSGIVING.	ORDINATION.
RETREATS, MISSIONS, ETC.	FOREIGN MISSIONS.
CHURCH WORK.	THE BIBLE.

OUTLINES OF CHURCH TEACHING: a Series of Instructions for the Sundays and chief Holy Days of the Christian Year. For the Use of Teachers. By C. C. G. With Preface by the Very Rev. FRANCIS PAGET, D.D., Dean of Christ Church, Oxford. *Crown 8vo.* 3s. 6d.

Oxenham.—THE VALIDITY OF PAPAL CLAIMS: Lectures delivered in Rome. By F. NUTCOMBE OXENHAM, D.D., English Chaplain at Rome. With a Letter by His Grace the ARCHBISHOP OF YORK. *Crown 8vo.* 2s. 6d.

Paget.—Works by FRANCIS PAGET, D.D., Dean of Christ Church.
STUDIES IN THE CHRISTIAN CHARACTER: Sermons. With an Introductory Essay. *Crown 8vo.* 6s. 6d.
THE SPIRIT OF DISCIPLINE: Sermons. *Crown 8vo.* 6s. 6d.
FACULTIES AND DIFFICULTIES FOR BELIEF AND DISBELIEF. *Crown 8vo.* 6s. 6d.
THE HALLOWING OF WORK. Addresses given at Eton, January 16-18, 1888. *Small 8vo.* 2s.

Percival.—SOME HELPS FOR SCHOOL LIFE. Sermons preached at Clifton College, 1862-1879. By J. PERCIVAL, D.D., LL.D., Lord Bishop of Hereford. New Edition, with New Preface. *Crown 8vo.* 3s. 6d.

Percival.—THE INVOCATION OF SAINTS. Treated Theologically and Historically. By HENRY R. PERCIVAL, M.A., D.D., Author of 'A Digest of Theology,' 'The Doctrine of the Episcopal Church,' etc. *Crown 8vo.* 5s.

POCKET MANUAL OF PRAYERS FOR THE HOURS, ETC. With the Collects from the Prayer Book. *Royal 32mo.* 1s.

Powell.—THE PRINCIPLE OF THE INCARNATION. With especial Reference to the Relation between our Lord's Divine Omniscience and His Human Consciousness. By the Rev. H. C. POWELL, M.A. of Oriel College, Oxford; Rector of Wylye and Prebendary of Salisbury Cathedral. *8vo.* 16s.

PRACTICAL REFLECTIONS. By a CLERGYMAN. With Prefaces by H. P. LIDDON, D.D., D.C.L., and the LORD BISHOP OF LINCOLN. *Crown 8vo.*

THE BOOK OF GENESIS. 4s. 6d.	THE MINOR PROPHETS. 4s. 6d.
THE PSALMS. 5s.	THE HOLY GOSPELS. 4s. 6d.
ISAIAH. 4s. 6d.	ACTS TO REVELATION. 6s.

PRIEST'S PRAYER BOOK (THE). Containing Private Prayers and Intercessions; Occasional, School, and Parochial Offices; Offices for the Visitation of the Sick, with Notes, Readings, Collects, Hymns, Litanies, etc. With a brief Pontifical. By the late Rev. R. F. LITTLEDALE, LL.D., D.C.L., and Rev. J. EDWARD VAUX, M.A., F.S.A. *New Edition, Revised.* 20th Thousand. *Post 8vo.* 6s. 6d.

Pullan.—LECTURES ON RELIGION. By the Rev. LEIGHTON PULLAN, M.A., Fellow of St. John's College, Lecturer in Theology at Oriel and Queen's Colleges, Oxford. *Crown 8vo. 6s.*

Pusey.—SPIRITUAL LETTERS OF EDWARD BOUVERIE PUSEY, D.D. Edited and prepared for publication by the Rev. J. O. JOHNSTON, M.A., Principal of the Theological College, Cuddesdon; and the Rev. W. C. E. NEWBOLT, M.A., Canon and Chancellor of St. Paul's. *8vo. 12s. 6d.*

Randolph.—Works by B. W. RANDOLPH, M.A., Principal of the Theological College and Hon. Canon of Ely.

MEDITATIONS ON THE OLD TESTAMENT for Every Day in the Year. *Crown 8vo. 6s.*

THE THRESHOLD OF THE SANCTUARY: being Short Chapters on the Inner Preparation for the Priesthood. *Crown 8vo. 3s. 6d.*

THE LAW OF SINAI: being Devotional Addresses on the Ten Commandments delivered to Ordinands. *Crown 8vo. 3s. 6d.*

Rede.—Works by WYLLYS REDE, D.D., Rector of the Church of the Incarnation, and Canon of the Cathedral, Atalanta, Georgia.

STRIVING FOR THE MASTERY: Daily Lessons for Lent. *Cr. 8vo. 5s.*

THE COMMUNION OF SAINTS: a Lost Link in the Chain of the Church's Creed. With a Preface by LORD HALIFAX. *Crown 8vo. 3s. 6d.*

Reynolds.—THE SUPERNATURAL IN NATURE: A Verification by Free Use of Science. By JOSEPH WILLIAM REYNOLDS, M.A., Late President of Sion College, and Prebendary of St. Paul's Cathedral. *New and Cheaper Edition, Revised. Crown 8vo. 3s. 6d.*

Sanday.—Works by W. SANDAY, D.D., Margaret Professor of Divinity and Canon of Christ Church, Oxford.

THE CONCEPTION OF PRIESTHOOD IN THE EARLY CHURCH AND IN THE CHURCH OF ENGLAND: Four Sermons. *Crown 8vo. 3s. 6d.*

INSPIRATION: Eight Lectures on the Early History and Origin o the Doctrine of Biblical Inspiration. Being the Bampton Lectures for 1893. *New and Cheaper Edition, with New Preface. 8vo. 7s. 6d.*

Scudamore.—STEPS TO THE ALTAR: a Manual of Devotion for the Blessed Eucharist. By the Rev. W. E. SCUDAMORE, M.A. *Royal 32mo. 1s.*

On toned paper, with red rubrics, 2s: The same, with Collects, Epistles, and Gospels, 2s. 6d; Demy 18mo. cloth, 1s; Demy 18mo. cloth, large type, 1s. 3d; Imperial 32mo. limp cloth, 6d.

Simpson.—THE CHURCH AND THE BIBLE. By the Rev. W. J. SPARROW SIMPSON, M.A. Vicar of St. Mark's, Regent's Park. *Crown 8vo.* 3s. 6d.

MEMOIR OF THE REV. W. SPARROW SIMPSON, D.D., Sub-Dean of St. Paul's Cathedral. Compiled and Edited by W. J. SPARROW SIMPSON. With Portrait and other Illustrations. *Crown 8vo.* 4s. 6d.

Strange.—INSTRUCTIONS ON THE REVELATION OF ST. JOHN THE DIVINE: Being an attempt to make this book more intelligible to the ordinary reader and so to encourage the study of it. By Rev. CRESSWELL STRANGE, M.A., Vicar of Edgbaston, and Honorary Canon of Worcester. *Crown 8vo.* 6s.

Strong.—CHRISTIAN ETHICS : being the Bampton Lectures for 1895. By THOMAS B. STRONG, B.D., Student of Christ Church, Oxford, and Examining Chaplain to the Lord Bishop of Durham. *New and Cheaper Edition.* 8vo. 7s. 6d.

Tee.—THE SANCTUARY OF SUFFERING. By ELEANOR TEE, Author of 'This Everyday Life,' etc. With a Preface by the Rev. J. P. F. DAVIDSON, M.A., Vicar of St. Matthias', Earl's Court; President of the 'Guild of All Souls.' *Crown 8vo.* 7s. 6d.

Whishaw.—THE CHILDREN'S YEAR-BOOK OF PRAYER AND PRAISE. By C. M. WHISHAW, Compiler of 'Being and Doing.' *Crown 8vo.* 3s. 6d.

Williams.—Works by the Rev. ISAAC WILLIAMS, B.D.

A DEVOTIONAL COMMENTARY ON THE GOSPEL NARRATIVE. *Eight Vols. Crown 8vo.* 5s. *each.*

THOUGHTS ON THE STUDY OF THE HOLY GOSPELS.
A HARMONY OF THE FOUR GOSPELS.
OUR LORD'S NATIVITY.
OUR LORD'S MINISTRY (Second Year).
OUR LORD'S MINISTRY (Third Year).
THE HOLY WEEK.
OUR LORD'S PASSION.
OUR LORD'S RESURRECTION.

FEMALE CHARACTERS OF HOLY SCRIPTURE. A Series of Sermons. *Crown 8vo.* 5s.
THE CHARACTERS OF THE OLD TESTAMENT. *Crown 8vo.* 5s.
THE APOCALYPSE. With Notes and Reflections. *Crown 8vo.* 5s.
SERMONS ON THE EPISTLES AND GOSPELS FOR THE SUNDAYS AND HOLY DAYS. *Two Vols. Crown 8vo.* 5s. *each.*
PLAIN SERMONS ON CATECHISM. *Two Vols. Cr. 8vo.* 5s. *each.*

Wilson.—THOUGHTS ON CONFIRMATION. By Rev. R. J. WILSON, D.D., late Warden of Keble College. 16mo. 1s. 6d.

Wirgman.—Works by A. THEODORE WIRGMAN, B.D., D.C.L., Vice-Provost of St. Mary's Collegiate Church, Port Elizabeth, South Africa.

THE DOCTRINE OF CONFIRMATION. *Crown 8vo.* 7s. 6d.
THE CONSTITUTIONAL AUTHORITY OF BISHOPS IN THE CATHOLIC CHURCH. Illustrated by the History and Canon Law of the Undivided Church from the Apostolic Age to the Council of Chalcedon, A.D. 451. *Crown 8vo.* 6s.

Wood.—THE STORY OF A SAINTLY BISHOP'S LIFE—LANCELOT ANDREWES, Bishop of Winchester, 1555-1626. By Lady Mary Wood. *Crown 8vo.* 1s. 6d.

Wordsworth.—Works by CHRISTOPHER WORDSWORTH, D.D., sometime Bishop of Lincoln.

THE HOLY BIBLE (the Old Testament). With Notes, Introductions, and Index. *Imperial 8vo.*
    Vol. I. THE PENTATEUCH. 25s. Vol. II. JOSHUA TO SAMUEL. 15s. Vol. III. KINGS to ESTHER. 15s. Vol. IV. JOB TO SONG OF SOLOMON. 25s. Vol. V. ISAIAH TO EZEKIEL. 25s. Vol. VI. DANIEL, MINOR PROPHETS, and Index. 15s.
    Also supplied in 12 Parts. Sold separately.

THE NEW TESTAMENT, in the Original Greek. With Notes, Introductions, and Indices. *Imperial 8vo.*
    Vol. I. GOSPELS AND ACTS OF THE APOSTLES. 23s. Vol. II. EPISTLES, APOCALYPSE, and Indices. 37s.
    Also supplied in 4 Parts. Sold separately.

A CHURCH HISTORY TO A.D. 451. *Four Vols. Crown 8vo.*
    Vol. I. TO THE COUNCIL OF NICÆA, A.D. 325. 8s. 6d. Vol. II. FROM THE COUNCIL OF NICÆA TO THAT OF CONSTANTINOPLE 6s. Vol. III. CONTINUATION. 6s. Vol. IV. CONCLUSION, TO THE COUNCIL OF CHALCEDON, A.D. 451. 6s.

THEOPHILUS ANGLICANUS: a Manual of Instruction on the Church and the Anglican Branch of it. 12mo. 2s. 6d.

ELEMENTS OF INSTRUCTION ON THE CHURCH. 16mo. 1s. *cloth*. 6d. *sewed*.

THE HOLY YEAR: Original Hymns. 16mo. 2s. 6d. and 1s. Limp, 6d.
    „   „   With Music. Edited by W. H. MONK. *Square 8vo.* 4s. 6d.

ON THE INTERMEDIATE STATE OF THE SOUL AFTER DEATH. 32mo. 1s.

Wordsworth.—Works by JOHN WORDSWORTH, D.D., Lord Bishop of Salisbury.

THE EPISCOPATE OF CHARLES WORDSWORTH, D.D., D.C.L., Bishop of St. Andrews. With Two Portraits. *8vo.* 15s.

THE HOLY COMMUNION: Four Visitation Addresses. 1891. *Crown 8vo.* 3s. 6d.

THE ONE RELIGION: Truth, Holiness, and Peace desired by the Nations, and revealed by Jesus Christ. Eight Lectures delivered before the University of Oxford in 1881. *Second Edition. Crown 8vo.* 7s. 6d.

UNIVERSITY SERMONS ON GOSPEL SUBJECTS. *Sm. 8vo.* 2s. 6d.

PRAYERS FOR USE IN COLLEGE. 16mo. 1s.

5000/4/99.

www.ingramcontent.com/pod-product-compliance
Lightning Source LLC
Chambersburg PA
CBHW021150230426
43667CB00006B/334